INSTITUTIONAL CHANGE AND INDUSTRIAL
DEVELOPMENT IN CENTRAL AND EASTERN EUROPE

Institutional Change and Industrial Development in Central and Eastern Europe

Edited by
ANNE LORENTZEN
BRIGITTA WIDMAIER
MIHÁLY LAKI

Ashgate

Aldershot • Brookfield USA • Singapore • Sydney

Published by
Ashgate Publishing Ltd
Gower House
Croft Road
Aldershot
Hants GU11 3HR
England

Ashgate Publishing Company
Old Post Road
Brookfield
Vermont 05036
USA

Ashgate website: http://www.ashgate.com

British Library Cataloguing in Publication Data
Institutional change and industrial development in Central
   & Eastern Europe
   1. Industrialization - Europe, Central 2. Industrialization -
   Europe, Eastern
   I. Lorentzen, Anne II. Widmaier, Brigitta, II. Laki, Mihály
   338.9'43

Library of Congress Catalog Card Number: 99-73314

ISBN 0 7546 1014 4

Printed in Great Britain

Contents

List of Contributors

Susan Berry Baca is Lecturer and Ph.D. candidate at the Department of Languages and International Studies, Aalborg University, Denmark.

Laszlo Czaban is Lecturer at Leeds University Business School, University of Leeds, UK.

Junior R. Davis is a Ph.D. from the University of London and is working as a Senior Economist at the Natural Resources Institute, University of Greenwich, UK.

Attila Havas is Project Co-ordinator at the National Committee for Technological Development (O.M.F.B.), and Research Fellow at Innovation Research Centre (I.K.U.), Budapest University of Economics, Budapest, Hungary.

Frede Hvelplund is Associate Professor at the Department of Development and Planning, Aalborg University, Denmark.

Niels Knudsen is working as an expert in energy planning in Central and Eastern Europe and is a Ph.D. candidate at the Department of Development and Planning, Aalborg University, Denmark.

Mihály Laki is Professor at the Department of Economics, Hungarian Academy of Science in Budapest, Hungary.

Maureen Lankhuizen is a Ph.D. candidate at MERIT, Maastricht University, The Netherlands.

Anne Lorentzen is Associate Professor at the Department of Development and Planning, Aalborg University, Denmark.

Henrik Lund is Associate Professor and Head of Department at the Department of Development and Planning, Aalborg University, Denmark.

Martin Myant is Reader at the Department of Accounting, Economics and Languages, University of Paisley, UK.

Hans van Zon is Professor at the School of Social and International Studies, University of Sunderland, UK.

Richard Whitley is Professor at the Department of Economic Systems and Organisational Change, Manchester Business School, UK.

Brigitta Widmaier is Senior Researcher at the Department of Work and Technology (IAT) in Gelsenkirchen, Germany.

Preface

ANNE LORENTZEN, BRIGITTA WIDMAIER, MIHÁLY LAKI

The processes of transformation in Central and Eastern Europe have represented a challenge for Social Science and Economic research. The changes were unforeseen, sudden and unprecedented and they implied a radical re-orientation of the economic, political and social order. New states emerged and cross-national economic and military blocks were dissolved. The European Union started to integrate new countries, contributing to the rapid development of a new social and economic division of labour in Europe.

The "first stage" of transformation was characterised by the installation of basic conditions for multi-party democracy and market economy. Accordingly research focused on issues that were both basic for the understanding of the process, but which were at the same time very general in their scope: The development of democracy, of market economy and of civil society. The observable changes, based upon values and institutions of the Western system, were measured by the degree of approximation to (more ideal than real) Western models.

The essence of the "second stage" in the transformation process, with economies privatised and institutional-legislative reforms in place, is different. It can tentatively be characterised as differentiated societal development processes widely influenced by endogenous forces. This second stage give rise to a host of more detailed research questions in relation to the development of regions, institutions, and branches as well as individual enterprises.

The contributions in this book refer to this second stage. The intention with the book is to characterise the capability of industries and single enterprises in Central and Eastern Europe to respond to the new conditions, and further to discuss how these conditions, in terms of institutions and economic structures, seem to form industrial development differently in the different countries.
In November, 1997, a group of researchers (economists, social scientists, and engineers) who are working on transformation processes in countries of Central and Eastern Europe were called together by Anne Lorentzen from Aalborg University for a workshop at Tannishus, Denmark. During two days the initial versions of the papers that now appear in this volume were presented

and discussed. As a result of the workshop, the publication of the contributions was envisaged, most of all because a commonly shared framework for research became obvious and proved to be fruitful in the discussions at Tannishus. This common framework is found in the focus on the level of branches and enterprises rather than on a macro-economic level, and the shared acceptance of the fruitfulness of case-studies and qualitative research methods. The book can be seen as a first step towards a much needed synthesis of research methods for the study of renewal and innovation in enterprises.

The people contributing to this book have done a great deal of work in not only revising but also rewriting their papers which we, the editors, thank them for. Language editing was important, since most of the contributors were not native English speaking people, and research fellow Susan Baca has made a tremendous contribution by doing much of the language editing of the book, together with our indefatigable secretary Dorte Madsen. The staff at the Department of Development and Planning, Aalborg University, Bente Vestergaard and Dorthe Andersen has worked hard on finishing the manuscripts. The Department of Development and Planning deserve our warm thanks for its financial contribution to language editing and indexing. Also the editorial meeting organised and hosted by the Institute for Work and Technology in Gelsenkirchen in October 1998 contributed to the successful realisation of the book project and to the opening of perspectives for future collaboration among the contributors.

Introduction

ANNE LORENTZEN, BRIGITTA WIDMAIER, MIHÁLY LAKI

This book is involved with the general topic of institutional change and industrial development in Central and Eastern Europe (CEE). The more specific focus is on the ways companies have responded to changing societal conditions in CEE through various processes of renewal, adjustment, and/or innovation.

The overall question, which we would like to shed light on by organising this volume, is how the patterns of industrial development and innovation emerging in CEE can be characterised and which possible problems and weaknesses are related to these patterns that seem to call for policy response. When analysing emerging patterns, as we suggest, it is important to be aware of different types of processes that have been going on in CEE after 1989. In a historical perspective the break down of the planned economy in 1989 has been followed by two major stages. During the first stage the basic conditions for multi-party democracies and market economies had to be installed. A second stage followed in which the basic institutions were more or less in place, and in which development processes influenced by endogenous forces started to take place. The contributions in this book refer to this second stage and ask how enterprises are able to operate and innovate under the new conditions – and what these conditions more specifically are.

The time that has passed since the gradual introduction of market economies in the formerly planned economies of Central and Eastern Europe nine years ago has been marked by shifts at ideological and economic as well as at scholarly levels. Ideologically the starting point of radical reforms in 1989 was a widespread belief in free market forces as a solution to most "evils"of the centrally planned economies. This was also reflected in a prevailing concern about macro-economic conditions. Transformation on the enterprise level was neither a political nor an academic subject. Privatisation, liberalisation and a reduced economic role for the state were main issues during the first few years. As the enterprises were in no way prepared to operate under market conditions, a very severe economic crisis swept over Central and Eastern Europe between 1990 and 1994. Life has become easier and less turbulent in

xiii

CEE since 1994, as new institutions have started to function, substituting for the abolished institutions of the centrally planned economy. The initial scepticism towards any interference in the economy by the state has been supplanted by considerations of where and how the government should contribute to development.

Thus in spite of initial frustration about the slow progress of the transition, the process has now gone so far that some even might say that the process of transition has come to an end. Consequently there should no longer be major differences in the economic and institutional conditions between East and Western Europe. We would not go as far as that. Two major differences that still exist between Eastern and Western Europe are that the labour market institutions and the social security systems in Western Europe are working as economically and socially stabilising factors. These institutions have not yet become well established in CEE. Seen from a company perspective such instabilities make it difficult to make decisions about company strategy and innovation.

Instead of declaring the end of the transition process, we would rather say that one phase of transformation seems to have come to an end: the major institutional changes have been widely achieved. Important areas of the economy have been privatised, only a few price regulations are still being upheld by the governments and most goods are traded freely across borders.

We maintain, however, that unsolved old and new problems abound, both politically and academically. Further, we insist that to some extent these problems have their roots in the conflicts arising from the systemic change from communism to capitalism and that they are thus "problems of the trans-formation process".

The evidence given in this volume challenges any simple and uni-linear perception of development in CEE. Research results thus seem to suggest that the history of communism in Central and Eastern Europe is very present in structures, institutions and attitudes, resulting in a considerable "path dependency".

It is important to note that we do not use the term of "path dependency" as a negative notion, as a barrier to development. On the contrary, competencies and capabilities accumulated through historical experience represent important potentials. Most CEE countries have a long industrial experience, high levels of education and social connections or networks that can be mobilised to serve the development of businesses in the new market economic context. However it cannot be denied that "path dependency" in relation to CEE also includes traits that are detrimental not only to company development, but also to political and economic development. The continuity of old power structures may block the emergence of new economic and political dynamics, and such is the role also of corruption and other forms of criminality.

We find that both in scholarly work, in planning and in management it is important to learn from history and to build on the good as well as to learn from the bad experiences.

The implication of this is that even if to a considerable extent the new market economic institutions form and stimulate innovation at company level, the same is true for the communist heritage. The continued presence today of institutions and attitudes dating from the communist period implies that it is probably erroneous to suggest that the conditions of operation are comparable for companies in CEE and Western Europe. Strategic decision making is sometimes made more complicated for companies in CEE by institutions offering conflicting incentives. For research it implies that features of the past represent explicatory factors behind the strategies of innovation at company level.

If history matters, as we suggest above, it is not in the form of the fingerprint of a "single type" of communism. The CEE countries each developed different types of planned economies, and differing histories represent differing points of departure for the development of modern capitalism in general and for developments at company level in particular.

A further complication in the study of innovation in the transitional economies is the necessary distinction between formal institutions and the incentives they produce on the one hand, and the response in terms of behaviour of the economic agents on the other hand. If institutions (rules of the game) can easily be changed on paper, the actual response (in terms of changed behaviour) to them may make slow progress, as behaviour is rooted in historically grown practices and attitudes. In a transition process an additional complication is that new and old institutions coexist, and may produce conflicting incentives. Further the span of influence held by the new institutions in CEE may be questioned, as well as the actual capabilities of single institutions.

Unquestionably, the processes going on in Central and Eastern Europe since 1989 have inspired and challenged researchers. Similarly to the above mentioned "stages" research can be characterised by different "waves" since 1989.

The first wave was dominated by mainstream economics, describing overall economic structural changes based on aggregate quantitative data, to the extent that such data existed. Crucial questions of competitiveness were addressed as changes in trade behaviour. With caution it can be said that the first wave of contributions ideologically welcomed the abolition of the communist system and the entry of a new one, implying a research focus on the processes of privatisation and liberalisation. Overall comparisons between the behaviour of the different countries could be made on the basis of aggregate statistics which were beginning to appear. Research was engaged with measuring degrees of similarity to the models prevailing in the West. The mentioned macroeconomic focus was further supported by the role of international monetary institutions, the interest of which was a one-sided focus on inflation rate management, leading to a general disregard of other problems and needs of the CEE economies.

Somewhat in opposition to the first wave of research a second wave has emerged. This wave has its roots in organisation and managerial studies, and in institutional economics and technology studies. The research focus of the second wave deals with socio-political and qualitative aspects of the economic and institutional developments in CEE. "The company" has become a focal point, and qualitative methods of empirical data gathering have gained importance. A variety of approaches are now being applied, making comparison more difficult, but nonetheless necessary.

This way this volume contains a selection of contributions which represent the second and newer wave of research. Empirical evidence from different branches in manufacturing is here brought together, the common denominator of which is interest in the changing conditions of innovation and the adaptability of companies in CEE.

We assume that technological progress and innovation in terms of new products and processes is a necessary condition for enterprises to succeed in a competitive global environment. Factors outside the enterprise codetermine the scope of change, and they may have supporting as well as challenging characters. They run from global modes of competition and international trade and investment, over conditions in the national environment to intermediary network structures.

In this book we seek to describe, compare and explain, to the extent that the present stage of research allows, recent developments at company and institution level in CEE. Based on our empirical evidence we scrutinise conditions for innovation within enterprises as well as possible policies in support of innovative industrial development.

We refer to the changes at company level (and in the relationships between companies) which are the result of more or less consistent choices taken in companies, and which include technological and organisational adaptation processes enhancing or hindering the development of innovative products and processes.

From an analytical point of view, we may distinguish between different development patterns characterising industry in CEE and, as can be seen in the contributions that follow, there is a marked difference between the east and the west of the region concerning the types of development taking place. With caution three patterns can be outlined as follows.

In the first, survival is the primary task. Companies react using different means, including dismissals and the sale of production units and stock at low prices, but without any prospects for co-ordinated and long-term strategies.

In the second pattern, short-term competitiveness is the main goal. Low wages are in focus and companies develop new roles as international sub-suppliers of comparatively cheap standard goods and components (a semi-peripheral position) in competition with newly industrialising countries.

The third pattern involves medium and long-term competition being considered and planned. Innovation is in focus and specialised niches are found where global competitiveness can be achieved (implying more or less "equal terms" with advanced Western countries).

The above three patterns may represent phases of industrial and technological development, but they also describe coexisting patterns in CEE today.

It goes without saying that the third pattern is an attractive goal, because it provides countries with more economic autonomy as well as comparatively higher levels of income than the other patterns do. It is therefore not surprising that this scenario is outlined in much detail in the industrial policy of, for example, Hungary.

Attractive as it is, the third pattern may not be achievable. Success in industrial development requires a combination of mutually reinforcing changes at company level as well as on institutional and political-economic levels.

The contributors to the present volume have researched the interplay of institutions, changing structures at micro, meso- as well as macro-level and the resulting innovation in enterprises. From different angles they shed light on the ongoing processes and assess the possibilities for the countries of CEE to attain and sustain a pattern that will allow them to compete on terms comparable to those in advanced market economies.

Section 1:
Continuity and Change of Industrial Production Enterprises

Introduction

ANNE LORENTZEN, BRIGITTA WIDMAIER, MIHÁLY LAKI

On the eve of transition it was assumed that liberalisation and privatisation would have an impact on the development of companies and industries. The external pressures arising from competition and hard budget constraints it was thought, would lead to company restructuring including a more central role for technological innovation as a parameter of competition. The overall change of institutions would, in other words, produce incentives in favour of innovation. Many theoretical arguments in favour of this overall hypothesis can be found, but has reality borne out expectations?

At the aggregate level it could be seen that during the first phase the impact of liberalisation was rather destructive, leading to steep drops in sales and investment as well as high levels of unemployment, inflation and interest rates. This conjuncture would make any renewal at company level involving more than tiny costs, close to impossible. Access to capital was thus a key problem in CEE industry. Privatisation in itself would only bring investment if the new owner was able and prepared to invest, and this was generally the case only with foreign investors. Often privatisation has proved to be a slow process, as in Hungary, where many state-owned firms continued deficit-making operations, with help from the state. Finding private investors for existing companies could be a time consuming procedure that postponed renewals of industry.

Whether privately, publicly or foreign owned, industrial companies faced one new condition that in any case necessarily would precipitate a change in be-haviour: Central planning was abolished; big companies gradually split up and privatised; and decisions concerning investment, wages, employment, personnel, sales, procurement and so on were transferred to the decentralised company management. The new structure and institutions of industry implied a scope for flexibility that was new to CEE industry. One question that we pose in this section focuses on how this new possibility was used in terms of technological innovation and improved competitiveness. Given the new possibilities and the new incentives, how did the companies behave, and what did they do to adapt themselves to the new institutional setting? Moreover what was the outcome of this in terms of innovation? Can different innovation paths be identified and if so, how are they related to other characteristics within and outside the companies involved?

Our point of departure was the general hypothesis that innovation would gain importance as a result of the new incentives. However this hypothesis is very simplistic indeed, as it is based on the abstract idea that the only incentive operative would be competition. Reality, of course, is more complex and regarding incentives, a lot of coexisting and even contradicting incentives are like-ly to be found in any economy, where assessment of economic profit may conflict with expectations of political benefit. This is even more the case in an eco-nomy in transition, where old and newly established institutions, attitudes and perceptions coexist.

Aggregate data might contribute with documentation of processes of change going on in industry in terms of output (production and sales) or input (investment and employment). But to understand processes of change and their characteristics more thoroughly it seems fruitful to study actual developments on the basis of detailed knowledge of companies' reactions to their changed environments. The general acceptance of this view is reflected in the fact that the scholarly interest has shifted to transformation processes on enterprise level, and case studies have gained momentum as research methods in innovation research in CEE. The contributions selected for this section are in accordance, based on in- depth studies of selected companies in Hungary and the Czech Republic.

In her contribution, *Lorentzen* focuses on the way in which innovation takes place at the company level in Hungarian manufacturing, and on the interplay between companies and their institutional environments. During Communism Hungarian industry was characterised by a preponderance of heavy industry, vertical integration of production, and standardised mass production, mainly intended for the eastern markets. The challenges facing Hungarian industry after 1989 included the disappearance of markets and of supporting institutions, as well as non-competitive production. The questioning *Lorentzen* pursues involve the types of responses that have been developed by companies in terms of innovation. In brief, she found that the response of companies consists mainly of a widening of the product range in order to meet new markets. Minor renewal of the generally very old machinery and equipment has been made, but funds for major changes have been lacking. Organisational and management styles continue largely unchanged, as steep functionally divided pyramids, and this, it is argued represents an important barrier to innovation because the innovative potential of the organisation is not mobilised and used. Even though a certain upgrading of qualifications could be seen, the specialised qualification profile in Hungarian companies is seen as poorly suited for a more dynamic innovation effort involving larger segments of the organisation. A change of this picture towards a more advanced and innovative type of production would require not only a change of company strategy, but also focused policies regarding R and D, investment credits, and education.

Whitley and *Czaban* report from a study of 18 Hungarian enterprises. Their point of departure was the hypothesis that substantial change in different aspects of the enterprises would be the outcome of institutional and market changes in Hungary after 1989. The sample included different types of ownership, and the impact of ownership on enterprise behaviour was used as an independent variable in the investigation. As a general trend the authors found that the split-up of big companies resulted in organisational and   production specialisation, but also that within the new decentralised structure, decision making generally stayed very centralised even though responsibility had been transferred to production units. Production continued to be narrow in the sense that the companies only had one major production line, mostly mass-production, and hardly any product innovation was made. Differences between state-owned and foreign-owned companies were comparatively small, and generally speaking continuities with the state socialist period were strong. Today the monopolistic market position of big enterprises, high sunk cost in machinery and types of expertise available thus seem to limit not only the speed but also the scope of change in enterprise behaviour. Consequently the authors foresee incremental rather than radical changes in products and production technologies, even in foreign-owned companies, in the future.

One important aspect of privatisation and liberalisation is the flow of foreign direct investment (FDI) into the CEE economies. In his contribution *Myant* discusses the role of (FDI) to enterprise development and innovation in the Czech automobile industry. He describes how FDI has had a limited quantitative impact, because the Czech government had no clear strategy with regard to FDI.

The approach of the Czech government was that Czech components were to be used, employment was to rise, there should be as much capital investment as possible and plans should include exports to the West. Volkswagen agreed to invest in Skoda in 1991, which was attractive because of a monopolistic situation and a well-known name. The story was different for the Czech lorry producers, who rejected the proposals made by Western investors because they thought they could do without them.

According to the author the government tried to pressure Volkswagen but, in the end, had to accept Volkswagen's own plans which did not include Czech sourcing. However, as a result of the co-operation employment increased, new investments were made and a new car model was launched in 1996. The extensive global Volkswagen network helped to increase sales. The positive outcome of Skoda investment may be explained more by the global approach of Volkswagen than by the efforts of the Czech government.

The extent of start-up investment or green field investments outside the car components industry has been disappointing in the Czech Republic but, even though the government has not been very successful in negotiating with foreign partners, the author finds the role of government in setting the terms to be indispensable.

1 Technological Change in Hungarian Industry after 1989

ANNE LORENTZEN[1]

Introduction

The transition in Central and Eastern Europe (CEE) from a centrally planned to a market economy generally expected to have a positive impact on industrial innovation and competitiveness. This was the point of departure for a research project on technological change in Hungarian industry after 1989, which was formulated and carried out by researchers at Aalborg University, Denmark. The aim of the research was to detect the impact of liberalization and privatization on the industrial technological capacity in a formerly centrally planned economy, with Hungary as a case.

Innovation may take place along different lines, and competitiveness may be obtained in different ways, so the outcome of the newly introduced competitive pressure on local companies is not predictable. Two opposing scenarios may be outlined: One scenario which offers the countries of CEE a role as sub-suppliers of relatively simple industrial products, which compete through low wage costs. The main competitors in this scenario are found among the newly industrializing countries of the third world. The other scenario is one in which the companies and industries of CEE constantly innovate and produce advanced and specialized products. The competitors in this scenario are found among the advanced industrialized countries. Which of the two scenarios will be realized depends on the way innovation takes place at the company level and on the interplay between companies and their surroundings.

Technology change (or innovation) at the company level was the focus of the research project, and the specific aim was to assess the capability of the companies to develop their production technology flexibly according to the new challenges arising from global competition and structural and institutional changes following 1989.

When we began our research in 1993, hardly any research on the topic could be found, and we literally felt that we were starting from scratch. In the meantime several works on related topics have been published. Without entering into a thorough discussion we draw attention to the following recent contributions

7

which, from different approaches, have studied changes at plant level in Hungary and elsewhere in CEE after 1989.

In 1993 Hare and Oakey (Hare and Oakey, 1993) published a study of the diffusion of new process technologies, in casu CNC machine tools in the Hungarian machine building industry, based on plant level investigation in 175 plants during the period 1989-90. They combine a macroeconomic survey with their plant level findings. Based on data up to 1994 Zon (Zon, 1996) identifies different development paths based on a study of three types of industries in six countries, with the intention of identifying the role of ownership, institutional change, marketing methods, human resource management, innovation and R and D. Hitchens et al (Hitchens et al., 1995) made a matched plant comparison of a cross section of manufacturing companies in Hungary and the Czech Republic covering 40 companies in each country collecting data referring to 1989 and 1992, and they found that productivity was comparatively low in the two countries due to a series of factors (old machinery, lack of management qualifications and so on). They combine a macroeconomic survey with a sample study. Whitley et al (Whitley et al, 1996) studied the changes that took place between 1989 and 1993 in ten formerly state-owned enterprises (SOEs) in Hungary, and found a prevalent continuity in their personnel, product lines and strategies. Whitley (Whitley, 1997) studied the consequences for enterprise structure and actions of the radical transformation of the political and economic institutions in Slovenia and Hungary, finding that the consequences have been much less radical than was expected by many in 1990. Inzelt (forthcoming) has made an innovation survey in 110 enterprises, mainly former SOEs or cooperatives in Hungary. She found that the level of innovation was relatively low, expenditure on innovation modest, cooperation weak, and so on, and she pointed at a series of factors hampering innovation, factors that are both internal and external to the enterprises.

Both quantitative methods based on economic approaches (Hare and Oakey, Hitchens, Zon) and qualitative methods based on organization theories (Whitley and Whitley et al) as well as a combination of the two (Inzelt) are represented among these contributions. Most of the contributions are more encompassing in terms of amount of data than is ours. However, our contribution may add both methodologically and empirically to the study of industrial change and innovation in CEE.

The development of Hungarian industry during Communism

The general features of Hungarian industrialization between 1948-89 which are of special relevance for the research project will be briefly outlined. Changes in branch structure and localisation of industry, the centralization or amalgamation of companies and changes in the institutional framework will be touched upon.

The industrial policy of the communist era can be divided into five phases of so-called 'socialist industrialization'. The first phases were based on an extensive development of industry and the absorption of manpower, while a focus on a more intensive industrial development including technological development characterized the industrial policy since 1969. Finally, in the 1980s economic efficiency became a major concern (Bernat, [1985] 1989:103-105). An important component of the strategy of rapid industrialization was trade and the social division of labour within CMEA (Council for Mutual Economic Assistance). In 1981 58.1 per cent of Hungarian exports went to other socialist countries and 51.5 per cent of the imports to Hungary came from them (Bernat, [1985] 1989:313).

The first five year plans favoured investments in heavy industry, including the machine building industry which, as a consequence, grew substantially measured in number of employees between 1950-1965. The food industry, on the other hand, stagnated during this period (Berend and Ránki, 1985, tab. 8.5 p. 265). The relative neglect of the food industry did not continue as the modernization of industry which took place after 1969 included the food industry, which was considered an important earner of foreign currency.

The 1980s were characterized by slow or negative growth rates, and new investments were scarce. As a result of the industrial policy after 1948, heavy industry therefore still dominated Hungarian industry in 1989, although mining and metallurgy have shown signs of being in crisis since the mid 1980s.

The company structure was also formed by the Communist governments. In the beginning of the 1960s companies were amalgamated into tröszts (trusts). The tröszts were created as a coordinating and governing instance, to take over some of the responsibilities from the ministries and central governing bodies (Nielsen, 1978:50). Thus in 1975 the 779 state owned companies consisted of 5,387 separate production units (Nielsen, 1978:243). In industry the company structure has been compared with the Fordist structure developed in the US in the 1920s, which the Soviet Union copied in the 1930s and exported to the CEE after the Second World War (Foti, 1993).

The institutional framework guiding intra-firm as well as inter-firm relations was thus very different from those guiding such relations in a market economy. Since the 1960s the production units functioned inside a tröszt, consisting of other production units related to each other in a horizontal or a vertical division of labour, units that took care of construction and maintenance of machinery, energy provision and repair and maintenance. The tröszt was connected to a trade company and to a branch research institute at ministerial level. In this institutional structure the managers were employees, the success of whom depended on their ability to bargain with their superiors about production quotas, equipment for the company and goods and services for the employees, while salaries (in a market economy used as incentives) and investment could not be decided at the company level (Kornai, 1992 and interviews).

The conditions of industrial development after 1989

The situation of the manufacturing industry changed considerably after 1989. The first few years were characterized by crisis: the Hungarian home market shrank, the CMEA market disappeared, capital for investment became scarce and expensive, prices rose, and competition got tough. At the same time new markets in the West opened, and many Hungarian enterprises succeeded there, thus changing the bulk of foreign trade from CEE towards the West. The economic downturn did not last, and a moderate but steady economic upturn could be seen from 1993-1994, when the GDP grew by 3 percent (WIIW:1996:78).

Institutional reforms towards a market economy had already started in 1968 in Hungary. Reform initiatives accelerated during the 1980s and speeded up again after 1989, with liberalization and privatization as main issues. Both were introduced gradually in Hungary, and in manufacturing this implied radical market changes as well as the emergence of new private economic agents. The private sector that had begun to emerge in the 1980s expanded quite quickly after 1989, and an abundance of small and medium-sized enterprises emerged, particularly in services, but also in manufacturing, where the number of industrial companies (mainly small companies) between 1992-1993 alone increased by 20 per cent (Bank Austria, 1995). Privatization, which in Hungary was organized as the sale of state assets at market prices, appeared to be a slow process, and state ownership is still important in industry.

Government initiatives directed towards industry have consisted of privatization policy, job saving measures mainly in metallurgy, and of the attraction of

FDI (Foreign Direct Investment). Hungary became the main receiver of FDI, due to political, economic and geographical reasons, and as a result FDI plays a considerable role in manufacturing today, where the largest concentration of FDI can be found in the category 'foodstuffs and tobacco', followed by machinery (Bank Austria,1995:26). Other sources of capital are scarce, however, as banks and credit institutions which can match the needs of private companies still have to be developed.

The two branches focused upon in this study have experienced the changes after 1989 in very different ways. Machine building suffered a lot during the beginning of the 1990s, both for structural reasons and because of economic recession in Hungary. However, the number of enterprises has grown considerably, the export share has grown to 48.7 per cent (Bank Austria,1995:32), and FDI has found its way to Hungarian machine building, where today it controls a fourth of the capital of this branch. As a whole, machine building has started to grow again after 1993, along with the economic recovery in Hungary.

Food processing seems to have lived quietly through the economic turbulence of the 1990s. Goods were mainly sold in Hungary, and a small part was exported to the West, as usual. State ownership was still important, and soon foreign capital represented a very large share, namely 31 per cent of the capital of this industry (Bank Austria,1995:34), concentrated in few, relatively large companies.

Renewed regional disparities add to the problems of industrial development in Hungary today. The most trouble ridden industries are concentrated in specific geographical areas in the northeast of Hungary, while the most prosperous ones are found in the west and in Budapest.

In sum manufacturing companies in Hungary were faced with the following changes after 1989: Production units turned into private enterprises, based on different kinds of ownership, which suddenly had to cope with competition, without the regulating and supporting institutions of the planned economy, while old markets disappeared. Their legacy was mass production of standardized goods, and the question was what technology change the companies would, and could, choose to develop competitiveness under the new circumstances.

Methodological and theoretical approach

The study of technology change in Hungarian industry is based on qualitative interviews in twenty production companies involved in machine building and food processing. We chose these branches because of their present and historical importance in Hungary, and because of our own professional backgrounds

(Lorentzen, 1985 and 1994; Bjerring and Rostgaard, 1987 and Rostgaard, 1993). The interviews were carried out in 1994 and 1995. The interviews regarded changes at different levels within the companies as well as changes in the relations between the companies and their surroundings, that is, in the trade and inter-enterprise relations as well as in the use of and need for infrastructure. A basic idea was to consider innovation at company level as a result of an inter-play between different factors, the priority of which could not be decided on beforehand. Concepts of 'the technological capacity of society' (Lorentzen, 1988) and Porter's Diamond (Porter, 1990) inspired the approach which focuses on qualitative aspects of technology change.

Economic development is a result of changes in many different areas of society. It can be perceived as the result of society's capacity to change its production of goods and services according to changing needs and according to changing circumstances. A term for this capacity is 'The technological capacity of society' (Lorentzen 1988). The technological capacity of society forms and determines the innovation processes in production. The focal point in the approach is *change of technology* at enterprise level. The concept of technology encompasses machinery and equipment, knowledge, organization and products.

Technology is embedded in socio-economic structures which determine the path along which technology is changed. Thus 'the social division of labour' (structure of production and market structure) determines the viable degree of specialisation and sophistication of products and processes. The 'infrastructure' is a lever or a barrier to the intensification of the social division of labour and the specialization and sophistication of technology. Banks, roads and schools are examples of infrastructure. Such structures are enabling or disabling for the change of technologies, including the emergence of new ones.

While structures are determining, actual changes depend on *agency*. When technology is to be changed, decisions must be taken , and these decisions must be implemented by social agents, for example by the enterprise management, as well as other social units. The capability of social agents to undertake technology change is mainly related to their *motivation*, their decision making capability and to their competence to install and operate the technology.

Motivation is not only related to the structural development paths but also to the institutions prevailing in society (Lorentzen and Rostgaard,1997:34). Institutions (the market, legislation) produce incentives (competition and profits, a subsidy) which encourage or discourage technology change. Correspondingly a change of institutions implies a change of incentives, and finally a change of the motivation of the social agents to change technology. In periods of transition old and new institutions may coexist, resulting in conflicting incentives (Nagy, 1994, Lorentzen, 1996).

In sum a variety of societal conditions interact and determine the direction of technology change. Using an approach similar to Michael Porter's (Porter, 1990), the focus here is on the company level, and the determinants we consider have parallels to the determinants suggested in 'the diamond'. By comparison, Porter's determinants are more specifically related to modern industry in the present phase of capitalism. In our study we have particularly drawn on his insights concerning the role of supplying and related industries as well as the demand conditions, and the interaction between societal structures and companies through the strategy (or agency) of the companies.

Boyer (1989) adds *phases* to the approach. With a focus on work organization and management forms he touches upon comparable societal determinants and the interplay between these and changing technology. Based on the argument that a sophistication of demand in the Western world exerts a pressure in favour of flexible production systems, he shows how a Fordist industrial model is being ousted by new industrial models based on information technology, flexible work organization, flexible supplier relations and new types of supporting institutions. The argument about the crisis of Fordism is important to bear in mind in a study of manufacturing in Eastern Europe, because Fordist principles have inspired the Soviet Union and later Central and Eastern Europe in relation to the planning of industry. In brief the Fordist principles of industrial production are a vertical integration of production, mass production, production of standardized products, centralization of decision making, hierarchic control and a specialization of tasks (Boyer,1989 p. 10). If this model is challenged in the West, it is likely to be under pressure in CEE as well, because these countries face the same changes of demand, exposed as they are to the world market.

In the following a brief overview of the main conclusions from our research will be given. The analysis is based on information from enterprise managers. In the first section the micro level technology changes are analysed, then follows an analysis of the changes in trade structure and in interfirm relations. The final part of the analysis detects infrastructural barriers to technological innovation. In the conclusion both branch specific, regionally different and general problems and potentials are listed.

Technology change in companies

Technology change at the company level was the focus of our research, and we intended to characterize the kind of technology change that has taken place in the companies studied since 1989, if any. One analytical guideline was a question of whether there were any signs that the companies moved away from Fordist inspired mass production towards more specialised production. The second question concerned the 'radicality' of innovation, and whether or not innovative activities (that earlier belonged to research institutes) took place at company level.

Product changes

First the changes in products will be characterized. In general product changes reflect the total innovative capability of the company, which arises from the combined application of technique, knowledge and organization. Moreover product changes reflect the ability of the company to respond to changes in its environment. We will first look at the changes since 1989 in terms of product range (number of different products) as a rough measure of whether there is a tendency to specialize. After that we will look at the quality of the changes made.

Our interviews showed that the product range was quite broad among the sample companies at the time of the interview. Table 1.1 illustrates the extent to which this situation had changed after 1989.

Table 1.1 Change of product range (number of different products) during the last five years, number of firms and *per cent*

	Decrease		Increase		No change	
All companies (20)	4	*20*	13	*65*	3	*15*
Machine building (11)	4	*36.4*	6	*54.5*	1	*9.1*
Food processing (9)	0	*0*	7	*77.7*	2	*22.2*

The table shows that, contrary to what we had expected, namely a certain product specialization, most companies had increased their product range. As the table shows, 65 per cent of the companies told us that they had expanded their product range since 1989. Only one fifth of the companies had decreased their product range (specialized). The companies that had specialized belonged to the machine building branch, but well over half the machine building companies had increased their product range. The increase of product range was most widespread among food producers, where 78 per cent of the companies reported an increase. In sum there was not a movement towards product specialization, but the contrary. As one company leader said:

'The number of products has increased, very considerably increased, during the last five years. Especially the domestic scope of various items increased at least by 40 per cent during the last five years. So we considerably extended what we could offer the potential buyers'.

Secondly, we wanted to characterize the changes in qualitative terms. In doing so, we divided the product changes into three categories. *Adaptation* is a change based on existing knowledge and technique, for example changes in size or proportions. *Development* denotes a change in existing products, based on major efforts in the company (research and/or development activities) whereas *alternative products* denotes the introduction of a new product, not previously produced, but based on the existing knowledge.

Table 1.2 Introduction of new products during the last five years, number of firms and *per cent*

	Yes	No	1. Adaptation		2. Alternative products		3. Development	
All companies (20)	18 *90*	2 *10*	10	*55.5*	5	*27.8*	4	*22.2*
Machine building (11)	11 *100*	0 *0*	5/11	*45.4*	4	*36.4*	3	*27.3*
Food processing (9)	7 *77.8*	2 *22.2*	5/7	*71.4*	1	*14.3*	1	*14.3*
Györ (7)	6 *85.7*	1 *14.3*	3/6	*50*	1/6	*6.6*	2/6	*33.3*
Budapest (8)	7 *87.5*	1 *12.5*	4/7	*57.1*	3/7	*42.9*	0	*0*
Miskolc (5)	5 *100*	0 *0*	3/5	*60.0*	1/5	*20.0*	2/5	*40.0*

N=20   N=18 (=Yes category)

Note: sums are more than one hundred as one company reported two types of product development.

From table 1.2 we can see that most companies, namely 90 per cent, had introduced new products since 1989. The branches differ in that all machine building companies had introduced new products, while less food producers had done so. Most of these changes were 'adaptations'. Alternative products had been introduced in 27 per cent of the companies, while new products had been developed in 22 per cent of them. The main difference between the two branches was that more machine building industries than food producing industries have introduced alternative products (36 per cent), and this is probably due to the problems of excess capacity in machine building. As one company expressed it:

> 'the Hungarian customers needed less spare parts, and therefore we have developed this gas container. It was in 1991-92. We were forced to use the capacity of the personnel.'

Looking at the regional differences, adaptation is in focus everywhere, but while Budapest companies prefer alternative products, the Miskolc and Győr companies prefer new products based on their own development efforts.

Machinery and equipment

Machinery and equipment make a difference when it comes to product quality and price, so part of our investigation was directed at changes at the level of production technique since 1989.

Age is used as a rough measure of how modern and up-to-date the production machinery is while another key indicator used is whether the machinery is computer-controlled or computer-assisted or not. This coincides roughly with the age of the machinery. CNC (computer numerically controlled) machines and modern machining centres are, especially in the machine building industry, a prerequisite for running a flexible and specialized production which is also cost-effective. To specialize is also a question of producing high quality products and therefore modern and up-to-date machinery is required. Below we will first characterize the existing machinery by using age as the basic indicator. Second quantitative as well as qualitative changes in machinery and equipment in the period 1989-1994/95 will be summarized.

Table 1.3 shows that the machinery in general is fairly old (more than 20 years). The oldest machinery was in general found in the machine building industry. There are, however, one or two exceptions to that. Especially one of the companies in the machine building industry had an assembly of machinery consisting of modern CNC machines. Some of the other companies had one or two CNC machines, while the rest of the machinery consisted of NC (numerically controlled) or conventional machines. The machinery in the food industry was in general newer, and may in the majority of the companies be characterized as fairly modern, traditional machinery. An analysis of regional differences clearly shows that the most modern and up-to-date machinery is to be found among the Győr companies. In general, however, we may conclude that the assembly of machinery does not constitute a basis for employment either of a modern flexible production nor of a specialized production. As one company describes it:

> 'Well, machinery level is very low. They are old and bad, very bad machines that we've got..I am sure that we have them for more than 20 years, more than 50 years. There are some museum pieces, and there are some newer ones..We have got two quite new machines..'

Table 1.3 Age of machinery and equipment, number of companies and *per cent*

	Below 10 years		10-20 years		More than 20 years	
All companies (19)	3	*16*	7	*37*	9	*47*
Machine building (10)	2	*20*	2	*20*	6	*60*
Food processing (9)	1	*11*	5	*56*	3	*33*
Győr (6)	2	*33.3*	3	*50.0*	1	*16.6*
Budapest (8)	1	*12.5*	2	*25.0*	5	*62.4*
Miskolc (5)	0	*0*	2	*40*	3	*60*

The changes in machinery and equipment which have taken place are summarized in table 1.4. In the table 'no changes' is a self explanatory category. 'Small changes' denote that a few pieces of new machinery or equipment have been added and 'considerable changes' denote that more pieces of machinery have been bought or, in some cases, that a renewal of a total department has taken place.

Table 1.4 Scope of change in machinery and equipment during the last five years, number of companies and *per cent*

	No changes		Small changes		Considerable changes	
All companies (20)	7	*35*	8	*40*	5	*25*
Machine building	6	*55*	4	*36*	1	*9*
Food processing	1	*11*	4	*44*	4	*44*

The table shows that a large part of the companies, namely 35 per cent, had made no changes, and that the changes in general must be characterized as modest. The exception is the one company in the machine building industry already mentioned and a number of companies in the food industry. The table shows that there is a remarkable difference between the two branches, as more than half of the machine building companies had not renewed their machinery since 1989, while most of the food processing companies had made as renewals, half of them even making considerable changes. This difference may be explained by the different economic situation of the two branches, as outlined above.

An analysis of the regional dimension (not included in the table) shows that four of the five companies with 'considerable changes' are located in Győr.

In the machine building industry the new machines added are normally CNC machines. There are different reasons for investing in new machines, one of which is that it is difficult to get reliable sub-suppliers and therefore it has been necessary to supplement the assembly of machinery (integration of production). Another reason stated is the desire to be able to produce products of superior quality. In the food industry the reasons stated for investing in new machinery are to save costs (labour and/or energy), to be able to produce a new special product (specialize), or to improve the quality of products.

As a whole there is a considerable dependence on old and outdated machinery, and this necessarily has got consequences for productivity and product quality.

Organization and personnel

The introduction of a market economy represents a challenge to the way production was organized until 1989, and the qualifications hitherto sufficient at plant level. This is so firstly because of the split up and the privatization of companies; secondly because cost efficiency has become a major requirement; finally because Fordist inspired management forms are challenged by new, more efficient management forms among competitors. One of the questions was how the companies responded to these challenges by organization changes, by changes in the qualification profile, and in the organization of innovative activities.

If we start by looking at changes in the organisational structure since 1989, sixteen of the twenty companies have made changes. The main form of change is a reduction in number of departments, and establishment of new departments in finances, sales, marketing and quality control. The reduction in number of departments is related to a reduction in staff. The new departments may be seen as necessary adjustments to the market economy.

There is a difference between the two branches. The companies that report no change all belong to machine building, while all food producing companies had changed their organization in one way or the other. The changes made included the establishment of new departments and the delegation of responsibility from top management level to punctional managers (Lorentzen and Rostgaard, 1997: 108-110). The resulting structure of organization can be seen in table 1.5.

Table 1.5 The organizational structure of the companies, number of companies and *per cent*

	Functional division	Hierarchic, 'top-down'	Delegation of responsibility	Horizontal coordination
All companies (19)	18 *94.7*	15 *78.9*	3 *15.8*	2 *10.5*
Machine building (11)	11 *100*	7 *63.4*	3 *27.3*	1 *9.1*
Food processing (8)	8 *100*	8 *100*	0 *0*	1 *12.5*

Note: No significant regional differences detected

Table 1.5 shows that almost all the enterprises are characterized by a functional division of labour and a hierarchic 'top-down' management style. Our data indicate that the food industry is more often hierarchically organized than machine building, where a delegation of responsibility and a more 'loose' organization can be found.

The general picture is however, that the type of organization prevailing in Hungarian industry is a Fordist type of organization with centralized decision making and a top-down management style. It is our impression that a 'strong' top management and direct control of decisions by the top manager in a number of companies can be interpreted as a necessary reaction to the new crucial role of enterprise management in a market economy.

At the shop floor level organizational changes can also be found. Unfortunately our data on work organization are relatively scarce, but findings related to the question of productivity may indicate the types of change in work organization that have taken place.

Table 1.6 How were changes in productivity achieved? Number of companies and *per cent*

	Machine building		Food processing		Total	
People work harder	0	*0*	2	*33*	2	*20*
Work harder/organization changes	3	*75*	1	*17*	4	*40*
Combination of org. and techn. changes	1	*25*	3	*50*	4	*40*

Table 1.6 summarizes our information about changes in work organization. The category 'people work harder/more' denotes an enforcement of discipline (for which a strong management is needed). Work harder in combination with organization changes denotes a change in work organization (e.g. that jobs have become multi-tasked and productivity increased (compared with the old one-man-one-job tradition). The last category means that machinery has been changed along with changes in work organization to increase productivity.

Table 1.6 shows that the organization of work has been changed in about half of the companies, and that the machine building industry mainly has done so by broadening the individual job profiles, whereas the changes that have taken place in the food industry seem to be more based on disciplining and efficiency obtained through a combination of technical changes and a taylorisation of jobs. Altogether the work organisation in the food industry seems to be a Fordist inspired type of mass production, whereas the machine building industry seems to have changed to a work organization which has become a little more flexible.

Qualifications have changed a great deal since 1989, both from a structural perspective and in terms of content. At present the qualification structure of the companies includes a high share of skilled workers, a relatively high share of white collar workers and a relatively heavy layer of management. Qualitatively speaking individual qualifications seem to be specialized or narrow. This implies an opposition in terms of qualifications between shop floor and management because most of the latter hold university degrees (Lorentzen and Rostgaard, 1997:83 ff). Since 1989 the share of skilled workers has increased, the share of white collar workers has decreased a little and top management has expanded. New skills have also been added. The two branches have undergone different kinds of change on this point. The machine building companies have increased the share of skilled workers, due to dismissals of redundant labour among the unskilled, and skilled workers have been retrained. In food processing the changes have taken place at management level, where new qualifications related to management in a market economy have been added. As a whole, modest changes in the qualification profile have been obtained, but it contains important Fordist principles and also potential problems, namely the narrow specialization of individual skills and the opposition of skills between different groups within the organization. However the high level of skills represents an important potential for innovation in products and processes.

This brings us to the innovation activities which, as previously mentioned, have only recently become a responsibility at company level. We wanted to know how this activity was organized today. We thus asked the companies who contributed new ideas, who made decisions and then how the new ideas were implemented.

Our interviews showed that top management level came up with 45 per cent of the ideas for product innovations, lower levels of management with 45 per cent of the ideas, while the shop floor level came up with only 10 per cent of the new ideas (Lorentzen and Rostgaard, 1997:p 124). Ideas for process innovations were not quite as centralized, as the shop floor contributed 25 per cent of these (op cit p. 133). The limited number of new ideas contributed from the shop floor level, seen in combination with the high level of skills at the shop floor, is an indication of an unused innovative potential at this level, which may be explained by the hierarchic, top down management style of the companies. Our impression was that also the implementation of new ideas was a very top-down process.

Changes in trade structure and inter-firm relations

The internal changes of the companies cannot be understood without reference to the external relations of the enterprises. In Hungary, the change of regulation system from planned and indirect supply and demand relations, managed, for example through trade companies, to market based and direct supply relations is an institutional change which was likely to have a great importance for the companies. The market-based supply and demand relations are thus more unstable and more direct than the planned relations were, and the ability to manage these relations are among the required capabilities of a company operating in a market environment.

Market changes

Our analysis shows that the geography of trade has changed considerably after 1989, and that both continuity and change characterize the trade relations of the companies we visited.

The open borders had been used by practically all companies to develop export contact to the West, but one third of the companies continued to export to Central and Eastern Europe.

The two branches studied have experienced the market changes in very different ways. Machine building companies, which on a whole have high export shares, point at changes in international trade relations, while there supposedly is continuity in the structure of the Hungarian market. Half of them have lost markets in CEE, and 64 per cent of them have increased exports to the West.

The food producing companies which sell their products mainly in Hungary, feel the changes mainly as a decrease in the size of Hungarian customers. The disappearance of centralized trading companies and big state-owned companies is perceived as a steep increase in the number of customers to be dealt with.

Regional differences can also be seen, as Györ companies, close as they are to the Austrian border, stress increased exports to the West. Around Miskolc, on the other hand, the loss of the CEE market is a serious problem for the companies, who try to compensate for this loss by exports to the West. Budapest companies also lament the loss of CEE markets and have increased their western exports instead.

Table 1.7 Principal market changes since 1989, as the companies see them, number of companies *and per cent*

	Competition		CE markets gone		WE exports increase		Branch diversification		Customer size decrease	
All companies (19)	3	15.8	7	36.8	7	36.8	2	10.5	6	31.6
Machine building	2	18.2	5	45.5	7	63.6	2	18.2	0	0
Food processing	1	12.5	2	25	0	0	0	0	6	75
Györ (7)	1	14.3	0	0	2	28.6	0	0	5	71.4
Miskolc(5)	0	0	3	60	2	40	0	0	0	0
Budapest(7)	2	28.6	4	57.1	3	42.9	2	28.6	1	14.3

Foreign owned companies might be expected to focus particularly on export to the West. The two examples we have of foreign owned companies belong to the machine building branch, and they were about to enter a role as subsuppliers to foreign companies, one directly linked as a machining department to the mother company abroad, the other as producer and supplier of simple parts to the open market in the West.

On the whole, liberalization has induced the companies to seek customers in the West, and this is likely to represent an important stimulus to technological change in the companies.

Inter-enterprise relations

While contact to final users was indirect before 1989, a change in relationship to customers necessarily had to develop as a consequence of liberalization and privatization. The companies might in principle choose between two approaches, namely to address the anonymous market or to address, and to establish contact with, the individual customers. The latter direct contact may represent an important source of information for the companies and may serve as an impetus for innovation.

Our interviews showed that the companies very quickly made their own direct linkages to their customers. This may have been the most obvious strategy in a situation where general market institutions were not developed. In machine building direct contact between customers and producers had existed before 1989, but the power balance has changed in favour of the former:

'Five years ago the customer who placed the order gave a present, and now the producers give the presents to the customers. So in Hungary the situation has changed.'

'I will tell you something about the old days. We had a system in which the Hungarian company only had the allowance to import, if it had an approval from us, that we could not deliver this product. Under such conditions the customer was the last. Today the customer is the king!'

In food processing the disappearance of trade companies and the split up of the tröszts meant that the companies for the first time have been able to establish direct links with the customers and their market.

The contact with the customers was used in different ways. As the machine building companies mostly produce customized products they discussed pro-duct specifications with the customers (75 per cent of the companies). The food producing companies discussed product specification to some extent, and in addition they stressed a process of feed back from the customers, mostly supermarket chains, as to the taste, package and so on, of their products.

'As I said, we have 400 partners, and new own shops. In our own shops we often make taste. We pose different questions and ask what they want, what they think of our product, is it cheap or expensive, is it good or not.'

Györ companies stressed continuous feed back from customers more than companies elsewhere, and Miskolc and Budapest companies mostly stressed the discussion of product specification with their customers. Both have a great importance as input of information to the innovation activities of the companies.

With some caution we can say that feed back from customers is new in a Hungarian context, while product specification is not. On this background we can say that in terms of branch food producers, and in terms of region the companies in Györ, have developed customer relations most radically.

Product development in a cooperation between customers and sample companies was not very widespread, as only 5 companies (3 from machine building and 2 from food processing) reported about such cooperation. There were no branch or regional characteristics of these 5 firms, but another important factor characterises them: Three of the cases were connected to requirements from foreign customers.

'We prepared certain samples, sent them out, and they made their remarks, they wanted a different shape, different taste, different composition, or slightly different, made their suggestions, and then again, price calculations and what ever. So this is cooperation really..that is a foreign customer, that is an export market.'

Supplies and suppliers

A change in the structure and quality of supplies is a precondition for a techno-logical change in terms of product development at enterprise level. Open bor-ders and the split up and privatization of companies after 1989 have challenged the supply structure of the planned economy, characterized by a high degree of internal integration of production in tröszts or big state-owned companies. We expected to find an increasing degree of out-sourcing as well as a focus on high quality inputs, including increased imports.

Table 1.8 summarizes the companies' comments on changes concerning the origin of their supplies.

Table 1.8 Changes concerning origin of supplies, number of companies and
per cent

	Change		No change		More imports		New supply structure		Other	
All companies	11	*96.1*	1	*8.3*	4	*44.4*	5	*55.5*	3	*25*
Machine building	5	*83.3*	1	*16.7*	(5) 3	*60*	2	*40*	0	*0*
Food processing	6	*100*	0	*0*	(4) 1	*25*	3	*75*	3	*50*

N=12   N=9

As table 1.8 illustrates, all companies but one had experienced changes concerning the origin of their supplies. Only one machine building company did not report any change, because the physical location of the supplier was the same, but the supplier had been privatized and split up since 1989.

The main change for the machine building companies was that they imported much more than before 1989. These companies benefitted from better import possibilities, both for quality reasons and because they could find cheaper inputs abroad. As a result, in 1995, 82 per cent of the machine building companies imported supplies from outside Hungary, and they wanted to continue their search for new and better suppliers in the future as well.

Food producers felt the change as an alteration of the supply structure. The suppliers of the food industry belong to agriculture, which before 1989 was organized as big agro-industrial complexes with stable internal supply relations. These agricultural complexes were gradually privatized, and instead of one stable supplier the food industry now had to address hundreds of small private farmers, who are less productive and have fewer resources than the state farms. This difficulty induced food producers to search for inputs from outside Hungary as well (33 per cent did that in 1995), but they hoped to increase their use of Hungarian supplies in the future.

Seen in relation to innovation at the company level, the changed supply structure is potentially favourable to machine building industries, while food processing industries have experienced great troubles in this area.

There were neither regional nor ownership differences in the above picture.

Apart from changes in the origin of supplies, a changed structure of supplies could have been expected as a consequence of the privatization and split up of companies. However, the companies we visited were mostly characterized by a very high degree of internal integration of production, implying that all production phases took place inside the company, and that most components were manufactured there as well.

Particularly the food industry based its production (of sausages, flour, frozen foods) exclusively on raw materials (which contrary to earlier are not grown 'in-house'). The machine building industry equally produces on the basis of raw material. Only half of them purchase components from other producers. Half of them subcontract part of the production, not because they intend to specialize, but because of capacity problems, as some of them reported. A regional difference is that companies around Györ seem to specialize more than others, while companies in Miskolc are more vertically integrated than others.

The high degree of internal integration of production may reflect an underdeveloped supply structure as well as a bias in the companies to continue as usual. In any case a high degree of internal integration of production is in contradiction with a focused strategy of product or process development which would allow the companies to compete in the area of high quality products.

Inter-enterprise relations

Suppliers, like customers, may represent an important source of innovation for production companies, depending on the way the two parties relate to each other. Before 1989 supplies were basically centrally regulated. In a market economy oducers have to address suppliers, either anonymously, as in a Fordist oduction system, or more personally, as in the 'new system'.

As expected most companies of our sample (86 per cent) had changed the ay they cooperate with their suppliers. The food producing companies had all anged the way they cooperate with their suppliers, while some of the machine uilding companies continued as before, as they already had personal contacts suppliers.

Apart from the fact that all companies had developed direct contact to ppliers, the most important changes in their relationship to suppliers were the llowing:

One third of the companies had externalized part of their production, namely raw materials, as the old company was split up.

As something new, contracts had been introduced between suppliers and the oducing company. It was mainly food producing companies that needed to :fine the obligations of the suppliers, because their supplier situation, as entioned above, looked more chaotic, while supplier relations were generally ore informal in machine building. Quality requirements to suppliers had also :en sharpened, and contacts to suppliers had become more frequent than :fore. In order to secure quantity and quality of supplies, one food producing)mpany gave assistance to suppliers. A manager in a machine building)mpany reported:

'We have not changed suppliers, but we made a remark that the supplier had to reach the quality if we were still to buy from him.'

he food producers were more formal, as they had more problems to solve:

'The written guide lines, spraying plans, preparation of the fields, the treatment of the harvest, this is written down so that you always know what quality comes from the field, and when it does not, then the problems can better be discussed. That is a double safety measure, that you have such things written down, because we can plan according to that.'

seemed from our interviews that the food producers had completed their change : supplier relations, while the machine building industries were just about to art. Those who envisaged changes pointed to continued quality control, long-rm supply contracts as well as an externalization of production to suppliers.

These changes have implications for product development, both quantita-vely and qualitatively, and they imply the possibility to specialize production. owever, direct cooperation with suppliers about changes in products also took place, namely in almost 60 per cent of the companies. Among machine building companies both new product development and quality changes sometimes involved supplier cooperation; among food producers suppliers were mainly involved in quality changes of the products.

In sum changes had occurred in the trade structure and in inter-firm relations which have importance for innovation at the company level: Exports to the West and requirements from foreign customers for product development, as well as the pressure to please customers, implies a focus on product quality and adaptation of products to customer needs. New institutions (for example feedback mechanisms) between customers and producers serve as a channel of information for innovation.

Access to imported inputs, which the companies benefit from, stimulate quality development in machine building, while a deconcentration of agricultural supplies represents rather an impediment to quality development in food processing. Both branches used suppliers as sources of information for innovation. Food processing did so in a formalized way, machine building in a less formal way.

Neither the structure of demand nor the structure of supplies seemed to invite the producers to specialize their production, and a high internal integration of production continues to be a characteristic of Hungarian companies, and a barrier to a strategy of focused product or process development.

Companies around Györ tend to specialize production more than others and they focus more on interfirm relations, both regarding customers and suppliers, as a source of innovation. On one point foreign ownership made a difference, as foreign-owned firms had found a role as international sub-suppliers to Western companies.

Infrastructural barriers to technological innovation

Technological changes taking place at the enterprise level also depend on the infrastructure. Infrastructure may act as a lever or barrier to technological innovation, and it may co-determine the direction of change at enterprise level. We have tentatively divided the infrastructure into technological, social (the education system), financial and physical (transportation and telecommunication) aspects and will in the following section summarize the most important findings from our company interviews.

The sample companies were in general satisfied with the *technological infrastructure,* that is institutions and organizations from which know-how and information about new types of machinery and equipment, product development and market trends are sourced. If we look at the patterns that have emerged since 1989 regarding utilization of the technological infrastructure, they differ very clearly between the two industries studied. The *food industry* makes rather intensive use of the central research institutes that existed also prior to 1989. In the food industry these research institutes have managed to transform themselves and thus live on, in spite of budget cuts and so on, as a valuable part of the technological infrastructure in Hungary, whereas the central research institutes in the machine building industry have disappeared. Altogether, many companies in the food industry seem to have developed sourcing of know-how and information into a rather systematic activity. As a spokesman from one company in the food industry told us:

> 'We are ordering every year or making a contract with them (the research institute) regarding....what is happening on the market in machinery and products. In product development we are giving them a guideline on what kind of products we would like to improve, and there are meetings where they show us what is the result of the [development] work, cutting the new products, and if the product has the right taste, on the first examination, we start industrial experiment. We try to produce a small quantity.'

The machine industry makes most extensive use of their customers and suppliers for acquisition of knowledge as well as information about possible product and process development. The extensive utilization of other companies/customers and suppliers as an important source may make the machine industry too dependent on chance. One company expressed it this way:

> 'We have made such containers earlier, but it was not pressure tanks, only ordinary containers. That meant that we had to learn a little more in this direction, or look a little on how we could make these pressure tanks...We looked in the literature. And we have visited some Hungarian manufacturers, and we have exchanged our experiences.'

According to the statements in the interviews the *education system* represents a more immediate barrier to technological change. A majority of the companies see a lack of employees with the right qualifications as a barrier to technological change as the summation in table 1.9 shows.

Table 1.9 Is it a problem to find people with the right qualifications?
Answers distributed by branches, number of companies and
per cent

	No	Yes	Yes, managers	Yes, workers
All companies 20=100%	8 40	12 60	5 25	7 35
Machine building 11 companies=100%	5 45	6 55	2 18	4 36
Food processing 9 companies = 100%	3 33.3	6 66.6	3 33.3	3 33.3

The table shows that a majority of the companies have had problems finding employees with the right qualifications. This picture is supported by Hitchens et al, (Hitchens et al. 1996:184) who points to a general mismatch in Hungary between the supply of and the demand for skills. Our research adds some details to that picture. Problems mentioned related to middle managers were people trained in financial management, people with sufficient knowledge of foreign languages and people with qualifications in programming and maintaining computer systems. Problems related to workers were specified as finding people with the right technical skills as well as people with the right social skills (such as work discipline, responsibility). The analyses of the regional dimension showed that problems in finding employees with the right qualifications were most marked in the economically more dynamic Győr area (86 per cent of the companies), whereas this issue was of less importance in the two other regions, where employment did not grow (Lorentzen and Rostgaard, op.cit. p.210, table 22.3). Qualitatively the requirements of the Győr companies to the employees may also have been different, thus accentuating the problem of recruitment.

The second most important barrier to technological innovation, according to the statements made in our interviews, was the *financial infrastructure*. Fifty per cent of the companies in the sample mentioned lack of capital as a barrier to change (Lorentzen and Rostgaard, op.cit. p.223, table 24.3). A majority or 67 per cent of the companies in the machine industry mention lack of capital as a barrier, whereas only 33 per cent of the companies in the food sector see lack of capital as a problem (Lorentzen and Rostgaard loc.cit.).This can be seen as a major reason for the fact that, as already mentioned, companies in the food industry have machinery which in general is newer than that in the machine industry. Our analysis also shows that the companies in the food industry to a large extent have been able to finance investments out of their own surplus, whereas the machine industry to a large extent has had to resort to bank loans (Lorentzen and Rostgaard, op.cit. p.222, table 24.2).

A natural question is whether or not foreign investment, of which there is a considerable amount in the two branches, makes a difference. This does not seem to be the case in our sample. The five companies with the most substantial investments are all Hungarian owned, (private, public or Hungarian majority of shares). Regionally speaking there is no difference, and this means that branch is the most important explanation for the differences in the financial situation of the companies. Contrary to what might have been expected the physical infra-structure does not represent a barrier to the activities of the companies, according to the managers interviewed. Apart from a number of Miskolc companies they all state that they are satisfied with the existing physical infrastructure.

Summary and conclusion

What kind of technology change could we observe in the Hungarian companies studied, and how could this change be explained? Did branch, regional location or ownership play a role in the process of change taking place in the companies? Were Hungarian companies developing an inferior role in the international division of labour or were they on equal terms with their competitors in Western Europe?

Our analysis shows that there are important similarities in the technological development among the twenty companies, regardless of branch, location and ownership. This resemblance is due, on the one hand, to a shared heritage of the Fordist inspired Soviet type production organization. On the other hand, they are due to common structural and conjunctural conditions. In brief this techno-logical development can be characterized in the following way:

The companies are characterized by a high degree of internal integration, both horizontally and vertically. On the product side the companies offer a wide product range, which, due to problems of excess capacity and in an effort to meet customer requirements, has been widened since 1989. This widening of the product range is made on the basis of in-house adaptations, while few compa-nies have had the resources and the necessary support from the technological infrastructure to undertake more demanding product development. Concerning machinery and equipment, most of it is old and outdated. Small changes have been made, but only a few companies have had the resources to invest in new production lines. Those who have made major investments have found the resources in their own economic surplus. The low quality of machines and equipment has implications for productivity and for product quality.

In terms of organization and personnel a hierarchical top-down kind of management prevails, and the rationalization of the overall organization and of the work organization which has been made has not changed this management style. An upgrading of management has taken place in terms of number and in terms of qualifications, so that the companies could cope with the new tasks related to financing, marketing and so on. Unskilled labour has been fired, so that the general level of qualifications in production, which was already quite high, has increased since 1989. Our analysis indicates that the capability of the companies to generate innovation is severely affected by the hierarchical management style and by the specialized qualifications of the staff, which means that the innovative potential existing in production is not used. The changed possibilities for international trade and the recession in Hungary have made the companies seek customers in the West, and for some companies contacts with foreign customers have implied joint product development.

As branch differences we would like to point at the following: *Machine building,* making not only standard but also customized products, has been used to product changes in terms of adaptation, which they still make use of. Excess capacity has forced them to find alternative products too, and they also have a capability to develop new products even though the machinery is much older than in food processing, and the changes in machinery small. The capability to generate new products may be seen in relation to the tradition for customized products and the fact that organization is less formal and hierarchical, and the level of skills on the shop floor is higher.

The machine building companies have been forced to increase their Western exports due to the recession of both the Hungarian and the CEE market, and they have welcomed the access to supplies from the West as an important input to their product development. In terms of infrastructure, the machine building industry is in dire need of a financial infrastructure that can support a much needed renewal of machinery. An adequate technological infrastructure is missing for the machine industry, as a supplement to the ad hoc type of product development taking place today. The recruitment of adequately skilled personnel is a problem too. In sum, the external barriers to technological development in terms of infrastructure are many for the machine building industry, while their trade relations seem to be stimulating.

Food processing, on the other hand, makes continuous product adaptations, in cooperation with research institutes. The branch has generated enough surplus to invest in new machinery, and while they have not considered skills at the shop floor very much, they have focused on increased productivity. Management skills, on the other hand have been much in focus, and this, together with the reasonable financial situation, has allowed the food industry to develop a more strategic focus on company development. Continuity characterizes the market of the food industry, although a strong focus on consumer taste has developed. Unstable supplies, on the other hand, represent a major problem, both for production volume and quality, which the food industry seeks to solve in different ways. An immediate problem for the food industry is found in access to adequate skills. In the long term a development of the financial infrastructure will also be needed. The research institutes, in close contact as they are with the old food companies, might have to develop access to new private companies in the branch. In sum, the supply structure and the supply of skills represent serious external barriers to the development of the food processing industry.

As a whole the changed institutions after 1989 have not affected the Györ companies negatively. They have had no major problems, as they were used to contacts with Western companies. They have been comparatively innovative in products and processes. In Miskolc, on the other hand, where integration in CMEA was strong, the changes in institutions caused great problems, and their location today is peripheral. Our analysis shows that the Miskolc companies have fought to survive by introducing new products, while other changes are few, and the very old machinery represents a serious disadvantage. The Budapest companies, maybe too used to their favourable location, seem to have reacted less to the institutional changes than companies elsewhere.

With caution we can thus point to the first scenario as the most probable for Hungarian industry: For many different reasons related to internal as well as external factors such as we have pointed out, advanced technological development in products and processes is hampered, and the technology change that takes place is relatively simple and inexpensive. The companies will then end up as suppliers of comparatively simple and low cost products. Clear examples of this are found in machine building already.

A change in this global trend towards the second, more attractive scenario, requires a focused policy of selective credits for innovation, a new structure of technological research and information institutes, a reformed education system and new management practices. The question is, would that be possible?

Note

1 This article takes its point of departure in Lorentzen and Rostgaard (1997). While Marianne Rostgaard declined from participating in writing this article, I thank her for her valuable cooperation during the empirical research, on which it is based.

References

Bank Austria (1995), *The Pioneer of Reforms, Hungary.* Vienna, December.
Berend, Ivan T. and György Ranki, (1985), *The Hungarian economy in the twentieth century.* Croom Helm. London and Sidney.
Bernát, Tivadar (ed.) [1985] (1989), *An economic geography of Hungary.* Akadémiai Kiadó, Budapest.
Bjerring, Bodil and Rostgaard, Marianne (1987), *Kvinders kvalifikationer, ny teknologi og fremtidens industrielle arbejdsmarked i Nordjylland. Delrapport II. Kvindeprofiler - Jobprofiler - Uddannelsesprofiler.* Institut for Samfundsudvikling og Planlægning. Aalborg Universitet.
Boyer, Robert (1989), New directions in management practices and work organization. General principles and national trajectories. Working paper. *OECD conference: Technological change as a social process - society, enterprises and the individual.* Helsinki. 11-13 December 1989.
Foti, Klara (1993), Lessons for Industrial Restructuring: Experiences of some Hungarian Enterprises. *Institute of Development studies. Discussion Paper 322.*
Hare, Paul and Ray Oakey (1993), *The diffusion of new process technologies in Hungary. Eastern European Innovation in Perspective.* Pinter Publishers. London.
Hitchens, D.M.W.N., J.E. Birnie, J. Hamar, K. Wagner, A. Zemplinerová, (1996) *Competitiveness of Industry in the Czech Republic and Hungary.* Avebury, Aldershot.
Inzelt, Annamária, (forthcoming), For a better understanding of the innovation process in Hungary. G. Hutschenreiter, M. Knell and S. Radosevic (eds): *Restructuring Innovation systems in Eastern Europe.* Edward Elgar, Great Britain.
Kornai, János (1992), *The socialist system. The political economy of communism.* Clarendorn Press, Oxford.
Lorentzen, Anne, (1985), *Capital Goods and Technological Development in Mexico.* CDR Research Report no 7. Copenhagen.

Lorentzen, Anne (1988), *Technological capacity. A contribution to a comprehensive understanding of technology and development in an international perspective.* Technology and Society Series no 5, Aalborg University Press. Aalborg.

Lorentzen, Anne [1992] (1994), *Teknologi og udvikling i den nordjyske maskinindustri.Rapport over en virksomhedsundersøgelse.* Aalborg Universitetsforlag, Aalborg.

Lorentzen, Anne, (1996), Regional development and institutions in Hungary. *European Planning Studies,* vol. 4, no. 3, pp. 259-277.

Lorentzen, Anne and Marianne Rostgaard, (1997), Technological change in Hungarian Industry after 1989 – results form empirical research in 20 Hungarian enterprises. Aalborg University, Department of Development and Planning.

Nagy, András, (1994), Transition and institutional change. *Structural and economic dynamics.* Vol. 5, no. 2 pp. 315-327.

Nielsen, Margit (1978), *Ungarn - økonomi og reform.* Sydjysk Universitetsforlag, Esbjerg.

Porter, Michael E (1990), *The competitive advantage of nations.* MacMillan, London and Basingstoke.

Rostgaard, Marianne (1993), *Changing Non-Skilled Women's Jobs in Industry.* Report from the Danish ATHENA Project. Aalborg University, AUC-Servicecenter.

Whitley, Richard, J. Henderson, L. Czaban and G. Lengyel, (1996), Continuity and Change in an emergent market economy: The limited transformation of large enterprises in Hungary. Richard Whitley and Peer Hull Kristensen: *The changing European firm. Limits to convergence.* Routledge, London and New York, pp. 210-238.

Whitley, Richard, (1997), State Socialist legacies and enterprise development in Eastern Europe: Hungary and Slovenia compared. Paper presented to the 13th EGOS Colloquium "Organizational responses to Radical Environmental Changes" held in Budapest 3-5 July 1997.

Wiener Institut für Internationale Wirtschaftsvergleiche(WIIW), (1996), *Countries in Transition.* Handbook of Statistics, Wien, Bratislava.

Zon, Hans van (1996), *The future of Industry in Central and Eastern Europe.* Avebury. Aldershot, UK; Ashgate Brookfield, Vermont, USA.

2 Continuity Amidst Change

Hungarian enterprises in the mid-1990s[1]
RICHARD WHITLEY AND LASZLO CZABAN

Introduction

The sweeping political changes and transformation of the institutional systems of the East European economies, together with the market shock created by the collapse of the CMEA in 1991, were expected to generate substantial changes in enterprise structures and behaviour. Privatisation, in particular, was thought by many observers to constitute both a necessary and sufficient condition for the transformation of existing enterprises into 'Western' capitalist firms (for a review of some of these approaches see Jackson, 1992).

However, some analysts have more recently (e.g. Tatur, 1995, Csanadi, 1997, Rona-Tas, 1997) pointed out that the relationships between these changes as well as the legacies of the past might limit the extent of radical and comprehensive transformations at the enterprise level. Not only have contradictions developed between the pace of change at the macro-level and at the level of firms, but also between the different roles of the crucial agent of the transformation: the discredited and fragmented state inherited from state socialism. The state in post socialist societies has been withdrawing from the management of economic relations at the same time as playing the leading role in the establishment of new institutions and behaviours in the economic sphere (Amsden et al. 1994, Whitley, 1996). The contradictory roles of the state, the co-existence of past and present institutions and patterns of behaviour and policy makers' inexperience in making macro and microeconomic decisions in an emerging capitalist economy that was quickly integrated into the world capitalist economy together led to confusion in the roles of other economic agents (Bunce and Csanadi, 1993; Csanadi, 1997) and created prohibitively high risks for those wishing to undertake radical enterprise transformations in many cases (Grancelli, 1995).

The ensuing deterioration of economic performance in the region, which to some extent undermined the legitimacy of the kind of capitalist economy that started to emerge in the region during the early 1990s (Gomulka, 1994), put pressure on governments to abandon the shock-therapy approach and introduce

37

the institutions of a market economy more gradually. All these factors led to a longer, more incremental and complex set of transitions at the enterprise level. In particular, they meant that the behaviour of managers in different kinds of firms, and of other economic groupings, could not simply be understood as the direct product of "designer capitalism" changes at the macro-level (Stark, 1996).

In Eastern Europe, Hungarian enterprises were among the most likely to have moved away from the state socialist past for two reasons. First, because of the increasing foreign ownership in manufacturing industry during the 1990s (Radice, 1995). Second, because the early but incremental market reforms between 1968-1989 led to a limited, though mainly formal, increase in managerial autonomy in state enterprises, direct contacts between these enterprises and their capitalist customers and suppliers, and to the growth of quasi-private and private firms in the small and medium sized firm sector (Berend, 1990). Additionally, because of the high external indebtedness of Hungary, the pressures of the international financial organisations on the government (Gowan, 1995) can be expected to have encouraged swift and continuous liberalisation of markets and privatisation of ownership.

In this paper we explore to what extent these contradictory changes in institutions, markets and ownership resulted in the transformation of Hungarian enterprises by the mid-1990s. After the turbulence of the early 1990s, marked by severe recession and high levels of institutional uncertainty, a more stable period ensued. By 1993, most of the institutions of the market economy were in place, the industrial recession had reached its nadir, some major enterprises had been privatised, and illusions of regaining the old CMEA markets had finally been lost. In the three year period between early 1993 and the end of 1995, the operation of the new institutions became more routinised and the governing rules of the game more transparent. By 1996, the new socialist-liberal government had, after the budget crisis and diminishing trust of foreign investors in early 1995, successfully completed the privatisation of the bulk of state property to (mainly) foreign investors and foreign ownership became dominant in the large company sector and in exports (EBRD, 1997). To some extent, then, we can contrast the highly fluid and uncertain business environment of the early 1990s with the more predictable one of the mid-1990s.

In studying the structure and behaviour of Hungarian enterprises in the mid-1990s, it is of course, additionally important to recognise that their controllers were active participants in constructing the sort of capitalism that is emerging in Hungary during this decade. Enterprises, their managers and employees were not, and are not, merely passive respondents to radical institutional and market changes, but in many cases were active agents seeking to structure outcomes to their advantages, albeit often with very short term objectives (Csanadi, 1997).

Information about enterprise ownership and control, products and markets, and organisational restructuring was obtained through detailed interviews with senior managers of 18 companies carried out in early 1996 (these companies were also interviewed in 1993 and 1994). To obtain further information and confirm our findings senior managers of another ten companies were interviewed in 1995 as well as employees and middle managers of 14 of the 18 companies. Furthermore, interviews were carried out with senior civil servants, politicians and representatives of interest representation groups. All these interviews were conducted in Hungarian. The results of this fieldwork were crosschecked by information obtained from secondary sources.

To clarify the legacy of the late state socialist period, we initially summarise the key characteristics of state owned enterprises (SOE) in the late 1980s in Hungary and suggest how the institutional and market changes of the early 1990s are likely to have affected them in the light of the conflicting pressures mentioned above. Then, we identify the changes in ownership that have taken place in 18 enterprises and how these were connected to changes in strategic and operational control. Finally, we describe how enterprises controlled by different groups and agencies restructured their organisations, and developed competitive strategies in the new environment.

The Expected Effects of Institutional Changes and Market Collapse on Hungarian Enterprises

In order to examine the effects of radical institutional changes and market collapse on enterprise structures and behaviour, it is first necessary to summarise the key characteristics of the typical late state socialist Hungarian enterprise. They were usually highly vertically integrated and undertook extensive component manufacturing because the scheduling and quality of supply of inputs were unreliable and because size was an important factor for gaining political support for additional resources (Grancelli, 1995, Szalai, 1991). Enterprises were also responsible for a number of welfare services and so a large number of units with no production function were parts of the company organisation. This combination of vertical integration, a large number of ancillary units, and in many companies, the geographically diverse allocation of plants during the industrialisation wave of the 1960s to create employment in the now mechanised rural areas, created a large number of sub-optimal company units (Devai, 1984).

Organisational and decision making structures were strongly hierarchical (Child and Markoczy, 1994), originally to ensure compliance with the plan, later because the pressures of the pseudo-market were not sufficient to change it. The party and trade union organisation of the company played an important role in formulating strategy, lobbying with central authorities and managing work force and welfare services (Hughes, 1994). Production units did not usually have any expertise or responsibility for dealing with financial or sales matters (Marosi, 1977).

The range of products and product lines of the large firm sector varied depending on the type of market served by the enterprise. Companies producing mainly for the guaranteed CMEA markets had very narrow product lines and within product lines made large batches of a few products with low or no customisation (Hitchens et al. 1995). These product lines were mainly finished products. Companies mostly serving the domestic market, though still having few product lines, produced a larger number of standard variations of products. Companies serving the markets of developed countries sold basic finished goods or components, usually according to the specification of the Western customer.

The political priority of full employment was ensured through wage regulations (Bonifert, 1987) and by the bargaining process and lobbying characteristic to bureaucratic planning (Szalai, 1991) which encouraged companies to grow and accumulate resources (including labour), while market pressures were subdued (Revesz, 1990). A large proportion of the workforce was made up of ancillary workers in non-productive units, and many other workers (mainly unskilled) were employed on low wages to reduce the average wage level of the company which was closely regulated by the state. By continuing to employ large numbers of low paid workers, managers were able to pay higher wages to their more skilled and useful employees (Bonifert, 1987). Many of the production workers were skilled workers (as a result of the large expansion of vocational schools in the 1970s) or gained skills through on-job experience (semi-skilled workers). The direct and indirect wage and labour regulations discouraged the mobility of labour and the combination of the weak external labour market and the skill related seniority system led to a strong internal promotion culture (Hethy, 1983). This was the case at all levels of employment: senior managers were usually promoted internally and had experience only within one or a few departments.

The political changes and economic liberalisation of 1989-1991 radically changed the environment in which enterprises operated. Severe cuts in subsidies and changing relations with banks, together with the liberalisation of trade and eventual privatisation resulted in stronger cost sensitivity and awareness of competition for customers. The transformed enterprises were supposed to develop strategies, structures and products appropriate to the emerging market economy.

As all companies were exposed to these changes, we could expect shifts from inherited structures, strategies, etc. in all of them, but the extent of the changes would depend on the strength of various pressures and their combination. The most visible changes were expected in employment levels and organisation structures. With the removal of the political priority of full employment and of restrictions on labour mobility, managers seemed likely to shed their surplus labour and cut production costs through large cuts in non-production workers. As import liberalisation and the liberalisation of market entry reduced companies' reliance on in-house component manufacturing and business services, a significant proportion of such cuts could be expected to be achieved through vertical disintegration and the reduction of welfare services carried out by companies (Hirschhausen, 1995).

We would also expect that top management teams of many of these enterprises would be replaced, especially in the privatised firms where external owners assumed control. As product lines changed and became more diversified, inside knowledge of the industry and markets would lose some of its importance and so outsiders could be appointed to senior roles. Foreign firm owners might be especially likely to replace significant numbers of managers with new recruits from outside the sector.

Considering the likely changes in product lines and innovations, we again need to distinguish between enterprises oriented to different markets. First, companies that produced mainly for the CMEA markets lost the bulk of these markets due to customer insolvency and Western competition. This also affected these companies' sales to other markets, as the large batches sold to CMEA markets covered a large proportion of their fixed costs. As these products were mainly finished products, companies would face intense competition if they were to switch to more demanding markets. These companies, then, seemed likely first to reduce employment and the number of sub-units. Subsequently they would have to upgrade their products and introduce new ones, or even move to new product lines, or go bankrupt.

Second, companies serving mainly the domestic market (excluding suppliers of domestic companies exporting to the CMEA markets that were in a similar situation to that of their customers) became fully exposed to import competition. These companies then would first attempt to compete on the basis of their low production costs. After initial downsizing, they seemed likely to focus on further reducing unit production costs, perhaps by limiting the number of product variations. Later on, perhaps, these firms might attempt to diversify their product range.

Third, companies selling their goods to Western customers can be expected to continue to compete on price and would upgrade their products. Those companies whose exports used to be helped by state subsidies or sales of large batches to the CMEA markets would face increasing pressure to cut costs. In nearly all cases, except for companies serving exclusively the markets of developed countries, enterprises had to reduce their output, then upgrade their products, introduce new products and enter new markets.

There were, however, a number of factors that countered these tendencies, especially in the early 1990s. Firstly, in some enterprises, high sunk costs made radical downsizing difficult as well as limiting diversification into new product lines. This was especially the case in capital intensive sectors and in sectors (such as the food processing industry) where existing supplier networks were crucial to the survival of the company. Even where such costs were not an obstacle to diversification or market change, the lack of knowledge of other products and markets inhibited such moves. Generally, upgrading products or developing new ones required resources that most companies did not have because of market loss, deteriorating cash flow and prohibitive loan conditions. Thus, changes of product lines can be expected to be a slow process in companies where resources from the non-domestic banking sector were unobtainable.

We would expect, then, that substantial changes in product lines would occur only in certain enterprises. These combined: a) access to resources from either the owner or a customer or a foreign bank, b) strong market pressure and/or, c) strong control by groups able and willing to implement strategic changes, and d) limited sunk costs. In the first part of the transition period, these conditions existed only for foreign firm owned companies and some of those that had undergone liquidation. Overall, changes in these firms seemed especially likely in the following areas: employment levels and structure, product innovation, suppliers and customers, organisational structure and procedures. In the mid-1990s, with the stabilisation of the institutional and market environment, more companies, controlled by various types of agents, can be expected to be able to carry out such restructuring as well.

Ownership and Control in 18 Hungarian Enterprises

These expectations were explored in 18 *leading* Hungarian enterprises that included the largest firms as well as some that had developed from small entrepreneurial partnership and medium sized privatised firms. In terms of sector composition, these firms represented the most important manufacturing branches of Hungarian industry, such as food processing, chemicals and engineering, including electronics. As can be seen from Table 2.1, they manifested a considerable variety of ownership types which were often quite complex, with strategic and portfolio investors including the state, local governments, employees, banks and firms.

There were two broad ownership categories: state owned (7) and privately owned companies (11). Within the group of privately owned companies in 1996, there were six companies owned by foreign firms, two by Hungarian private managers, one by its employees and two companies without a clear dominant owner, that is, no stake exceeded 5 per cent of all shares. Ownership *per se* does not, of course, necessarily imply control over strategic decisions or company assets. In a period of transition, when property relations are new and not established, when the institutions that ensure and regulate these relationships are new and when the rapid and sharp market changes create high risks, control over the key decisions can be more important than ownership in legal terms (cf. Kotrba, 1995 on the Czech privatisation). Because of the high indebtedness and the deteriorating profitability of many companies, the financial position may be as important in the way control is exercised over companies as formal ownership.

An important initial distinction in terms of type of control can be made between 'inside' and 'outside' control. Companies whose non-owning top managers exercise substantial effective control over strategic decisions and the way these are implemented, together with those whose managers became owners, can be considered to be under 'insider' control. Such insider control does not necessarily require large managerial shareholdings or a very hands-off approach by outside investors. One of the insider-controlled firms, for example, was privatised under the Act on Employee Share Ownership Programme of 1993 (ESOP). In such firms the majority of shares are owned by a fund that represents the shareholding employees. As most employees do not have the cash to buy these shares, the Act permits payment for them to be made from the taxed profits of the company. No dividends may be paid until these shares are fully paid for. The combined lack of internal accumulation of resources and the reluctance of banks to lend to enterprises whose profits are pre-assigned as payment for shares limits the capacities of these companies to change.

Outsider controlled firms consisted of state owned enterprises (SOE) and those dominated by external private owners. Most privately owned and controlled firms, especially those under foreign ownership and control, can be expected to

Table 2.1 Classification of 18 Hungarian Companies by Type of Control in 1996

Type of control	Type of largest owner						Employment				Sector
	State	Foreign firm	Management	Employees	Fragmented ownership	Bank	0-500	501-1500	1501-3000	3001-	
Crisis SOEs	2	0	0	0	0	0	0	1	0	1	Machinery (2)
Stable SOEs	4	0	0	0	0	1	0	0	0	5	Chemicals (3), Metals (1), Machinery (1)
Management controlled	0	0	2	1	2	0	1	1	2	1	Electronics (2), Food (1), Chemicals (2)
Foreign firm controlled	0	6	0	0	0	0	1	1	2	2	Chemicals (1), Electronics (2), Telecoms (1), Building materials (1), Metals (1)

pursue growth and profit goals. State controlled ones, on the other hand, are likely to pursue more varied and contradictory objectives, as political pressures and connections fluctuate (Henderson et al. 1995, Voszka, 1995). Private controllers were therefore more likely to implement changes systematically than state agencies.

It should be pointed out here that in the first period of the transition, until their merger in 1995, two different state agencies (State Property Agency, State Asset Management Company) exercised ownership rights. In the course of the bank consolidation programme, a third institution, the Hungarian Development Bank also acquired stakes in SOEs. Although there were differences between the way these agencies developed strategies and controlled companies, in the longer term the effects of these differences appear to be negligible. Finally, distinctions should be made between Hungarian private controlled firms and foreign controlled firms since it is the latter ones that had more ready access to financial means to implement changes in company development.

We explored the roles of different owners of the 18 Hungarian enterprises by asking top managers about the formal powers and informal influence of dominant owning groups. The formal role included their veto powers (on investment and divestment decisions, top management appointments, product introductions), and the membership and powers of the Board of Directors. The informal role included owners' involvement in operational decisions and strategic issues, for example banking relations, customer-supplier priorities, investment decisions, pricing and wage policies and obtaining information on company performance and management decisions.

We distinguished between four types of owner control in this research on the basis of the type and degree of owner involvement in strategic and operational decision making and the financial position of the enterprises. As all but one of the privately controlled companies were financially stable, that is made profits or were breaking even and had limited debts, financial position was a classification factor only for SOEs in our sample in the first half of the 1990s. Thus, we divided SOEs into two categories: 'stable' and 'crisis' depending on their profitability and debts.

The two crisis SOEs in 1996 had accrued large losses during the first half of the 1990s and had large debts. They had lost many of their markets (both domestic and foreign) and were unable to switch to new markets at a sustainable level. As a result, their size fell significantly, and in 1995 they were still not viable without outside support. Their likely fate is either a rapid privatisation in which the new owner takes over parts of the companies or continuing divestment that may result in the disappearance of the viable units too. Stable SOEs, in contrast, managed to reduce their outstanding debt, either with the help of the state (debt forgiveness) or from their own resources, and were able to break-even after interest and tax payments. A common characteristic of these companies has been that while they stabilised their position or even improved it from 1993 onwards, they lacked significant investment resources.

'Combining the formal role of large owners with their informal influence, it is clear that the two manager owned companies, the ESOP owned company and the two companies with fragmented ownership, were substantially insider controlled. Not only in operational matters, but also in formulating strategy the senior management team was the de facto controller of these enterprises. In the case of the SOEs it was equally clear that state agencies exercised considerable, though declining, control over enterprise behaviour especially in those making losses. Where, however, foreign firms had taken a substantial shareholding and the state intended to sell the rest of its stake to those firms, it appeared that the foreign shareholder had already become the dominant partner. The first of these companies was privatised in 1989 and acquired by the current owner in 1990, the last one in 1995.

The close control exercised by outside controllers over Hungarian enterprises characteristic of the early 1990s declined significantly by the mid-1990s, except for crisis SOEs. The day-to-day control exercised by non-executive members of the Board of Directors appointed by the owners declined as the Boards met monthly or even less frequently at the end of 1995. Crisis SOEs, however, still had to report very frequently (weekly or fortnightly) to their owners and had to obtain prior agreement of the owners even on day-to-day decisions. This general decline in owner control of operational issues in most outsider-controlled companies appeared to result from the more stable market and institutional environment, the clearer rules of the game and the advance of privatisation. It did not mean, however, that owners were developing an Anglo-Saxon type remote relationship with companies. In the mid-1990s, owners were still intensively involved in strategic issues, especially in investment and divestment issues and appointments of top managers.

This overwhelming importance of large shareholders on company strategy in Hungarian companies is reflected in senior managers' view of the importance of other institutions and organisations. While two stable SOEs mentioned ministries as somewhat influential institutions (through economic regulations) and three companies (two stable SOEs and one manager controlled firm) mentioned the actions of their strategic partners as being influential, a closer look at the type and level of influence reveals that companies did not consider these to be important in strategic decision making. Considering the general under-funding of Hungarian companies, it is surprising that only one of the crisis SOEs considered the banks to be influential. It contradicts the widespread opinion of the early 1990s that bank-company relationship would become an important factor in the Hungarian economy and would lead to the banks developing large holdings in companies or to mutual ownership.

Although in the beginning of the 1990s some banks indeed owned shares in the companies we studied, our findings did not indicate strong and close relationships between banks and enterprises. Interviews with senior managers of banks showed their clear intentions to reduce their holdings in companies and develop a more distant relationship with them. The bank consolidation programmes of 1992-1994 created the basis for such arm's-length relationships, as it allowed for the removal of large non-performing debts from the banks' balance sheets. This, and the establishment of more standardised, 'Westernised' accounting systems, more developed risk assessment methods and the less chaotic market situation enabled banks to obtain the data on companies needed for lending decisions in a more routinised way and less frequently and less extensively by the mid-1990s. The exceptions are, of course, for the crisis SOEs. These companies had to report on a wide variety of business developments ranging from cash-flow to prices and cost, sales and order-stock. While other companies typically reported to their main lender quarterly, crisis SOEs and the foreign owned firm bought after bankruptcy had to do so weekly.

While in the early phase of the transition bank ownership was encouraged by the government as a substitute for the lack of domestic savings, the advance of privatisation and the acquisitions by foreign investors in particular, made this government policy unnecessary. The crisis in the banking sector in 1992-1993 (Bonin and Szekely, 1995) encouraged banks to reduce their investment. Subsequent government decrees made the reduction in banks' ownership in companies prudent as after 1993, banks had to accumulate risk provisions for their investments too. The privatisation of the banking sector and the increasing foreign ownership in the company sphere also discouraged the re-emergence of interlocking bank-company relationships after 1995.

Organisational Restructuring

Changes in overall employment

Considering first changes in employment since 1990, Table 2.2 shows that, while 14 of the 18 companies had cut their work force, some of them very significantly, four had actually increased theirs, albeit mostly by not very much. In general, we found that the main source of these increases in overall employment was the acquisition of other companies. One of the firms that increased its employment in the 1990s was a large stable SOE that acquired one of its customers. Another one had to develop new skills as it had belonged to a horizontally co-ordinated trust before privatisation, and also acquired one of its major competitors. Two of the owner controlled medium sized firms increased their employment as they moved to new markets or product lines.

Although the largest employment losses occurred in the crisis SOEs, exceeding 50 per cent, two of the stable SOEs suffered similar decrease in employment compared to 1990. The most severe cuts were made by the firm that was liquidated in 1991. However, towards the mid-1990s this company had restructured many of its operations and markets and substantially increased its workforce between 1993 and 1996. In the case of some of the SOEs, these cuts happened only after 1993 when the remaining political pressure to maintain employment disappeared. Most of the companies interviewed seemed confident that they would be able to maintain, some of them even increase, their employment in the second half of the 1990s. The common factor of companies losing a very large proportion of their workforce, therefore, was not so much the type of control, but very difficult financial situations because of large inherited debts and market losses.

In terms of changes to the structure of employment, Table 2.2 also shows that cuts in the work force occurred disproportionately among non-direct production workers, especially in foreign firm owned companies and crisis SOEs. These were mostly clerical workers and support staff, including those assisting skilled workers. Contrary to the expectation that Hungarian firms under severe market pressures would replace full time skilled employees by part time or casual semi-skilled workers to reduce costs and/or gain flexibility, the enterprises we studied did not do so. This finding corresponds to statistics from the Hungarian Ministry of Labour that show a negligible use of part time workers in manufacturing firms in the mid-1990s. Besides the continued use of highly specialised and often worn out machinery in many firms, this reliance on skilled workers can be explained by the abundance of relatively cheap skilled labour, agreements with trade unions in the large firm sector. The relatively expensive redundancy payments stipulated by collective agreements also constrained companies in replacing their existing work force. For example, in one of the stable SOEs, the average redundancy payment would have been 18 months salary, which, according to the Chief Executive Officer, who was reluctant to make large-scale redundancies in a company town, rendered a large reduction in the workforce unfeasible.

Table 2.2 Control Type and Employment Changes in 18 Hungarian Enterprises[2] between 01/01/1990 and 31/12/1995

Change in Employment	Control Type				Total
	Crisis SOEs	Stable SOEs	Manager Controlled	Foreign Controlled	
Total Employees					
Increase		1	2	1	4
1-20% decrease			1	1	2
21-40% decrease		2	1	3	6
>40% decrease	2	2	1		5
Direct Production Workers					
Increase		1	2	1	4
1-20% decrease			1	2	3
21-40% decrease		2	2	2	6
>40% decrease	2	2			4
Line Management					
Increase		2	2	3	7
1-20% decrease		1	1	2	4
21-40% decrease	1		1		2
>40% decrease	1	2	1		4
Non-Workflow Employees					
Increase		1	2		3
1-20% decrease				1	1
21-40% decrease		2	2	2	6
>40% decrease	2	2	1	2	7

Finally, we briefly consider changes in the intensity of supervision as measured by the proportion of first line supervisors to production workers. In both crisis SOEs and all foreign firm controlled companies, this ratio increased between 1990-1996. This corresponds to our findings from interviews carried out with production workers in 13 Hungarian companies (Whitley and Czaban, 1998a), that showed supervisors in these groups of firms exercising closer control on less skilled production workers than did those in stable SOEs. Overall, it seems that privatisation, *per se*, did not have a significant impact on employment structure, and certainly not more than financial crises. Some differences between foreign firm controlled enterprises and stable SOEs were noticeable, however, and these were echoed in other aspects of firm behaviour.

Changes in the overall organisational structure

Some of the above mentioned changes in employment were the results of disposals of organisational sub-units. Companies sold, separated and closed both 'core' (typically factories) and ancillary (units with functions such as transport, construction, maintenance, etc.) units in the first half of the 1990s. While there were quite a number of firms that retained all their core units throughout this period, all of the 18 companies studied here closed or sold ancillary units as a response to the more readily available and reliable supply of such products and services. Nevertheless, control type was an important factor, as foreign firm controlled companies were the most willing to cut these activities. Together with the crisis SOEs these firms continued to close such units in the mid-1990s, while the stable SOEs and the manager controlled firms tended to sell them. Sale, besides genuine transfer of ownership, often meant setting up the unit concerned as a subsidiary, sometimes with outside investors. This sometimes facilitated becoming a subcontractor for multinational companies, which seems to be a common feature in East-Central Europe (see for example Havas, 1997 for the automotive industry), but it also improved the use of excess capacity (because of the general decline of output) and reduced risk exposure.

Overall, differences in the number of closures and sales of various types of organisational units were related to combinations of type of control, company size and financial position. Foreign firms emerged as the group that more readily cut non-core units, and the continuing disposal of such units resulted in a more specialised organisation than the stable SOEs. Stable SOEs and foreign owned firms are also the largest firms in the sample, they had the resources to implement the expensive closures (e.g. redundancy payments, long notice periods) or to set up these units as subsidiaries, perhaps with outside investment. The larger size (and the related cash flow) also allowed for phasing out production or services rather than closing or selling them. In the crisis SOEs, the extent of the restructuring required was so large that without additional resources it would have been equivalent to liquidation of the company, which the owner (the state) would not authorise at that time and only provided the necessary funding after 1993.

By 1996 almost all companies claimed that they had a new organisational structure with some of them implementing a new structure several times during the first half of the 1990s. When asked about the nature of the new organisation, almost all CEOs (Chief Executive Officers) responded that the new organisation was a divisional one. However, an enquiry into the characteristics of these 'divisions' revealed that in most cases they were very different from American ones. In most companies they were cost centres whose products were similar or supplied inputs to each other. As a result, these 'divisions' are not self-contained. For example, in 1996 production units had no financial function in five of the six foreign owned companies. This was also the case in the crisis SOEs, in the two manager controlled firms and in two stable SOEs. Considering the financial, especially cash flow, problems in most state owned companies, this centralisation of the financial function is not surprising.

As the financial position improved in many enterprises, this extreme centralisation (in one of the large stable SOEs, which had a large outstanding debt, all payments had to be authorised by the financial director in 1993) was eased and, except for one stable SOE, 'divisions' were allocated a finance department. The close connection between financial position and centralisation of the finance function is clearly shown in the crisis SOEs, where formerly devolved financial functions were recentralised by 1996. In foreign firm controlled companies the centralisation of the finance function was a way of controlling the acquired organisation in a strange economic environment. In three of these the two top managers who were not local Hungarians were the CEO and the finance director. In another one the only non-local member of the top management team was the finance director who had significant powers to set budgets for various management levels.

The continuing centralisation of commercial functions is also strong evidence that these enterprises did not establish genuine profit centres. Production units in five of the foreign owned companies, in all the crisis SOEs, in two of the manager controlled companies and in two stable SOEs had no commercial functions. The centralisation of these functions is especially striking in foreign owned companies as three of them had centralised these functions since acquiring the Hungarian firm. Production units were not only non-self-contained, but also operated under close supervision of the centre of the company or the top management team. Typically, the units reported fortnightly to the CEO. These reports were very detailed, including output, input, production, stock, cost, employment etc., and so even the claim that these 'divisions' were independent cost centres should be taken with a considerable pinch of salt.

The enduring strong degree of centralisation of control is also clearly reflected in the decision making structure in these companies. We asked senior managers to identify the level at which decisions on various strategic and operational matters were taken both formally and in practice. The levels ranged from supervisor (1) through workflow manager (2), factory manager (3), business unit/director (4) to CEO (5). The level of centralisation of decision making was especially high in state owned companies, partly because of their financial difficulties and their attempts to meet the demands of state agencies. However, the high level of centralisation of decision making was characteristic in all control types. Company headquarters clearly retained the right to make decisions on all strategic issues and also on many operational issues. Decentralisation and centralisation could also depend on whether the controller of the firm had the people in decision-making positions it could trust. Thus, we briefly have to discuss the changes taking place in the group of people who made or implemented the decisions, the top management team.

In all but two companies the CEO was replaced at least once between 1990 and 1996, in many firms more than once. Although the replacement of the CEO was due to a number of reasons, in the case of foreign owned companies post-privatisation replacements were justified by 'changed circumstances' in most cases and 'inability of achieving targets' in one case. Whatever the reason might be, foreign owners usually recruited the new CEO from outside the firm, thus breaking with tradition and differing from the other types of companies (except for crisis SOEs). Nevertheless, expertise in the particular branch seems to be still important, as only one of the CEOs came from outside the industry.

Not only CEOs were replaced, but top management teams too, at least in the first phase of the transition. The proportion of new members of these teams exceeded 80 per cent in all control groups except the owner-managed firms. Most of these top managers, however, were still insiders, thus the apparently large shake-up was a result of the general advance within the company hierarchy, speeded up by the political and institutional changes. Towards the end of the first half of the 1990s top management teams became more stable in spite of continuing replacements of CEOs. Except for the crisis SOEs, where the frequently changing CEOs brought and took their direct collaborators, and one stable SOE, where the change in government resulted in the replacement of most senior managers, such changes declined during the stabilisation of the transformation.

Foreign owned companies, however, continued to recruit more of these top managers from outside the firm. In three of these five companies the majority of senior managers in 1996 were external, while in state owned companies, after the initial increase, the proportion of senior managers recruited from outside the firm dropped towards the end of the first half of the 1990s. We were unable to verify whether this change was a result of the resistance of 'insiders' or of extensive knowledge of the company still being regarded as a crucial factor for managerial success in SOEs.

Changes in Product Lines and Markets

These changes in organisational structures and personnel, albeit more limited than many anticipated at the time, were easier to implement than major shifts in product lines and markets. This is because of the narrow base of managers and workers' expertise in existing product lines, the sunk costs of machinery, lack of knowledge of new markets and how to access them and difficulties in obtaining new capital on feasible terms. We now explore the remarkable stability of product lines and business partners in these Hungarian companies in the 1990s.

Hungarian companies continued to operate in very narrow product lines: No company had more than three product lines with more than 10 per cent of turnover at the end of 1995. Most concentrated on a single major product line, such as buses or particular kinds of drugs, that contributed over 75 per cent of total sales turnover. At the start of 1996 nine of the 18 firms studied had only one major product line. Indeed, the actual proportion of total turnover contributed by the largest product line remained remarkably stable between 1990 and 1996 and many companies became more specialised in terms of their major outputs during the 1990s.

This high level of product specialisation and stability in the nature of outputs was consistent across the control types considered here, although there was a small tendency of the manager controlled firms to change their degree of specialisation as the business environment stabilised, mostly increasing it. Foreign firm controlled enterprises, in particular, were just as specialised as SOEs, indeed they became more so in the mid-1990s. Similarly, size and sector effects appeared negligible in these respects. Most product lines were mass-produced with the largest product line in 10 companies consisting of standard outputs with standard modifications and in four companies it consisted of standard outputs with modifications to customers' requirements.

This low level of customisation was related to the dominant positions many firms had in the domestic market and the concentration of many of them on making relatively low value added, standardised capital goods. By 1996, 13 firms had main product lines with over 67 per cent of the domestic market share with the SOEs and foreign controlled firms dominating the domestic market. While the latter mostly produced consumer products for both domestic and European markets the former tended to produce basic capital goods and their export products were component inputs for their traditional Western customers.

This concentration of many SOEs on the production of standardised components was difficult to change in the absence of major new sources of capital and technological upgrading. For example, one of the crisis SOEs produced components for other companies and for its competitors, but lacked the reputation and capability to make them with the special, higher value, modifications required by some customers, and was locked into a very competitive, low value added, shrinking market segment. Although the other crisis SOE made products to customers' specification with components from its suppliers, a large proportion of the value added in these products came from the components. The small batch sizes of these customised products together with the losses incurred by the standardised products of the company forced it to continuous downsizing. As a result, it became less and less competitive leading to the break-up of the company in the longer term.

Differences between control types were more noticeable when we examined changes within product lines, especially product upgrading and innovations. Some of the foreign owned companies started to introduce new products or upgrade existing products already in the beginning of the transformation and by 1996 such innovations accounted for all these firms' sales. On the other hand, innovation was much slower in SOEs and only in two of them did upgraded products account for more than 60 per cent of sales by 1996.

Access to resources for product innovation was clearly a crucial condition for relative market success in Hungary during the second phase of the transition. The companies that improved their financial position were the ones that managed to introduce new products (or product lines) and improve existing ones, while the least successful ones, the crisis SOEs, were selling basically the same products as in 1990. The examples of the stable SOEs show that ownership alone was not the crucial factor behind these innovations. From the interviews with these firms it was clear that the upgraded products these companies introduced towards the end of the first half of the 1990s were already available in the early 1990s, but because they did not have access to investment resources on feasible terms, managers were unable to begin their production.

Thus, by the time these products appeared in the market, they were not so 'new'. This, in turn, limited the ability of these companies to accumulate internal investment resources.

These differences in the rate and extent of product innovation were not reflected in R and D expenditures. These were largely due to sectoral differences, with the pharmaceutical firms clearly investing more in this area than other companies. This suggests that a significant factor behind the introduction of new products and upgrading existing ones in many foreign firm controlled enterprises was the transfer of expertise and technology from the parent firms. Indeed, in 1996 many senior managers of the foreign firm controlled companies stated that they co-operated with their mother company on R and D matters.

The limited changes in product lines were also reflected in the relative stability of customers and suppliers of these companies. Three firms still had the same three largest customers in 1996 that they had had in 1990 while nine companies had altered one of their three largest customers and four firms changed two major customers during this period. Thus, only two companies, one manager controlled and one foreign firm controlled, changed their three major customers. The former did so because it moved to new product lines, and the latter because of the transformation of its 1990s markets.

Changes of major suppliers of these companies were even more limited. Six companies did not change any major supplier between 1990 and 1996 and another six changed only one. Those companies that changed three major suppliers (one stable SOE and one manager controlled firm) did so because of the disappearance of traditional suppliers (CMEA and domestic) and changing product lines. Limited changes in product lines, high domestic market share and cost considerations may explain the small shift in the supplier base of foreign controlled firms. These exhibited substantially higher overall stability in this respect than any other control type of these Hungarian firms (three of them did not change any major supplier and three changed only one of them).

Conclusions

The results of our research can be summarised as follows: Many firms in Hungary, especially those controlled by foreign firms, have, after six years of radical institutional and market changes, a more specialised structure in terms of major outputs and fewer employees. Production units have become more responsible for operational matters, but only senior managers and the CEO are responsible for the outside relationships of the company. These top management teams have mostly changed completely since 1990, but only in foreign firm controlled companies have substantial proportions of their members come from outside the organisation. The foreign owned firms also tended to transfer at least one of the senior managers (the CEO or the financial director) from the parent company or recruited them abroad (though many had Hungarian ancestors). In the course of the interviews it became clear to us that the appointment of expatriates was intended more to tighten owner control than to bring new expertise into the company.

Narrow product lines, little customisation and little change in the proportions in which products are produced remained characteristic features of most of these Hungarian companies. Market pressures eliminated companies and plants rather than forcing them to move to new product lines or diversify. In most cases, companies did not have the resources to innovate and where these were available, in foreign firm owned companies, the market situation and the very fact that most of these companies were acquired because of their products and their dominant market position reinforced existing patterns.

Thus, the expected large changes in firm structure and behaviour as a result of hard budget constraints, market pressures and privatisation have proved to be small and incremental. While institutional changes, the more competitive business environment, the spread of Western management techniques and foreign investment have started to challenge the deep structural characteristics of the Hungarian economy and business, continuities with the state socialist period, strong domestic quasi-monopolies and high sunk costs in machinery and expertise have limited the scale and speed of corporate change. Competing mostly on price with machinery that is expensive to replace, many of these Hungarian firms concentrated on cutting costs and increasing output without making large investments in restructuring production technologies and work systems.

This pattern may eventually be broken by foreign investment. Although the changes in the organisational structure, product lines, labour relations (Whitley et al. 1997), work organisation (Whitley and Czaban, 1998a, Czaban and Whitley, 1998 were limited in the foreign controlled firms studied here, they were more substantial than in state owned companies. However, such changes do, of course, take time (Whitley and Czaban, 1998b): The acquired company has to be restructured, it has to be made profitable and effective, structures have to be changed, people have to be trained. Furthermore, all these actions require large investments of money and energy. While there are some signs that foreign owned companies are beginning to restructure their production lines, introduce new products and reorganise work systems, these changes are essentially incremental. As the large number of similarities between foreign firm controlled companies and stable SOEs in this research showed, this kind of restructuring does not necessarily lead to a new business development path.

In conclusion, then, the responses of Hungarian enterprises to radical shifts in their business and institutional environments in the 1990s were more complex and incremental than many observers expected. The combination of high levels of institutional and market uncertainty with high sunk costs in specialised technologies and organisational capabilities, and limited resources for new developments, inhibited radical changes. Most top management teams focused on short term survival in the threatening and unpredictable environment, while attempting to ensure that their interests were not ignored in the struggle to establish new rules of the game. The very openness of political and economic arenas during the transition made it difficult for actors to take and implement strategic decisions since the nature of competing groups and processes governing outcomes were very fluid, as Csanadi (1997) has emphasised. In this situation, most managers carried on doing the same thing in much the same way, while reducing costs by disposing of units and non-core employees. Major investments in new facilities, products and markets were simply too risky in this period, even if the money could have been obtained.

The companies taken over by foreign firms exemplify this limited nature of enterprise change in the face of major societal upheavals. Despite having, at least in principle, access to new capital resources and managerial expertise, most remained highly specialised in terms of their products and markets and concentrated on increasing production efficiency and market domination. Indeed, since their new parents acquired most of these because they had desirable assets in their existing product lines and control over distribution channels, radical changes in their activities and capabilities seem unlikely. Rather, incremental innovations in products and production technologies, including work systems, are more probable as the new owners seek to earn some return on their investments.

Changes in ownership and market environment, then, may encourage the reproduction as much as the radical reshaping of enterprise structures and strategies in the former state socialist societies. The effects of institutional changes on business organisations are often contradictory and by no means unidirectional, as the examples of the postwar Allied occupations of Germany and Japan also indicate.

Notes

[1] This research was supported by the Economic and Social research Council under grant number R 234422.
[2] One of the foreign firm controlled companies has been omitted from comparison of employment figures to 1990 as it was an integral part of a large state organisation and could not be separated from it.

References

Amsden, A., Kochanowicz, J. and Taylor, L. (1994), *The market meets its match: Restructuring the economies of Eastern Europe,* Cambridge, MA, Harvard University Press.

Berend, T. I. (1990), *The Hungarian Economic Reforms 1953-1988,* Cambridge, Cambridge University Press.

Bonifert, M. (1987), *Berszabalyozas* (Wage regulation). Budapest, KJK.

Bunce, V. and Csanadi, M. (1993), 'Uncertainty in the Transition: Post Communism in Hungary', *East European Politics and Societies* 7, 240-275.

Child, J. and Markoczy, L. (1994), 'Host Country Managerial Behaviour in Chinese and Hungarian Joint Ventures: Assessment of Competing Explanations' pp. 211-231 in Boisot, M. (ed.), *East-West Business Collaboration.* London, Routledge.

Csanadi, M (1997) 'The Legacy of Party-States for the Transformation', *Communist Economies and Economic Transformation,* 9, 61-85.

Czaban, L. and Whitley, R. (*1998*), 'The transformation of work process in emergent capitalism: The case of Hungary' *Work, Employment and Society* 12:1 47-72.

Devai, K. (1984), 'Erdekeltseg es a vallalati meret [Interest and the size of companies]' *Politikai gazdasagtani fuzetek,* 59.

EBRD (1997), *Third Report on Transitional Economies,* London: European Bank for Reconstruction and Development.

Gowan, P. (1995), 'Neo-Liberal Theory and Practice for Eastern Europe', *New Left Review, 213,* 3-60.

Gomulka, S. (1994), 'Economic and political constraints during transition', *Europe-Asia Studies,* 46(1), 83-106.

Grancelli, B. (1995), 'Organisational change. Towards a New East West Comparison', *Organization Studies,* 16, 1-26.

Henderson, J., Whitley, R., Czaban, L. and Lengyel, G. (1995), 'Contention and confusion in industrial transformation. Dilemmas of state economic management', pp 70-108, in Dittrich, E., Schmidt, G. and Whitley, R. (eds), *Industrial transformation in Europe,* London, Sage.

Hitchens, D.W.M.N., Birnie, J. E., Hamar, J., Wagner, K. and Zemplinerova, A. (1995), *Competitiveness of Industry in the Czech Republic and Hungary.* Aldershot, Avebury.

Hughes, S. (1994), 'Of monoliths and magicians: Economic transition and industrial relations in Hungary' *Work, Employment and Society,* 8, 69-86.

Jackson, M (1992), 'Constraints on systemic transition and their policy implications' *Oxford Review of Economic Policy,* 7(4), 407-429.

Kotrba, J. (1995), 'Privatisation process in the Czech Republic: Players and winners', pp. 112-146 in Svejnar, J. (ed.), *The Czech Republic and Economic Transition in Eastern Europe,* London, Academic Press.

Marosi, M. (1977), *Hatekonysag, osztonzes (Efficiency, motivation),* Budapest, KJK.

Radice, H. (1995), 'Organising markets in Central and Eastern Europe, Competition, governance and the role of foreign capital', 109-134, in Dittrich, E., Schmidt, G. and Whitley, R. (eds), *Industrial transformation in Europe* London, Sage.

Revesz, G. (1990), *Perestroika in Eastern Europe, Hungary's economic transformation 1945-1988,* Boulder, Westview.

Rona-Tas, A (1997) 'Social Engineering and Historical Legacies, Privatization and the Business Elite in Hungary and the Czech Republic', pp. 126-141 in B. Crawford and A. Lijphart (eds) *Liberalization and Leninist Legacies, Comparative Perspectives on Democratic Transitions*, Berkeley, University of California Press.

Stark, D. (1996), 'Recombinant property in Eastern European capitalism', *American Journal of Sociology,* 101(4), 993-1027.

Szalai, E. (1991), 'Integration of Special Interests in the Hungarian Economy, The Struggle between Large Companies and the Party and State Bureaucracy' *Journal of Comparative Economics,* 15, 284-303.

Tatur, M. (1995), 'Towards corporatism? The transformation of interest policy and interest regulation in Eastern Europe', 163-184, in Dittrich, E., Schmidt, G. and Whitley, R. (eds), *Industrial transformation in Europe,* London, Sage.

Voszka, E. (1995), *Agyaglabakon allo orias. Az AV Rt letrehozasa es mukodese* (The giant with feet of clay), Budapest, Penzugykutato Rt.

Whitley, R. (1996), There is no alternative: The necessity of state coordination of East European reindustrialisation. *Competition and Change* 3. 321-332.

Whitley, R., Henderson, J. and Czaban, L. (1997), 'Ownership, Control and the Management of Labour in an Emergent Capitalist Economy: the Case of Hungary', *Organization,* 4(3), 409-432.

Whitley, R. and Czaban, L. (1998a), 'Ownership, Control and Authority in Emergent Capitalism: Changing Supervisory Relations in Hungarian Industry' *The International Journal of Human Resource Management,* 9:(1), 99-113.

Whitley, R. and L. Czaban (1998b), 'Institutional Change and Enterprise Transformation in an Emergent Capitalist Economy: The Case of Hungary' *Organisational Studies,* 18, 259-280.

3 Inward Investment and Structural Transformation[1]

MARTIN MYANT

Introduction

The aim of this contribution is to explain the course of inward direct investment in the Czech Republic and to assess its impact on that country's post-1989 economic transformation. The focus is on transformation at the micro- level, in enterprises and individual sectors using data mainly from the automobile sector. Czech experience can then be compared in broad outline with that of other countries. The conclusions are compatible with those of comparative studies which show the impact of inward direct investment depending on the type of inward investment undertaken, the structure and capabilities of the host country and, to a very great extent, the policy framework established by the country concerned (Dunning and Narula, 1996, p.13, and Dunning, 1993). It is therefore appropriate to ask whether a different policy approach could not have led to, or could not in the future lead to, a significantly different outcome.

Thus some countries have been able to follow a path of development very heavily dependent on inward investment in high-tech industries, Singapore and to a lesser extent Ireland being examples. Others have given very general encouragement to inward investment and this has provided a valuable means to replace employment in declining heavy industries, as has been the case in parts of the UK. Generally, again, the infrastructure, the policy framework and the environment of an advanced market economy have been enough to attract firms bringing the most modern technology. Other countries have pursued policies to attract inward investment only in specific areas for which domestic firms were ill-equipped, but as part of a conscious and clear strategy of developing a technologically advanced industrial structure. South Korea and to a lesser extent Taiwan are examples. Finally, a number of countries have made no particular effort to encourage inward investment, or have actively discouraged it. This may be incompatible with rapid growth for low-income countries, but it seems to be fully consistent with high levels of income in a number of advanced market economies, such as Japan and, to a lesser extent, Sweden. One attempt to classify this uses a three-fold distinction between a

61

passive, open-door approach, a pro-active approach seeking out the most beneficial inward investors and a selective approach using inward investment as a means to advance technology only where needed (Lall, 1996a, p.440).

The striking point is that the Czech Republic does not fit easily into any of these categories. Governments, despite some internal conflicts, have shied away from a systematic industrial policy and there has not been a clear conception of a strategy for raising the technological level of industry or for replacing declining industries with new investment. Attention has centred almost exclusively on creating the basis of a market economy by the privatisation of the enterprises inherited from the past.

This has left policy makers with a very limited conception of the place of inward investment. It has never been spelled out in detail, but much of government activity was focused on finding foreign 'partners' that could help solve the problems of specific Czech enterprises, and often with the maintenance of existing production programmes. In only a very few cases was a wider view taken, for example of how multinational companies could help transform or modernise a whole sector. There was certainly no conception of creating a welcoming environment that could attract completely new investment as a basis for the development of new, modern sectors. Thus the aim was as much to preserve the economic structure of the past as to create a new one.

This has inevitably strongly influenced both the kinds of firms that have come and their impact on the course of the economic transformation. Above all, it has left the Czech Republic as a country with a relatively low share of foreign ownership when set against its overall level of development. Those firms that have come have provided only a limited basis for overcoming the past weaknesses of industry, as inherited from central planning.

The result has been a transformation process exhibiting a very high degree of continuity with the past. The detailed sectoral structure within manufacturing industry has undergone remarkably little change.

The one great exception to this, the passenger car sector, could be seen to some extent as an example of what a different policy approach might have achieved. That, however, should not be exaggerated. A firm base had already been laid before 1989 and other branches had less potential to benefit from direct inward investment.

The policy approach to inward investment also points to the need for a slightly unusual bias in the focus of an analytical account. Thus much existing literature concentrates on the motives of inward investors as that clearly is the principal determinant of investment for countries pursuing the 'open-door' approach. For the Czech Republic it is at least as important to understand the decision-making process on the side of the host country. In effect, it is as if the Czech government were pursuing a highly selective approach in which firms are attracted only when an appropriate Czech enterprise already exists and is itself looking for outside help. This account therefore begins with an outline of the Czech transformation and privatisation processes which created the framework within which inward investment has taken place.

The Czech Transformation

The essence of Czechoslovak, and subsequently Czech, government policies was to ensure the free play of market forces by opening the economy, freeing prices and privatising state-owned enterprises. The initial assumption was that this alone would provide a satisfactory basis for rapid growth, raising the per capita GDP from its 1989 level of around half of the European Community's average when measured by purchasing power parity.

The key steps towards liberalisation were taken in January 1991 with the freeing of prices, apart from those of housing, energy and transport, a sharp currency devaluation, the introduction of partial currency convertibility and an associated package of fiscal, monetary and wage restraint. It coincided with the collapse of trade between the countries of the former Soviet bloc and was followed by a sharp fall in output across most of industry (Myant, 1993).

Table 3.1 shows the broad figures.

Table 3.1 The course of the Czech transformation

	1991	1992	1993	1994	1995	1996	1997
GDP	-11.5	-3.3	0.6	2.7	5.9	4.1	1.0
Industrial output	-21.8	-7.9	-5.0	2.3	8.9	6.1	4.5
Real exports				6.7	10.1	3.0	10.2
Balance of payments surplus as per cent of GDP			0.4	-0.1	-2.7	-7.6	-6.1

All figures are percentage change on previous year unless otherwise stated.

Source: Czech Statistical Office.

The post-1991 recovery was somewhat delayed, with stagnation even in 1993 due to the effects of the break-up of the Czechoslovak federation. The main stimulus for the renewal of growth came from three sources (Myant, 1996). The first was the service sector based often on very small firms. This was under way already in 1990 and expanding employment opportunities helped to absorb much of the labour released by decline in industry. It was, however, to a great extent a one-off change, reflecting the poor development of the service sector under central planning. Its contribution to growth therefore tended to decline.

The second was a growth in exports of less sophisticated products and semi-manufactures. This was stimulated by devaluation and trade liberalisation and gave a new lease of life to much of industry. Again, however, growth subsequently tended to slow, reflecting a gradual real currency revaluation and the relative stagnation of markets for basic products such as steel and raw materials.

The third was industrial expansion stimulated by inward investment, particularly in the motor vehicle sector. This has become increasingly important as the other sources of growth have tended to reach limits. It is, however, insufficient to ensure a continuation of high rates of growth, as the figures for 1997 indicate.

The slowdown in 1997 was an inevitable result of the limited nature of these sources of growth. Sectors of industry can broadly be divided into three categories. The first, made up mostly of light industry, has experienced continuing and steady decline in the face of competition both from low-wage countries and from producers of high-quality products in western Europe. The second, including sectors serving a safe domestic market, such as food, and producers of basic materials, such as steel and heavy chemicals, have shown stability or even some growth. The third, centring on the motor vehicle sector, has been able to grow rapidly thanks, as will be argued, largely to inward investment. Thus output from the broader transport equipment sector fell by 48 per cent between 1990 and 1992, by a further 4 per cent up to 1995, but then grew by 37 per cent over the next two years.

The tendency towards overall stagnation by 1997 was accentuated by the need for the government to respond to growing balance of payments difficulties, indicated by the high deficit relative to GDP shown in Table 3.1, following a faster growth of imports than exports. Pressure on the currency and strong criticisms from the IMF led the government to implement austerity packages aimed at cutting demand (EIU, 1997, pp.12-14). This can be expected to lead to slower growth over the following few years, but expansion should continue in export-oriented sectors.

When set against initial hopes at the beginning of the transformation process, these economic results must be seen as a major disappointment. They indicate a consistent failure to reach a satisfactory level of competitiveness, understood to mean the ability to achieve a satisfactory level of exports to pay for the consumption standard accepted as normal by the population. Behind this lies a weakness in modern industrial sectors, such as electronics and pharmaceuticals, which are growing rapidly in the most advanced economies. In so far as they existed up to 1989 they have been hit extremely hard by the failure to compete with powerful foreign firms. There is also a continuing weakness in the more sophisticated or fashionable products even in lower-tech branches. Thus the opening of the economy has brought aspirations for Western European standards of consumption, but the structural transformation has not created the basis for a high-wage economy that could support those aspirations.

Two Forms of Privatisation

A key step towards raising the economy to a 'Western European' level was to have been privatisation. There were, however, two essentially distinct conceptions of how this was to be implemented and of how it could be expected to lead to an improvement in economic performance. One, derived from neo-liberal or neo-classical economic theory, saw improvements coming from private ownership irrespective of who the owners were. This, along with hard budget constraints, would force restructuring within enterprises, leading to rapid improvements in efficiency. The issue was essentially one of incentives, with state ownership seen as leading naturally to complacency and inefficiency.

This was very much the thinking of Václav Klaus, Federal Minister of Finance from December 1989 to June 1992 and subsequently Prime Minister of the Czech Republic. He gathered a group around his ministry from early 1990 who worked on ideas for privatisation almost entirely by vouchers, whereby existing enterprises would be transferred very quickly, and without significant charge, to private owners. State ownership would thus be replaced by individual private ownership and the new private owners, it was assumed, would quickly start to exercise their ownership rights, putting pressure on previously unresponsive managers and forcing a speedy restructuring process (Myant, 1993). Tomás Jezek, one of the enthusiasts for this conception, headed the newly-established Ministry for Privatisation from June 1990 to June 1992.

The alternative conception emphasised linking privatisation to a search for foreign partners that could bring expertise, new management methods, contacts to the outside world and investment in new technology. For advocates of this view the specific identity of the new owner could be extremely important.

It was this latter view that initially dominated the practice of government ministries in charge of industrial enterprises. It pointed to a key role for direct inward investment and was continued in various forms in the Czech Ministry of Industry and Trade, headed by Jan Vrba, from June 1990 to June 1992. Beginnings had been made even before November 1989 with a law allowing the formation of joint ventures with foreign companies. The aim had been to encourage export-oriented production, with a hope that more advanced technology might diffuse through the economy, but very little was achieved (Štěpánek, 1989). At the same time, views were being expressed on the need for far more substantial inward investment if industry was to reach a reasonable level of competitiveness, with possibly a third of the engineering industry passing into foreign ownership. That, it was openly suggested, would be likely to mean the disappearance of traditional Czech brand names such as Tesla or Skoda (Kolanda, 1989).

Although no such clear view came publicly from the government in the period after November 1989, the Czechoslovak and Czech governments definitely encouraged enterprises to follow the example of a few pioneering companies that were seeking solutions to their difficulties with the help of a foreign partner. These were generally companies that had established international links beforehand, such as the Avia lorry producer that manufactured under a Renault licence from the 1960s and had already been discussing modernisation with its former associate. Thus initial approaches were often made by enterprise managements, particularly after warnings from the government that no more help from a central planning body could be expected. Managements similarly dominated the early course of negotiations, although the ultimate authority rested with the government.

This remained an important part of the approach to restructuring, particularly for the engineering and vehicle industries, and to a certain extent to privatisation in general, in the Czech Ministry of Industry and Trade up to June 1992. Rather than emphasising privatisation as a panacea, irrespective of who was to become the new owners, the ministry under Jan Vrba was looking for solutions related to estimates of the strategic options that would give enterprises a clearer chance of a long-term future. That involved some serious analysis of their particular problems. In some branches, such as much of light industry, the view was taken that enterprises should be able to survive on their own. In others, a link-up with a foreign partner was seen as absolutely essential.

The factors that determine the success or otherwise of these negotiations are discussed in a following section. However, a crucial limitation to the extent of inward investment was the partial success of the alternative conception of privatisation referred to above. The aim of finding 'any' owner as quickly as possible led to the emphasis on voucher privatisation, although the final outcome was a substantially watered-down version of the original abstract idea.

The decision-making procedure allowed for an input from the ministry controlling an individual enterprise, usually the Ministry of Industry and Trade, and from enterprise managements whose influence was particularly strong owing to their knowledge of local conditions and the priority they could attach to the issue. The Ministry for Privatisation processed all individual enterprise proposals, but could be overruled by the full government and, especially in the first voucher wave, had time for little more than a formal check on documentation produced elsewhere (Myant, 1993).

The final outcome was therefore a compromise between a pure and abstract concept, the needs of individual enterprises and the views within various ministries. Enterprise managements were generally happy with a substantial body of shares being offered for vouchers, but they also in some cases assured sale of shares to themselves or to a chosen foreign firm. Some enterprises were even left in state ownership, such as the 'strategic' companies mainly in energy and transport. Some shares, often in these strategic companies, were transferred without charge to local authorities. The voucher scheme was implemented in two waves over 1992-1993 and 1993-1994, in which vouchers were exchanged for shares with the price of the latter determined by an iteration process of balancing supply with demand.

Voucher privatisation has come in for increasingly strong criticism as a possible source of subsequent Czech economic difficulties (EIU, 1997, p.14). For present purposes, two negative features are particularly relevant. The first is that it brought nothing new to the enterprises. The second is that the voucher method at least in part cut across the approach to privatisation that emphasised inward investment.

The two voucher waves required preparation of detailed proposals by set deadlines and that often disrupted negotiations with foreign partners. Moreover, foreign companies were often suspicious of the unpredictable results from this untried method. The figures in Table 3.2 show the results of privatisation of enterprises after conversion into joint stock companies, the precondition for participation in the voucher waves. They indicate the very small proportion of shares that went to a foreign buyer. In many cases a proportion of the shares was left in state ownership for a prospective foreign partner that then never materialised: these make up a major part of the 5.44 per cent 'other' unsold shares, down from 7.60 per cent in 1995. They are gradually being sold off to domestic, or very occasionally foreign, purchasers.

Table 3.2 The fate of shares in enterprises converted into joint stock companies, percentage of total by 31 December 1996

Privatised	70.10
by sale	9.60
by sale to foreign buyers	1.92
exchanged for vouchers	47.84
other forms of free transfer	12.66
Not privatised	29.27
strategic companies	23.83
other	5.44
Unaccounted	0.28

Source: Statistical Yearbook of Czech Republic, 1997, p.513.

The greatest successes in gaining inward investors came independently of the voucher privatisation waves, although even then aggregate figures are modest. Fully or partly foreign owned firms accounted for 4.0 per cent of industrial employment in 1993, rising to 9.4 per cent in 1996 (see Table 3.3). The most important single case was the link-up between Volkswagen and the Skoda car manufacturer. This was conceived within part of the Czech government as a step that could bring modernisation to a whole branch, with a positive impact across a range of component suppliers. A number of further deals were reached that brought major foreign companies into the Czech economy, completely dominating a particular product. Examples are in sheet glass, tobacco, telecommunications and petrochemicals. In no case, however, were there such substantial spillovers beyond the single firm concerned. Results in other sectors have been less impressive.

The Determinants of Inward Investment

The linking of inward investment to privatisation meant that its scale and form depended on the motives and actions of three parties involved, meaning the foreign company, the Czech government and the management of the Czech enterprise. Their attitudes partly reflected the objective position of that industry, but there was also a subjective element that could make agreement more or less easy to attain. The determinants of inward investment can therefore be followed around a summary of the aims and actions of these three actors, with the two on the Czech side treated together.

The aims of the multinationals

In all cases the most obvious and absolute precondition for inward investment was the desire of a prospective foreign partner to come. This is the angle most frequently pursued in literature on multi-national enterprises with attempts to define motivation around specific objectives such as gaining access to markets, benefiting from cheap labour or broader strategic aims (eg Estrin, Hughes and Todd, 1997). In the Czech case, the nature of the privatisation process and often complex negotiations involved strongly discouraged any firm with a single simple objective.

In general, multinational companies were attracted by the range of possibilities that might arise in the future. They were frequently attracted by the possibility of sales on the domestic market, at least as a fall-back if other plans fail, and of possible exports into Eastern Europe or other parts of the world. The extent to which they intended to integrate a Czech subsidiary into a global network was often very flexible.

As will be indicated later, there was very wide variation in the objectives of specific inward investors, but those interested in a large-scale commitment were most likely to be attracted where one Czech firm had more or less total dominance in the domestic market. That gave the investors security even if other plans, such as further expansion with exports to the East, prove unrealistic. The same logic meant that they were also more likely to accept the risks involved where the sector was enjoying expansion across the world. These factors pointed to about as favourable a position as could be imagined in the case of passenger cars. For goods vehicles the position was not hopeless from the start, but in all respects it was less favourable. The successful attraction of a foreign partner would therefore have been possible only with a more active role from the government.

The aims from the Czech side

The Czech government and individual enterprises themselves had a decisive influence on whether or not an inward investor came, but probably less influence than they thought over the precise terms attached. If the terms they were demanding did not fit with the thinking of a potential investor, the result was likely to be a failure to agree at all.

The Czech government's attitude was decisive where it concluded that a partner was not necessary, irrespective of interest from abroad or of the views of the enterprise management. This was particularly true where domestic demand had not been hit by the 'shock' of 1991 or where, for some other reason, financial results remained good.

This reluctance to sell was strengthened in a few cases into the vaguely-defined notion of the 'family silver', referring to firms that were so central to Czech pride that they could not be allowed to pass into foreign hands. Supreme examples were the brewers Plzeňský Prazdroj of Plzeň and Budvar of České Budějovice.

In some cases the Czech government was generally willing to sell, but has frequently insisted that it will not give any extra help to inward investors. This reflected its free-market credentials plus a degree of public suspicion at the motives of foreign companies. In practice, however, this principle was not ri-gidly maintained. Some firms have been given very favourable terms while others have been sold off at surprisingly low prices.

In other cases the Czech side has seemed very tough in its demands. This was most common in well-established engineering enterprises where enterprise managements were particularly strong. The desire for a foreign partner was frequently conceived around rather narrow objectives, such as overcoming immediate financial difficulties. Serious prospective partners typically had rather different objectives relating to their own global thinking. The result could be prolonged negotiations with the Czech side trying to set the most precise terms possible so as to preserve as much as they could of past employment and production levels. The most important case here was the possible link-up of the Škoda-Plzeň heavy engineering combine (no relation to the car manufacturer) with Siemens, which fell through completely in the autumn of 1992 as it became clear that Siemens was interested only in some parts of the Škoda operation.

At round about the same time, a string of other potential deals ran into the ground in the motor vehicle industry. This effectively closed the door on 'brownfield' investment, in which a new owner could use an existing enterprise as little more than a base for a vigorous rationalisation completely changing the production profile. A number of major deals were agreed in the following years, particularly in oil refining and telecommunications. In these cases, however, the aim was to continue with and gradually modernise existing operations. There was even strong opposition from within the Czech companies' managements around arguments that necessary resources for investment and modernisation could be found from internal sources.

Successes and Failures

The successes and failures in the motor industry, in terms of attracting inward investment, can serve to illustrate the factors that determined the outcome of an attempt to find a foreign partner. Most important a proud Czech company with a powerful management essentially wanted to continue with at least as substantial an operation as in the past, but faced immense immediate financial difficulties and a longer-term threat to traditional markets both from imports and from the collapse of demand in former CMEA countries. The outcome depended on the approaches taken both by the Czech side and by the prospective foreign partners.

Success with cars

The clearest success was the case of the Škoda car manufacturer of Mladá Boleslav. Urgency on the Czech side stemmed partly from the immediate need to overcome the financial difficulties of the state-owned enterprise, but the primary motivation was derived from a solid assessment of the prospects of the whole sector. This had been developed throughout the late 1980s, with a growing recognition that the Czech motor industry's problems could only be resolved by cooperation with one or more foreign companies. The logic was impeccable.

Output of passenger cars had reached about 180,000 by 1976 but remained roughly stable from then on. Despite a massive level of investment associated with the development of the new Favorit model in the late 1980s, capacity was still limited above all by the engine plant, built in 1963. Its product was also considered the weakest part of the Favorit. Attempts at cooperation with East Germany had proved unsuccessful and ideas of manufacturing engines under licence from a western company also appeared expensive and risky: such deals could only be justified if there were a guarantee of adequate sales in the West to cover the costs of the licences plus imported equipment. The industry was therefore left facing the seemingly insurmountable problem of raising annual output to over 400,000 vehicles, the level required to begin approaching car ownership levels of Western Europe, when the country could not provide the resources for the necessary investment.

Thinking in the government after December 1989 was largely a continuation of this approach. A foreign partner was sought, but around a set of clearly-defined objectives. The key points were that output was to be doubled, that Czech and Slovak components were to be used, that employment levels were if anything to rise, that there should be as much capital investment as possible, that there should be plans for exports to the West to cover hard currency imports and that the Škoda name should be retained. In a sense the aim was a contradictory one of bringing in a foreign partner so as to maintain and develop a specifically Czech motor industry.

This was to lead to tensions both during the negotiations and in the following years, but the Czech aim was far from an impossible dream. It was made realistic by the highly competitive nature of the passenger car sector, with a number of experienced multinational companies eager to expand into CEE. This gave the Czech side considerable power to bargain with prospective inward investors over the terms.

By August 1990 the choice had been narrowed down to just Renault and Volkswagen. The latter had been in tune with the Czech aims from the start. It offered to keep the workforce of around 20,000, to build an engine plant with a capacity of 500,000 by 1995, to raise car capacity to 400,000 by 1997, to encourage investment in the Czechoslovak components industry, to produce an improved version of the Favorit over the 1995-1998 period and to launch a completely new model in 1998. Although some persuasion may have helped Volkswagen to accept these terms, none of them were in conflict with a plausible business strategy. Thus Volkswagen was happy to retain the Škoda name, not least because it could be used for cheaper cars for sale outside Western Europe without damaging the image of existing names. It was keen to develop the Czech components industry because, once it had accepted the logic of continuing the production of existing Škoda models, it also needed to maintain the production of specific components.

The agreement was signed with Volkswagen on 28 March 1991 and the latter formally took a 31 per cent stake in a new company on 15 April. This was initially established as a joint venture between the old car manufacturer and Volkswagen, as that was the only appropriate form allowed by Czechoslovak company law at the time. Its share was to rise to 70 per cent in 1995, following payment of nearly DM 2 bn and investment of DM 8.2 bn. It would have no responsibility for the company's past debts, estimated at Kčs 1.4 bn, which would be covered from the later sale of the remaining 30 per cent share.

Further details of the agreement included the joint venture having the right to set its own prices, protection from the possible application of new laws for the protection of economic competition, a two-year tax holiday, a promise of a cut in turnover tax on new cars, a commitment to maintain a 19 per cent duty on imported used cars, a commitment to use further non-tariff measures should the domestic market come under threat and the duty-free import of investment equipment (Lidové Noviny 31 May 1991).

There were criticisms that the price had been set too low and that the terms had been too generous. Škoda was even later penalised for allegedly exploiting its monopoly position. It is conceivable that the deal could have been better, but the key point was made by the government minister responsible for the negotiations; 'without a foreign partner Škoda would have been condemned to bankruptcy' (Grégr, Rudé Právo, 27 May 1991). With the agreement, he claimed, 20,000 direct jobs had been saved, plus another 40-60,000 in supplying firms. Set in more general terms, it did seem that the danger of being downgraded into a 'mere' assembly operation had been avoided and that there was a real likelihood of modernisation across the whole sector.

The great contrast here is with other enterprises in the vehicle industry. A combination of factors, including the attitudes of managements, the failure of the government to press through with a strategic vision, the structure of the industry and the approach of potential partners, led to far less favourable outcomes.

Disaster for lorry producers

Three Czech lorry manufacturers had a combined annual output during the 1980s of about 45,000 vehicles. The Czech government had recognised the branch's weaknesses, both in the 1980s and during 1990, drawing the general conclusion that the individual enterprises could not survive alone. The need was for a vi-gorous rationalisation – they tended even to use quite distinct components – before a serious foreign partner could be attracted (Myant, 1993, p.250). The Czech government did not impose so radical a change from above. Although the Ministry of Industry and Trade favoured a more interventionist approach than Klaus and his allies, it restricted itself to giving general advice. The dominant view at the time was that rationalisation and reorganisation was not a task for government and managements were left to seek solutions to their own problems. Those of the three lorry manufacturers, partly reflecting long-standing rivalries, preferred to carry on in isolation.

Their stubborn optimism led them to turn down overtures from potential foreign partners who anyway had only a limited interest in a risky venture that need contribute little to their global plans. Thus the Liaz enterprise, producing long-distance road vehicles, turned down a possible deal with Mercedes Benz which would have given hope for only part of the operation. Tatra, claiming to produce an excellent lorry ideal for rough terrain, similarly insisted that it would ultimately prosper alone and rejected a possible joint venture to assemble Iveco lorries. It opted instead for predominantly voucher privatisation, ensuring its safety against attempts from the government at rationalisation across the sector or at a possible sale to a foreign firm.

Avia, producing lighter goods vehicles under a Renault licence from the 1960s, shunned an approach from Renault in favour of one from Mercedes Benz. There were long delays during the negotiation of terms, with Mercedes Benz demanding strong protection for the domestic market. The German firm finally pulled out in 1993 without a clear explanation of the reasons. Its decision may have resulted in part from the reduction in the size of the market after the break-up of the Czechoslovak federation.

The cases of lorry manufacturers show a substantially different picture from that in passenger cars. The Czech government offered less attractive terms while the level of interest from potential western partners was also much lower. Production in the Czech Republic could have made sense if it had been a precondition for penetrating a new market, but there was no interest in taking the Czech brand names or using technology previously developed there. There was also little interest in incorporating a Czech plant into a global operation, unless it were to be confined to a very low-status role. That was highly unattractive to the Czech side.

The Impact of Inward Investment

The result of these complex negotiations was a level of inward direct investment into the Czech Republic that leaves its cumulative share small in relation to that of domestic ownership. Table 3 shows its overall importance in industry in terms of the available quantitative indicators. Where it has occurred, foreign ownership has frequently brought substantial benefits in terms of higher investment and partial or full foreign ownership is associated with higher labour productivity. Its greatest impact has been in transport equipment, with an average inward investment of $11,000 per employee against an average for the economy as a whole of $1,500. This high figure obviously reflects an even higher level per employee in passenger cars alongside substantially lower figures for some other products.

It is impossible to quantify the effects of inward investment in the Czech Republic across different sectors of industry in any serious way. Nevertheless, a rough gradation can be identified from the case of the transformation of a whole branch through cases of transformations of individual enterprises to cases where it has contributed the kind of 'second-best' strategies forced on many Czech enterprises whereby they produce simple products under contract to western European firms that require minimal new investment or technological advance (Myant, 1997). There are cases where its impact may have been negligible or even negative. This section provides an overview of these different cases starting with the case of the most substantial transformation, that of the passenger vehicle industry.

Table 3.3 Czech industry by types of ownership, percent of total

	Enterprises		Output		Employment	
	1993	1996	1993	1996	1993	1996
Private	40.9	49.4	15.3	25.3	17.6	31.4
State	39.4	9.3	66.8	9.9	68.1	9.3
Partial and full foreign ownership	5.4	8.6	6.5	15.9	4.0	9.4
Mixed forms of domestic ownership	3.7	22.7	9.2	44.6	6.7	45.0
Other domestic ownership	10.6	10.0	2.2	4.3	3.6	4.9

Source: Statistical Yearbook of Czech Republic, 1994, p.258 and 1997, p.382.

Škoda cars

Despite some of the criticisms referred to earlier, the broad results from the Škoda car manufacturer confirm a tendency towards an increase in output, along with the promised development of new models. As Table 3.4 shows, output has experienced hiccups, with the depressed domestic demand in 1991 and a drop in 1994 due to disruption during the launch of the new Felicia model.

The 1997 figure indicates that, at least in terms of output of finished vehicle, Škoda was not far short of the level originally promised in 1990 while employment had risen to exceed 22,000. Volkswagen has been vital to this growth. It has made possible investment equivalent to 10 per cent of turnover in 1993, rising to 13 per cent in 1994 and 1995 and 18 per cent in 1996. Although this was less than originally hoped for, it is considerably more than could have been contemplated under Czech ownership. It has also made possible the development of the completely new Octavia model, with engine sizes of 1.6 to 1.9l, launched in November 1996. The planned output of 90,000 for 1998 is below initial Czech hopes but, again, above the potential of a Czech-owned firm.

Table 3.4 Output of Škoda cars

	Output in thousands
1989	183
1990	187
1991	172
1992	201
1993	220
1994	174
1995	208
1996	263
1997	357

Source: Škoda auto.

Above all, Volkswagen has made possible continuing sales. The period after March 1991 did not see an ordered shift to new, stable markets. On the contrary, any hopes of stability were shattered by threats to the domestic market, first from imported used cars and gradually also from imports of new cars, and by events in Eastern Europe. Sales to the former Yugoslavia rose and then fell. Sales to Poland boomed, reaching 40,000 in 1991, and then almost disappeared after customs and tax barriers added 41 per cent to the price of imported cars. Selling cars therefore depended on seizing opportunities around the world and the Volkswagen connection was extremely valuable, with exports providing 63 per cent of revenues in 1997.

Assembly of Škoda cars started in Volkswagen's Poznan plant in 1994, with output reaching 15,000 in 1996. Sales to China, where Volkswagen already has assembly facilities, started in 1991 and had reached 3,643 in 1995. Assembly is planned in an Indian plant, jointly with Audi models, and production started in a plant in Sarajevo in August 1998. It has been more difficult to penetrate the former Soviet Union, where Škoda claims to be taking the lead among 'Western' European car manufacturers. Plans for assembly work in Russia have faced continual problems, but pilot assembly began in a plant in Belarus in early 1996.

Despite this broadly positive picture, Volkswagen's relations with the Czech government went through a very stormy period which, for a time at least, strengthened public doubts over the benefits of inward investment. The focus of dispute stemmed from a change in Volkswagen's overall strategy during 1993. This included a decision to cut costs by reducing planned levels of investment and by standardisation of basic components across the group. For Skoda that was translated into a 40 per cent cut in investment plans, a decision to drop the plans for the new engine plant and a cut in the output target for 1998 from 450,000 to 390,000 cars. The revised investment plan for Škoda involved total spending of only DM 3.7 bn, instead of DM 8.2 bn referred to in 1991. DM 1 bn of the reduction in investment was said to reflect lower costs, but the bulk was a result of the new intention to use common components.

There was an issue of national pride involved here. The momentous decision was being taken in Germany and without reference to the Czech government, although the latter was still the major shareholder. It was not obvious that even the new plans could be fully trusted. Rather than helping the Czech motor industry to prosper as an independent entity, the way seemed clear for Škoda to become a minor assembly works in the Volkswagen group. The prominence of Volkswagen personnel, 70 in 1991 rising to 150 in 1994, was also attracting some adverse comments.

There was some bluster from the Czech government about asserting the power conferred from being a majority share owner. Ministers even took up a demand for legally binding commitments from Volkswagen. In the end, however, an agreement was signed on 19 December 1994 which committed Volkswagen only to ensuring a total capacity of 340,000 vehicles by 1997, with a possible subsequent increase to 390,000. There was to be no discrimination against Czech component suppliers, provided they satisfied demands for price and quality: that was hardly a major concession. The Czech government was to have a power of veto over strategic decisions up to the year 2000. In exchange, Volkswagen acquired a majority share more quickly than previously agreed.

Thus, the final agreement broadly reflected Volkswagen's plans. The government's scope to negotiate a better deal had always been very limited. Skoda was a tiny part of the Volkswagen group, accounting for barely 2 per cent of total turnover. The Czech market was relatively minor and prospects of becoming a base for exports into Eastern Europe were not materialising. Moreover, the Czech government had little political leverage in Germany. In short, there was very little chance of persuading Volkswagen to do anything that was not a logical part of its overall business strategy. Despite the formal appearance of a renegotiation of the agreement, all that really happened was a slight delay in the harmonisation of Czech expectations with the realities of multinational business.

Component manufacturers

A somewhat analogous adjustment of hopes took place in the motor components sector which had developed purely to supply the Czechoslovak motor vehicle industry. With a few exceptions, it exported a negligible proportion of output in 1991. This was a weak basis for a long-term future within such a globalised industry. Firms were producing on too small a scale to compete internationally and, whatever might be promised, could not survive indefinitely as suppliers to the Czech motor industry alone. The depth of problems faced by vehicle manufacturers apart from Škoda only served to emphasise this point.

A successful component industry ultimately had to be able to export and supply other manufacturers. For that it needed new technology and investment which almost invariably required linking up with a foreign partner. By 1996 this had, at least in many cases, been achieved with exports of $350mn, equivalent to 1.6 per cent of total Czech exports. Behind this lies a major transformation which was largely, but not totally, stimulated by Volkswagen.

Volkswagen was committed from the start to developing, as well as just using, Czech and Slovak component manufacturers. This was a logical business strategy as the Favorit, and its successor the Felicia, were specific Škoda models with production runs too small to interest major outside component manufacturers. Over 80 per cent of their components were of Czech or Slovak origin.

Already in March 1991 Škoda was inviting its 250 suppliers to a 'congress' to discuss what would be required of them. The initial Volkswagen reaction was tactfully polite. Czech firms were complimented on their ability to improvise where past hard currency restrictions had made ideal solutions impossible. That, however, was all irrelevant for the future. Improvements were now sought both with threats – foreign suppliers could now be used if appropriate – and with promises of help. Thus Volkswagen set up courses on quality improvement and general management techniques and put local firms in touch with potential foreign partners. Reaching an adequate standard was rewarded with the possibilities of long-term contracts, to run over up to 8 years, and of supplying the whole Volkswagen group.

By 1995 there were said to be 42 joint ventures with foreign participation and 17 new greenfield investors supplying half of the value of Škoda's components, while only 30 per cent came from Czech- or Slovak-owned firms and 20 per cent from imports (V Köhler, Hospodářké Noviny 17 February 1995). The cost of those imports was almost covered by exports of components to supply Volkswagen and Audi cars.

The launch of the new Octavia model marked a major break. This could be seen as the inevitable moment of truth when the Czech components industry had to start proving itself against wider competition. In view of the new Volkswagen strategy, much of the car was the same as others in the Volkswagen group and would therefore fall under the unified sourcing strategy. Under one third of the car's components were specific to that model and they alone could be almost certain to come from Czech firms. The result was a near massacre of orders from many Czech firms, including a number that had been praised in the past and enthusiastically sought out foreign partners.

The effect this had on Czech suppliers to the motor industry varied very much between firms. Three broad groups can be identified. The first are those that kept their place as Skoda suppliers. In some cases that meant an extremely strong position with the possibility of supplying throughout the Volkswagen group. Generally speaking, these firms were producing on so large a scale that they were anyway not dependent on a Škoda contract alone. Among them were the glass manufacturer Glavunion, owned by a Belgian subsidiary of a Japanese company, and Akuma, a firm making batteries which had eagerly absorbed Škoda's advice and modernised its production, thanks to investment from its Geneva-based owner.

The second group is made up of firms that lost contracts for the Octavia, but had undergone substantial modernisation and were not wholly dependent on a Škoda contract. There were firms here that had linked up with major western partners, such as Lucas or Siemens, through which they could find new export opportunities.

The third group contains firms under Czech ownership. With a few exceptions, particularly of firms with products that did not require a high level of technology, these were increasingly excluded from any major role in the motor components industry. It should, however, be added that Czech component manufacturers had been relatively small and weak enterprises before 1989 and few were proud or stubborn enough to believe that they could prosper without a foreign partner. That approach was more typical of the manufacturers of final products with a well-known brand name. Those that had remained alone frequently behaved more like the typical Czech-owned engineering firm, continually trying new, technologically simple products, often outside the motor industry, to compensate for lack of resources for investment and for technological and other weaknesses.

The general conclusion on the motor industry must be that Volkswagen's acquisition of Škoda played an enormously important role. Events, however, did not unfold precisely in line with some of the more naïve hopes from the Czech side. It did not lead to the continuation of a Czech motor industry as a distinct entity. It did, however, provide an impetus to change across the whole sector that enabled a number of firms to play a role within a wider, European motor industry. The spillover effects have been very clear, in terms of technology and management methods, not least because they were consciously and deliberately fostered over a crucial transition period by the Škoda management.

Those that never came

Any overall assessment of the impact of inward investment is often hampered by the difficulty of judging what would have happened without the multinational companies (cf Lall, 1996b, p.64). The specific nature of Czech inward investment, coming overwhelmingly into firms that already exist, makes possible some comparison between enterprises in the same country. There are an enormous number of Czech firms that considered the possibility of linking up with a foreign partner and even set some shares aside in the voucher waves in the hope that a favourable deal could be sorted out. Perhaps the most remarkable disappointments are in the motor vehicle industry, where the search began very early and options were available, albeit not on terms that the Czech side felt it could accept. The story of those vehicle producers that found no partner contains some of the clearest disasters in the Czech transformation.

Liaz's lorry output fell from 14,500 in 1990 to 443 in 1995. Output of Tatra lorries fell from 14,585 to 422 over the same period, with employment down from 17,000 to 7,500. There was some subsequent recovery, with hopes of producing 3,000 vehicles in 1997, but there is no real chance that the firm can prosper. Avia did rather better, with a drop from 16,533 to 3,096 between 1990 and 1995. It even found a possible rescuer with a takeover by the South Korean firm Daewoo in August 1995. There are ambitious plans for expansion, but annual output has barely risen above 5,000 vehicles and the company continued to make losses through 1996 and 1997. There are still occasional optimistic claims from the Tatra management, but also voices suggesting that they should have looked more favourably on the deals on offer in the past.

Greenfield investments

The story can be completed with reference to investment from scratch, usually on greenfield sites. In the Czech case this has been relatively unimportant in relation to other aspects of the transformation process. The most significant cases in the early period were in the motor components industry. Some were linked to Volkswagen's acquisition of the Škoda car manufacturer while others were quite distinct. Particularly in these latter cases, investment was based around very specific, and therefore often rather limited, objectives. It could bring very welcome employment opportunities and some export earnings, but little further impact on the transformation as a whole.

An example is the investment by Siemens in a firm that started production of wiring for Opel cars in December 1992 in a Škoda-Plzeў plant in Stribro. It invested at a rate equivalent to roughly 30 per cent of turnover in new equipment and reconstruction of the building. By 1994 it was employing 900 and was facing a serious labour shortage. Further expansion was undertaken with investment in a plant in Plzeň, set to employ 500 producing the wiring for the BMW 5 series. This was a very simple case of taking advantage of cheap labour with an adequate level of skill for a labour-intensive part of car component manufacture. The choice of location, close to the Bavarian border, reflects an advantage of the Czech Republic that need not be related to its established motor industry.

Completely new investment outside the car components industry has been rather disappointing with, for example, little activity in the electronics sector. The experience of many other countries with a similar income level suggests that its contribution to economic development can be enormous, but the Czech Republic's ability to attract these kind of firms is limited by three important factors. The first is the relatively poor knowledge of English. The second is the low level of financial incentives for greenfield investments. The third is the weakness of the industrial infrastructure. These reflect partly past history and partly the extremely low priority attached to attracting this kind of investment.

There has been one major success with a Japanese electronics firm. Construction work began outside Plzeň in July 1996 on a television assembly plant for Matsushita and the factory opened in October 1997. A total investment of $66mn is planned with a target employment of 1,200 and an output of 1mn televisions per annum. Nevertheless, over 90 per cent of components will be imported, reflecting the low level of the electronics industry in the Czech Republic. Some further new investment was announced during 1997, but a flood of electronics firms is yet to materialise.

Conclusion

Czech experience is consistent with the argument that an investment development path is 'idiosyncratic and country specific' (Dunning and Narula, 1996,
p.22). The idiosyncracies in this case stem above all from the policy framework
which could be said to include two distinct elements. The first element has been
an open door approach to inward investment in general, but linked to minimal
general incentives or efforts to attract firms that could develop completely new
activities. This has attracted a few firms that can benefit from relative low wages
and a location close to industrial centres in Germany, but the impact has been
small.

The second element has been the close links between inward investment
and privatisation in which the Czech side has sometimes been very selective in
allowing foreign firms in. The implicit precondition has often been the likelihood
of a continuation of roughly the same level and form of activity as in the old
enterprise. This has set clear limits to the extent of inward investment, meaning
that it comes largely into the parts of the economy that were already reasonably
strong. It means, for example, and contrary to a widely held expectation (eg
Estrin, Hughes and Todd, 1997), that foreign ownership has typically not been
associated with vigorous restructuring and job losses. Foreign companies that
had such intentions were unlikely to be invited in and firms that needed such
surgery were left to struggle on under domestic ownership.

Nevertheless, where inward investment has occurred its impact has often
been very substantial. An attempt at precise quantification would be unrealistic,
but the peculiarities of the Czech process make it possible to contrast the fates
of enterprises and sectors under different forms of ownership. A mechanical
comparison would not be completely sound, as starting conditions and potential
were to some extent specific to every case. It is, however, clear across much of
industry that foreign ownership was the only way to overcome immediate
financial difficulties and to gain access to world-wide sales networks. The
success and potential of the motor industry is a clear illustration and there can
be no serious question that much of this was a result of foreign ownership.
There are, however, numerous cases where comparison is possible between
firms within the same sector and the conclusions are in many cases very similar.

It would, however, be wrong to conclude automatically that more inward
investment would be beneficial irrespective of the terms. The process whereby
firms came generally ensured that only those bringing clear benefits were allowed
in so that their subsequent performance can give a biased impression. Moreover,

there are also cases where the impact has been less clearly positive and some where it may even have been negative.

The real point, to judge from experience elsewhere in the world, is to devise a policy framework that incorporates inward investment into a general conception of economic development, based on an assessment of what is possible. The takeover of the Škoda car manufacturer by Volkswagen was the result of such strategic thinking, but it was an exceptional rather than a typical case. Good results also reflect the previous strength of that sector. The problem for the future, if the Czech Republic is to create a modern, technologically advanced market economy, is to find the means to develop sectors in which it did not have such favourable starting conditions.

It may be possible and appropriate in some sectors to support Czech-owned companies or to encourage inward investment only as a supplement where absolutely necessary. In other cases, such as electronics, domestic firms may be too weak to play a prominent role, but experience of countries at a similar level of development points to the importance of providing a range of infrastructural, educational and scientific preconditions even for the development of a sector around foreign firms. An important step was taken on 29 April 1998 when the Czech government finally approved a coherent package of incentives to inward investors. That may lead to a new upsurge in inward investment, particularly as accession to the EU becomes imminent, but it is unlikely on its own to lead to the emergence of strong high-tech sectors.

Note

[1] The research for this contribution was undertaken with support from the European Commission's Phare ACE Programme 1995. The particular project included case studies of the transformation of Czech enterprises using predominantly published material from Hospodárské noviny, Ekonom, Lidové noviny, Mladá fronta dnes, Rudé právo, Práce and Právo over the period 1989 to 1997.

References

Dunning J. (1993), *Multinational Enterprises and the Global Economy*, Addison-Wesley Publishing Company.

Dunning, J. and R. Narula (1996), 'The investment development path revisited', in Dunning, J., and R. Narula (eds), *Foreign Direct Investment and Governments: Catalysts for Economic Restructuring*, London: Routledge.

EIU (1997), Czech Republic, Country Report, 3rd quarter 1997, London: *The Economist Intelligence Unit.*

Estrin, S., K. Hughes and S. Todd (1997), *Foreign Direct Investment in Central and Eastern Europe*, London: Royal Institute of International Affairs.

Hiospodářké Noviny 17 February 1995.

Kolanda, M. (1989), *Strategie rozvoje strojírenského a elektrotechnického promyslu*, Politická ekonomie, 37.

Lall, S. (1996a), 'The investment development path: some conclusions', in Dunning and Narula, 1996.

Lall, S. (1996b), 'Transnational corporations and economic development', in UNCTAD, *Transnational Corporations and World Development*, London: International Thomson Business Press.

Lindové, Noviny 31 May 1991.

Myant, M. (1993), *Transforming Socialist Economies: The Case of Poland and Czechoslovakia*, Aldershot: Edward Elgar.

Myant M. (1996), 'Towards a policy framework in east-central Europe', in M. Had (ed.), *Economic Policy Framework in CEECs for the Process of Moving Towards the European Union*, Prague: Foundation for the Study of International Relations.

Myant, M. (1997), 'Enterprise restructuring and policies for competitiveness in the Czech Republic', *Ekonomický casopis*, 45, pp.546-567.

Rudé Právo 27 May 1991.

Štěpánek, V. (1989), *Společné podniky v socialistických zemích*, Prague: Ekonomický ústav Ceskoslovenské akademie ved.

Section 2:
The Change of Energy Systems

Introduction

ANNE LORENTZEN, BRIGITTA WIDMAIER, MIHÁLY LAKI

The development of an efficient infrastructure belongs to the determining factors behind the economic and social development that the CEE countries aim towards. Means of communication and transportation, systems of education and the production of goods and services in the energy sector belong to the necessary infrastructure of a modern society, whether centrally planned or based on market principles.

After the decline of the socialist system in CEE, privatisation was considered a main issue not only in industry, agriculture and trade, but also in the production of public goods and services, hitherto in state hands. In addition to the general goal of reducing the economic power of the state, privatisation was seen as a means to modernise outdated infrastructure systems as well as a preferred way to diminish public deficits. Not only from within, but also from the outside, pressure was put on the newly emerging market economies to privatize and liberalize a number of areas. The World Bank, for example, argued strongly in favour of privatisation and liberalisation, within the energy sector.

The energy sector is characterised by its complexity, consisting of several production and service units based on different kinds of technology related to the provision of fuel, production of heat and electricity, as well as their distribution. This complexity also implies that many different social agents representing different interests, authorities and competencies coexist in the sector. It is different from other industrial sectors in that it provides a basic commodity, namely energy, on which other producers and households depend. Further more it is important that production is continuous or at least follows the fluctuations in demand for energy. A stoppage of electricity supply can cause great damage in all the areas depending on it. A sufficient, stable and a cost-effective supply of energy should thus in principle be the general purpose of the energy sector.

Apart from the risk associated with an unstable energy supply, the production of energy gives rise to other problems. The provision of fuel as well as the transformation of fuel into electricity and heat can impact very negatively on the natural environment. Forests disappear, landscapes are turned into deserts, water is poisoned and the air is polluted. While the prevention of pollution has been on the agenda for the last 25 years in Western Europe, environmental protection received little attention in CEE before 1998. In Western Europe technology development in the energy sector has included both an improvement of energy efficiency in electricity and heat production, and better pollution control and recycling, not to mention energy saving measures among energy consumers. Environmental damage is considerable in some parts of CEE, and a renewal of the energy sector could be expected to include a move towards environmentally sound technologies.

The energy sector is also of strategic importance, and, consequently, a one-sided dependence on other countries through fuel imports or foreign ownership is politically unattractive. This is a strong argument in favour of continued public intervention in the energy sectors of CEE countries.

In the present phase of development there are two types of questions to be raised. One concerns the actual development of energy sectors in CEE since 1989: Which institutional and technological changes have taken place, and how can the changes be explained? Which types of privatisation are observable, and which new investments have been made? Do the new investments include environmentally best practice technologies?

A closer look at these factors leads to another question, more normative in nature: Through which institutions can cost efficiency and environmentally sound technological solutions be reached? Is privatisation the simple answer to this question and, in case it is, which types of privatisation and which organisations and companies are involved? In processes of privatisation, what should be the role of the local or national governments? The chapters of this section discuss these questions from different angles.

Davis provides a very useful overview of reform issues in the electricity industry of CEE. Firstly, the author looks at the dominant forms of trading and electricity structures emerging in the transition economies. Secondly, electricity price development and price setting mechanisms are considered and thirdly, economic regulation is reviewed.

In CEE the generation and distribution of energy has traditionally been publicly owned and vertically integrated, but today the countries differ concerning whether or not the generation and distribution of electricity is separated. They also differ in terms of type of ownership. While the World Bank sees the differences as stages and welcomes independent (private) power producers as the most efficient, this may not necessarily be a correct assumption since ownership and structure are linked to different local circumstances, and privatised ownership may be combined with lack of competition.

Formerly, pricing was used in CEE countries to subsidise industries or households, leading to high energy use. However, prices are now in focus during the adaptation of the sector to EU structures, where prices follow costs. This is difficult in CEE, where costs still cannot be calculated, but all CEE countries are in the process of phasing out energy subsidies, leading to substantial increases in electricity prices.

The World Bank agenda, however, is not necessarily being realised. The wish of governments to control this important sector, the felt need for subsidisation, as well as continued pressure to maintain pre-existing social structures, for example in the area of employment, counteract the liberal trends exerting world wide influence.

Hvelplund and Lund analyse changes in the East German energy system after 1990, when the two Germanys were united. The article analyses how specific clusters of techniques that are not environmentally optimal are being favoured by the new owners of energy production systems, techniques which do not fundamentally differ from the old East German ones. In other words, a path dependency at the institutional level exists, which results in a mere re*building* of the East German energy system, at a time when a genuine re*structuring* would seem optimal.

The strategy that is being implemented today is, according to the authors, to update the old techniques, and rebuild the system based upon brown coal. There will be some improvements in the energy system, but there is no fundamental re-orientation as far as energy production is concerned towards environmentally sustainable techniques. Taking into consideration that the installations have a lifetime of 20 to 40 years, East Germany will be bound to brown-coal-based high pollution technologies for more than a generation. The organizational structure of German energy production also reflects the existence of strong political influence which tends to impede choices in the direction of the most cost efficient and ecologically sound constructions.

Also in Hungary an urgent need to restructure the power sector has been felt. *Knudsen* characterises the Hungarian energy sector on the eve of transition as strongly centralised, having old and out-dated capital stock, and technology based on the extensive use of labour and fuel, much of the latter imported from Russia. Energy supply at low prices was considered a social good, and making changes in pricing was therefore a touchy issue. Environmental concerns, on the other hand, were not in focus.

Between 1994 and 1996 the goal of privatising the Hungarian energy sector was widely achieved. But even though there was competition in the tenders, and investments and some modernisation were made, no substantial change of technology took place. The social agents are bound by old perceptions which, to a large extent, form their interests and define their possibilities to act.

Even though market mechanisms had only worked to a very limited degree, leaving most processes to planners, *Knudsen* shows how, in the Hungarian electricity sector, the market economic discourse has been able to link lines of action which were otherwise likely to be incompatible.

4 Restructuring Hungary's Electricity Sector

Modernisation discourses and technological determinism

NIELS KNUDSEN

Introduction

During a brief period after the break-down of the communist system in Eastern Europe, there was a certain openness as to the possible directions of economic and social reform. The discourse of 'shock therapists' was balanced by discussions of 'a third way' between socialism and market economy, or by the point of view that a guided transition might prove less painful (and indeed less costly in economic terms) than the radical introduction of market forces in all sectors of the economy (Samson, 1993, pp 59–70).

In the recent years, the transition discourse has changed. On the one hand it became clear, at least to most scholars, that 'shock therapy' was unrealistic for the simple reason that social inertia prevented a rapid shift in production mode. On the other hand, the welfare benefits defended in the 'third way' approach have come to be regarded as expensive habits of a spoiled and under-productive middle class. The aim for today's reformers seems to be the securing of a steady turn towards market economic practices in all areas of the economy.

In the laborious process of transforming social institutions, this goal seems to provide an effective indicator of the direction which the reforms must take, at least in areas where the functioning of the market mechanism is easy to install and monitor. In more practical terms, this goal is far more complicated. For in the 'real existing market economies' of the West, the functioning of the market mechanism is indeed strongly restricted, by tangible institutions (such as legal and regulatory systems) as well as tacit institutions such as fair behaviour in business.

The rude market mechanism, balancing supply and demand, in fact works in a marketplace which is strongly restricted in what is on offer as well as in the ways in which it can be traded. In the case of raw materials where a large number of suppliers offer the same product to a large number of buyers, the

91

market mechanism is a good description of economic practices. But in the case of for example infrastructure, the market mechanism has little influence on development.

The fact that the ideal market economy does not exist, and in most cases never could, is a dilemma for the understanding of the transition process: Is the market economy a means for obtaining the welfare of Western countries, or is it a goal for the transition, being itself an indication of a well accomplished modernisation process? And in those cases where the market mechanism is not effective, should the transition economies imitate western practices (though not consistent with market principles), or should they introduce regulatory practices which emulate the functioning of a perfect market (which will in reality mean the re-introduction of a degree of centralised resource allocation)?

In the following it will be argued that the market has become an ideal for the transition process, and that it has achieved this partly because it lends legitimacy from the concept of the Modern. (This is a concept which is not alien to the thinking of centrally planned economic systems either.) Much of the discussion has come to address the problem of 'how' to progress towards a market economy, 'how' to overcome so-called 'market imperfections', thus ignoring that the understanding of the real existing market economies is rudimentary, and that these are far from representing ideal market economies. (Cf. Dilley, 1992 pp 1–27, Jameson, 1990, 260–278.) It is particularly worthwhile to notice that minor distortions in an otherwise effective market can lead to major mis-allocation of resources, as the market is bound to reinforce the effect: only players who exploit the opportunity will survive.

Yet in the real transformation process, indigenous and foreign actors pick up different elements of the largely incoherent 'market economic' concept, and fit them to their own notions. The result is a string of related actions and concepts which all reflect different constituents of the market economic ideal, but in the totality of which the market mechanism at best works arbitrarily.

This chapter summarises the development of the power sector in Hungary after the break-down of the central planning system. The outcome of the 'market' reforms in this field lead to a result which is far from optimal in a market economic sense. However, the chapter aims to demonstrate how each of the agents in the process take in some of the contrasting elements of the market economic principles, which then provides legitimacy, meaning and direction to his actions.

Methodology

The theoretical background for the research presented in this chapter is partly institutional economic theory, and partly neo-institutionalism in sociology and organisation theory.

New institutionalism in economics (such as North (1990)) stresses the way in which institutions guide economic transactions, thus concluding that economic actors not only behave 'rationally' in the narrow economic sense, but that an economic regime[1] is as much based on tacit as on tangible institutions. These range from legal regulations, which ensure that competition takes place on equal terms, to tacit agreements about, for example, fair practices in negotiating and fulfilling contracts. Much of the work with economic institutionalism has been based on the assumption that transaction costs (documented to be an important and growing cost in modern economies which are based on complicated economic transactions) depend on the degree to which economic agents can be expected to follow the same rules without necessarily enforcing them. In the opposite case, transaction costs such as negotiating and enforcing contracts would claim an even larger share of the added value of production, and in the end make many transactions impossible. The conclusion is that the market economy is not only defined by the rational choice of free and fully informed agents, but that the actions of economic agents are restricted by a set of rules and habits which are only partly tangible.

Even though economic institutionalism questions the total rationality of the free agent, its vision is still materialist. As opposed to this, new institutionalism in sociology and organisational theory questions even the possibility of basing social theory on a materialist view. Rather, the reality to which the social (and economic) agent is reacting is already interpreted, and therefore already shaped by his perception. Reality is socially constructed. Thus, the importance of material realitity becomes less: social agency is formed by the perceptive structure which is shared by the agents, and which to a large extent forms their interests as well as defines their possibilities to act. Thus, what becomes relevant to social science is not so much the relation between social agents and material reality as it is the agents' own interpretation of this relationship (See for example Berger et al, 1966, pp 1–18 and 185–9; DiMaggio et al. 1991, pp 1–40).

In this theoretical context, economic theory becomes particularly interesting as a study object, as it indeed fulfils some of the functions ascribed to institutions in the sociologist traditions: It forms our perception of our relation with the 'real' (material), it defines which actions we can take (such as profit-oriented economic transactions), and is the most developed common reference (social reality) in debates about social reform, policy, performance of government, etc. In this chapter, economic theory is mostly treated as such a common cognitive reality.

In the developed market economies, the relationship between agency and the shared image of reality is disguised by unconscious practices (habits), which allow for large inconsistencies. This is necessary, as the shared reality includes conflicting norms and concepts, which are in this way balanced (An example could be the conflict between the concepts of 'citizen' and 'economic actor', which in principle do not have the same interests, rights and obligations). The balance is often disturbed and readjusted, but most often in a continuous and partly unconscious manner.

In transition economies, the readjustment of practices is suddenly made conscious because of radical, discontinuous social change. Therefore the influence of economic theory as a common reference, providing a cognitive model for in-terpreting reality and reforming social practices, becomes of major importance. At the same time, the influence of this shared, socially constructed reality becomes easier to grasp, as it is very often made explicit.

The methodology used in this chapter uses the following steps: It identifies a development trend in the reform of Hungary's electricity sector. It then compares the trend to an alternative trend, which would be more economically efficient, and therefore should come closer to a 'market economic' development, if the argument that the perfect market would allocate resources optimally is accepted.

On this background, the chain of direct and indirect influences which form the current development is traced. For each major element, the chapter then explores how this influence relates to the image of the market economy (shared cognitive reality), and tries to point out which other forces are balanced with the principles of market economy. The approach could be termed 'relationist' (Latour 1993, 1994), as it puts more emphasis on the chain of actions and chain of arguments than on the situation and actions of the individual agent.

The research is largely based on interviews with representatives of the relevant organisations, and on analysis of the large body of documents which accompany the reform of the sector, largely consisting of laws, regulations and technical analyses.

The outlined approach has an intrinsic paradox: On the one hand, it is based on a materialist assumption ('that an alternative development path can be outlined and its performance analysed') and on the other hand it insists that material reality is secondary and pre-interpreted, and that cognitive reality is the primary object for social research. Therefore, the alternative development trend which is outlined by the author must be seen as an alternative interpretation (or even narrative) of material reality, whose claim to be more efficient than the present development is confined to the cognitive sphere of energy planning and economic forecasting.

Economic transition and the Modern

The concept of modernisation can lead to an understanding of the above paradox. In a time when most social researchers acknowledge that Modernity is something of the past (or even an illusion of the past, see e.g. Latour (1994, pp 23–71)), how can we speak of 'modernisation' of the former centrally planned economies? And how can the West, with its fairly pragmatic governance practices, talk about 'modernisation' of a system, which is based on such rationalist ideas as central planning — far more 'hard-core' modernist than most thinking about the market economy (see Ruthland, 1985, pp. 24-67)?

On the surface, this is explained by the two different meanings of the word modern. The Modern, with a capital M, contains the whole idea of Modernity, with its ideal belief in the rational, in progress, and in the victory of an enlightened humanity. As opposed to this, in common use modern would simply mean 'up-to-date'. And it would be in this sense that the transition economies would be modernised.

However, a closer look at the transition discourse shows a deep influence from Modern concepts in the larger sense, and it is worthwhile to enquire into this modernisation debate. The standard economic model is indeed the locus where the belief in progress, rationality, and the next-to-unlimited possibilities possessed by the individual are maintained. It is thus rooted in ideas of Modernity. This paradigm has suffered remarkably little impact from theoretical as well as empirical difficulties, ranging from Coase's critique of the market (1937), via Simons critique of the concept of rationality (1957) to the latest critiques from neo-institutionalists and the 'new micro-economy' (Cahuc, 1993, for a review).[2]

In its role as means-and-goals, the market economic 'Modernisation' model comes to function as a common reference in the more locally situated reform discourses. The market economic language has become the language of Mo-dernisation, and certainly possesses some qualities which make it suit this role. On the concrete level, it is a language of the rational and efficient. The intrinsic (Modern) values of this language claim to be universal, and therefore thwart or overrule the more cumbersome debates over 'local' values and interests which are at play in the process of radically changing society. Further, market economic language has ideological references to the 'free' and democratic West, even though the theoretically 'free', rational agent of market economic theory actually has little to do with the free subject of a democratic state.

Thus, in the reform process in former centrally planned economies, 'the M/ modern' includes two principles, which tend to merge into one mental category. On the one hand there is the image of the Modern, which carries the values of freedom (the free subject) and efficiency/prosperity (the rational). On the other, the 'modern' is the opposite of what was inherited from the past. It often takes inspiration from what exists in the West (and is hence 'opposite' of the existing) and can take very concrete forms (transfer of technology, regulatory principles, etc.). This concept is often a guide for concrete actions, and the relation to the concept is very theoretical. In the conclusion of this chapter, we will see how the confounding of the two concepts has played a role in the formation of techno-logical change in the Hungarian power sector.

It follows that the image of the market economy has different but related functions in the stabilised market economies and in the transition economies. In the market economies, the image of the perfect market is used as a reference for real practices, for instance in the case of measuring and correcting market imperfections. On the concrete level, the functioning of the market mechanism is sustained (and restricted) by a number of institutions (such as regulatory bodies, courts), and by the practices of companies and consumers, which together ensure a stable regime in which the market mechanism plays some allocative role.

In the transition economies, the image of the market plays a much more radical role, as there is no stable economic regime needing only corrections. In the actual functioning of the economy, therefore, the incoherence of the concept becomes more apparent: On the one hand, reformers adopt institutional forms and practices from the market economies, not taking into account that these lead to grave market distortions. On the other hand, new or existing economic actors emerge, who openly exploit the capitals at their disposal (including political capital, force, etc.), without producing new riches. Table 4.1 summarises the difference between the real functioning of market economic principles and their value as cognitive reference.

In reforming the actual functioning of the economy, external forces are active in several ways: The imitation of institutions and practices is promoted very actively by the European Community, for example by way of its Acquis Communautaire, a set of legal and organisational requirements which all member

Table 4.1 Market principles as a cognitive reference and as functioning allocation principles.

	'Market' economy	'Transition' economy
Theoretical understanding of the market	Competition and Pareto-optima[3] as a guide for real (regulated or imperfect) practices	Meta-language of transition. Teleogy
Actual functioning of the market	Productive and transactional practices embedded in institutions, habits, 'regime'	Imitation of institutions and practices. Exploitation of possibilities (opportunity)

countries must meet. The role of consultants who live from implementing their adapted or pre-fabricated concepts must also be stressed. For example, the privatisation of power systems is a global industry for such companies as Andersen Consulting (probably the world's leading consultancy firm in the field, advising both governments ('sellers') and private clients ('buyers') on electricity sector de-regulation and privatisation).

Foreign companies actively exploit the new possibilities, often without benefiting the national economy accordingly. For example, many reformers had hoped that liberalisation of the economy would lead to foreign investment in production. These reformers were surprised when the first wave of foreign investment largely focused on retail businesses. This has added to the already considerable debt burden of the 'new democracies' by boosting the consumption of imported goods without increasing the domestic production of wealth.

In the following example, we shall look at the way in which the market economic principle was conceptually interpreted and practically implemented in the specific example of Hungary's power system.

Background

When Hungary broke with the central planning system in 1990, it had inherited an industrial structure which was unfit for the new, market-oriented environment. The problems related to power production and distribution were typical of these problems (IEA, 1993; MVM 1995a; Valentiny, 1994; interviews):

- Technology was optimised for other criteria than efficiency, as labour and primary energy were abundant in the communist economy. Thus, energy production was very labour intensive and utilised the energy sources poorly.

- The capital stock was old and under-maintained, largely due to an increasing capital scarcity in the 1970s and 1980s.

- The institutional structure of the sector was strongly centralised, had a high degree of integration between economic, technical and political decision making and a high degree of autonomy. This created a high degree of inertia and little incentive for structural change.

- The sector was dependent on Russia as a supplier of primary energy, and infrastructures such as pipelines and a high voltage grid linked the country with the former Soviet Union.

- During the central planning period, environmental concerns had been less than the concern for accelerating economic development. Therefore, the environmental impact from the power sector was very high as compared to West European standards.

- Under Communism, the population had come to regard energy, which was strongly subsidised, as a social good. Therefore, the introduction of higher (ultimately cost reflective) energy prices has been a politically sensitive issue during the transition period.

Given this background, the need for restructuring the power sector in almost every respect (physical, financial, organisational and operational) was very urgent. External pressures from very different sources (ranging from environmentalists to the nuclear lobby), added to the necessity.

The Present Standard of Hungary's Power Sector

During the last years of the period of central planning, Hungary had come to rely on electricity imports from the Soviet Union (largely the Ukraine). Therefore, the dramatic decrease in power consumption from 1990 onwards did not create over-capacity in the national supply system, as opposed to most other transition economies of Central and Eastern Europe. As it was politically decided to reduce imports of electricity (in order to reduce dependency on Russia and Ukraine), capacity largely matched demand in 1993-1994, when the trend in power consumption was stabilised (interviews).

The power production units are old. Calculated as a balanced average, the service life (time in operation since commissioning) of existing power plants was 19.6 years by mid-1995. For coal fired plants, the figure was 26.6 years. Average efficiency is about 30 per cent, the average for coal fired plants is approximately 27 per cent.[4] This should be compared with 'best technology' values of approximately 45 per cent for coal fired plants and 55 per cent for oil or gas fired plants based on combined cycle technology.[5]

The low efficiency, coupled with very poor environmental performance, means that much of the existing capacity must be replaced. The National transmission company, Magyar Villamos Müvek Rt. (MVM), assesses that only 2,000 MW oil and gas fired capacity, and the four existing nuclear units of 460 MW (of a total generation capacity of 7,200 MW) can be retained beyond 2010. Even this requires substantial investments in upgrading technology (specifically investments in flue gas cleaning). Before the year 2000, 800 MW of coal fired capacity must be abandoned, in the following decade another 3,000 MW must be retired.

In the basic MVM scenario, this will require the construction of 4,000 MW new capacity before 2010. The combined pressure from environmental regulation and the demand for efficient operation creates a huge demand for new investments in the power sector (MVM 1995a, 1995b, 1995c).

Table 4.2 Development plan of the MVM strategy department; all figures are MW capacity (Compiled from information in IEA, 1995, MVM 1995a)

Year	1995-7	1998 - 2000	2001	2002	2003	2004	2005	2006	2007	2008	2009	2010
Available capacity			7340	7440	7480	7560	7760	7890	8000	7960	8080	8030
Installed capacity	7290	7600	7880	8230	8170	8090	8020	8150	8260	8220	8340	8290
New capacity												
Coal		200	310			200	200	200	160		160	
Oil				550	470							
Gas	380	500	250	100		150						
Retirement	100	390	280	300	530	430	270	70	50	40	40	50

A further demand for new investments has been induced by Hungary's aspiration to join the West European Union for the Coordination of Production and Transmission of Electricity (UCPTE) network co-operation. Joining the UCPTE will allow Hungary to be connected directly to the network of the members (by operating the network synchronously with these). This will make it easier to increase the imports and exports from UCPTE countries, and to draw on their generation reserves. But UCPTE has requirements for the total capacity and availability of the power plant park. Fulfilling these standards has demanded the erection of two peak load gas turbines[6] (financed with the participation of the World Bank), and UCPTE standards form the basis of MVM development plans. Hungary was temporarily connected with the UCPTE network in 1997, which demonstrates the success of Hungary's modernisation effort on the technical level (Valentiny, 1994; interviews).

Hungary has at its disposal some indigenous energy sources, particularly coal, lignite and gas. But gas production has peaked, and much of the coal production is un-economic and will be gradually reduced. Hungary is linked with Russia through oil and gas pipelines. Oil-based power plants have been erected in connection with the oil refineries, and are fuelled with residual oil. In order to reduce fuel dependency, the National gas supply company (Hungarian Oil And Gas Company, MOL), is building new transmission pipelines, connecting Hungary with the West European gas network.

In the past, emphasis was put on fuel diversification, and this trend will be continued. For historical reasons, Hungary is particularly keen on avoiding dependency on Russian energy supply. This means that the capacity based on oil and natural gas cannot expand.

A large part of the Hungarian heat market is supplied by district heating. The power supply utilities have supplied much of the heat to the district heating networks. In the statistics, many of Hungary's power plants therefore appear as 'co-generation units'[7] (nearly 30 per cent of the total capacity (MVM, 1995a.). However, the sense of co-generation in these statistics is by utility (heat and power production by the same utility is 'co-generation'[8]). In technical terms, only a few per cent of power generation is co-generated which becomes apparent from an inspection of district heating production statistics.

Reform of the Hungarian Power Supply Sector

Like the rest of the planned economies, Hungary developed a highly integrated energy sector during the period of central planning. In the reform process, electricity supply was separated from direct state control (through corporatisation), and was split up into separate companies responsible for generation, transmission, and distribution. The aim of this unbundling was partly to improve public regulation and control over the performance of individual sub-sectors, and partly to enable the privatisation of the new companies.

The need for public control stemmed from the fact that the electricity company had a monopoly and thus opportunities for cross-subsidising specific consumer groups and for hiding profits. The unbundling was also intended to allow a precise cost allocation between generation, transmission and distribution of electricity. Here it is important to notice that electricity distribution is a natural monopoly, which cannot be regulated by the market mechanism. Countries (such as England) which have highly liberalised electricity markets still have a strong regulation of this monopoly.

A first attempt at privatisation of the distribution and generation companies in 1992 was unsuccessful. It was acknowledged that the failure was largely due to the inappropriate regulatory framework: Pricing and cost allocation was opaque, and political control over the sector was not sufficiently well defined, thus placing a high political risk on possible investors. For this and other reasons, a thorough reform of Hungary's energy legislation was initiated in 1992, and the resulting Electricity Act, which lays down the principles for pricing of electricity and for the granting and withdrawal of licences, was finally approved by Parliament in 1994. The new regulatory framework (see below) gave the investors more confidence in the sector. Privatisation of distribution and generation companies was re-initiated in 1994. All of the distribution companies and a number of production utilities were almost instantly privatised.

Privatisation of the companies has taken place through competitive bidding. In all cases, the investors have bought a minority of the shares (typically 40 per cent), but with an option to buy majority, and with the right to chair the board. The bidders had to present a realistic business plan and to demonstrate experience from similar activities in the tender.

For strategic reasons, the State will retain ownership of the transmission company and of the Páks nuclear power plant. The transmission company, which is a residue of the original electricity conglomerate, also has a central role in the planning of power sector expansion.

In all cases, privatisation took place through a sale of shares, rather than the issuing of new shares. In this way, privatisation generated a benefit for the central budget, rather than a recapitalisation of the companies.

In all but a few cases, privatisation was carried through between 1994 until autumn, 1996. The few exceptions were small power plants which had been merged with coal and lignite mines with uncertain prospects. The last privatisation round, planned for the autumn of 1996, failed, probably due to political intervention in the regulation of electricity and heat tariffs during the same period.

In the research for the present chapter, the impact at plant level has been explored on the basis of only a small sample of production and distribution companies. In none of these cases had privatisation led to a radical change of organisation, reduction of staff or modernisation of capital equipment. Introduction of computerised operation statistics, modern management tools and accounting happened gradually. Privatisation and licensing procedures specify that a business plan for the plant must be presented, and in many cases there is a specific demand for new investment. In the first phase after privatisation, change seems to be centred on the introduction of these new investments, rather than changes in the existing (management and shop-floor) organisation.

Regulation and Institutional Set-Up

The institutional and regulatory frameworks are designed to meet a number of contrasting goals, namely:

- Attracting new investment to the sector,

- Ensuring the optimal allocation of new investments, and preventing over-investment,

- Gradually introducing competition in the sector, without threatening stability,

- Ensuring a fair pricing of electricity, relating to the ideal of cost reflective prices and the abolition of cross subsidies.

The best way to describe the regulatory framework is to demonstrate the stages of planning and tendering new capacity.

The first step in this process is the elaboration of a strategic investment plan. This is a long-term capacity development plan, generated with the aid of computerised models (the OECD 'WASP' tool, which selects a 'least cost' sequence of investments under set pre-conditions). The elaboration of this plan is the task of the planning department at the transmission company (the MVM Rt.). With a given set of criteria, the model generates an 'optimal' investment sequence by use of the present value of future costs. The electricity planners correct the results of the model to meet political goals, such as fuel mix.

Plants which become economically obsolete are retired. However, many retirements are due to the inability of old plants to meet environmental requirements. A combination of the two can occur where plants can be retrofitted to meet requirements, but this is not economically feasible.

The outputs from the model are an investment sequence and a retirement scheme, which are optimal given a specific set of assumptions, and often referred to as a 'least cost' investment plan. The inputs are partly the general as-sumptions (such as demand prognoses, interest rate, etc.), and partly a specific set of 'candidate' plants with given characteristics, from which the model can choose.

The strategic investment plan serves two major purposes: It is the reference for the negotiation of power purchase contracts with generators, and it is the basis of the Government's establishment plan. This plan is based on the strategic investment plan, but Government has been known to make minor adjustments (such as advancing the establishment of a particular plant, a step which can be interpreted as an attempt to increase the value of assets due for privatisation).

When approved by Government, the establishment plan serves as a basis for a competitive tendering procedure: The establishment plan describes the main criteria for the individual plants. Tenderers are offered to bid for the licence to construct these plants, specifying investment, performance, technical details and business plans for their proposals. Thus it is ensured that licensing is in harmony with the least cost investment plan.

Prices and licences are regulated with reference to production costs. On the basis of a survey of necessary costs (carried out to avoid hidden profits), prices are regulated to allow investors an 8 per cent profit on their investment as a minimum. Efficient generators may earn up to 12 per cent of their investment as a profit; above that, they must split their earnings with the consumers (in the form of reduced tariffs). These regulatory principles are specified in the Electricity Act.

The new regulatory framework should promote improved efficiency in the sector, and it should be possible to obtain a performance comparable to that of existing market economies. In the case of Hungary's electricity supply, this will first of all be obtained through investment in new technology. Therefore, the new regulatory framework must first of all be judged by its ability to create change in technology, and not least to allocate investment in new technology, and to promote the most efficient technology available.

It should be clear from the above that the planning and regulation of technological development is designed to emulate the performance of a market, but that the market mechanism is operational only in a very few cases. Moreover, even where the market mechanism operates, the scope of competition is very narrow. There is not competition between generation and energy savings, as the demand curve is set; there is not competition from alternative technologies, as the 'candidate' plants are selected by the planners on the background of their knowledge and tradition;[9] and there is not competition between different organisations, types of ownership, etc., as these factors are specified in the tender conditions.

The result is a 'selection sequence' which determines the technological development in the electricity sector. Each step bears in it elements of the market, together with elements of a programmed development. The resulting sequence has proved effective (it ensures new investments), but inefficient (it is strongly conservative to technological change, and eliminates effective competition in a number of areas). The elements of competition and planning, respectively, are illustrated in the table below:

Table 4.3 Elements of market and planning in the chain of technology choice in the renovation process

	Element of planning	Element of market
Strategic investment plan	Pre-selected criteria: Demand, interest rate, plant type (candidates)	Emulates Pareto optimum under static conditions
Licensing	Pre-selected criteria for bidders (e.g. experience from similar projects)	Selects the lowest investment costs for a given plant (competitive bidding for licence)
Prices and tariff setting	Long-term price regulation based on necessary costs	Incentive for efficiency at plant level

It must be remarked how the elements of planning have priority over the elements of the market, as they define the playing field of competition. In this way it is clear that technological development is largely determined by institutions. However, each of these include or allow an element of competition. In that way, the planning becomes legitimate: The market only determines minor details of the development, even though the market *is* at play in the process. The market mechanism does prevent excessive abuse of a monopoly situation, but does nothing to shape development in terms of choice of technology.[10]

We have now seen that the 'market orientation' of Hungary's power sector is effective (new capital is attracted), but that the market only works in very limited fields. In the following, we shall discuss how the restructuring of Hungary's power sector is largely driven by three discourses with very little interference, but with a shared reference in the modernisation and (more vaguely) market orientation of the sector.

Three 'Modernisation' Discourses

Attempts at reforming the electricity sector have mainly been driven by three different rationales, carried by different organisations, and which have been institutionalised in different (partly competing) forms.

1. The privatisation discourse

At a very early point, the objective of privatising Hungary's electricity sector was articulated in policy. The powerful Minister of Privatisation was a driving force behind the aspiration to privatise. The desire to privatise was the background for the first electricity sector reform, which led to an unsuccessful privatisation attempt in 1992. Modifications of this reform (eventually leading to the Electricity Act in 1994) were designed to make privatisation possible. For example, potential buyers and their consultants were consulted during the formulation of the Act.

From the point of view of market economic theory, private (or rather external), profit-seeking ownership of an enterprise is necessary to secure the accountability of management, which will otherwise have an incentive to 'misdirect' their effort, for example by disguising profits as employee benefits. (See for example Frydman et al. (1994) pp. 10-14 and pp. 100-102).

This part of the privatisation discourse constitutes the 'overlap' between efforts at privatisation and the market economic rationale from which, we argue, it gains legitimacy.

There are other obvious purposes of privatising the sector, such as:

• attracting foreign capital, and thus reducing the deficit of the central budget;

- breaking the monopoly of the national power production company;

- creating links to Western power utilities which would facilitate investment and the transfer of technology.

Each of these purposes had some weight in the privatisation debate. But most interviewees, including staff and consultants of the privatisation agency, acknowledge that the motor behind privatisation has primarily been the desire to reduce the public deficit. The success criteria for the privatisation agency seems from the beginning to have been the income which could be obtained from, and the privatisation effort is linked to the debate about the central budget deficit, which dominates much of the public debate.

One indicator of the 'income generation drive' is the chosen form of privatisation. If the argument for privatisation is to improve sector performance, the obvious solution would be to issue new shares. This would ensure (needed) new capital to the companies in the form of new equity, but would not generate in-come to the central budget. In the chosen model of privatisation, shares have been sold off through a tendering procedure in which the highest price has been the main criteria. This has secured an income to the State, but has not provided the companies with needed capital (interviews).

Rather, much of the physical capital would be technically outdated if exposed to genuine competition, and what has really been sold is thus rather the right to produce and develop the companies — a de facto monopoly, very contrary to the rationale of privatisation. It is significant that investors who operate in competitive markets (such as English and American companies) have shown very little interest in the tenders, whereas power utilities in continental Europe have obtained ownership of most generation and distribution companies. Those investors who have been interviewed for this survey refer to the investments as 'strategic'.

The privatised generation companies are doubly vulnerable. On the one hand, they are sensitive to price and tariff regulation which might set prices lower than production costs. There has been extensive debate over the Government's tariff setting in the near past. Some of the new, Western European investors admit that this risk is settled at the political level: If the Hungarian Government continues to set unattractive electricity prices, the utilities consider themselves strong enough to create pressure from Western Governments on Hungary which will correct the prices. It must be noted that the electricity utilities in continental Europe (which represent the larger share of the investors) are closely connected with Government in their own countries, such as the EDF (France),which is a state-owned company, and RWE (Germany), which is a shareholder company largely owned by local governments.

In addition, the reconstructed companies are sensitive to open competition which would allow for direct competition from alternative technologies (such as co-generation, see Co-Gen Europe (1996 pp 64–70) and Knudsen (forthcoming)). In many cases, alternative supply structures could create remarkable gains in efficiency, but these are excluded from the market by the regulatory system.

The conclusion is that the theoretical aspect of ownership reform — that of creating external ownership which in turn would hold management responsible for efficient operation — supplements a real agenda of selling off shares in Government owned enterprises at the highest price. This has only been possible through the introduction of a non-competitive (or rather, selectively competitive) regulatory framework. It is by nature conservative of·the existing structure (they are the elements of this structure which must be sold off). The theoretical argument of establishing external ownership relates to the rational (and hence 'Modern') principles of economic theory, and claims to represent an enlightened rationality. The real practice rather points to modernisation in the opposite sense: to do something which will cause the existing to change in a given direction. However, the real changes are presented as the introduction of market economic principles, thus gaining legitimacy from the 'rational' market logic.

2. Technical modernisation

This discourse is largely carried by the National Electricity Company (the MVM), which has been given the role of electricity transmission company after the unbundling of the sector. Through its department for strategic planning, the company still plays a key role in deciding the future of the electricity supply sector.

Through the elaboration of the strategic investment plan, the planners of the MVM largely design technological change in the sector. In practice, the Government's investment plan and the actual licences have deferred very little from the strategic investment plan thus far.

In many respects, the least cost investment plan represents the ideal of central planning. The structure of the sector is decided by the planner, and competition only takes place at a very late stage (bidding for the planned licences), with very little scope for innovation or competition between alternative technologies or supply structures. In some cases, competition is not effective at all, such as is the case when new capacity must replace an existing coal or lignite fired plant to which coal production is linked.

In principle the scenario model 'emulates' market competition, but puts more weight on long-run total costs of production than competitors in a market would. This rules out some of the failures of the market mechanism (short-sighted investments, uncertainty about the future), but introduces others:

1. Supply alternatives are indicated by the planners, and it is up to them to introduce competition from alternative supply forms. The choice of competing technologies in the plans has been very conservative, which in effect limits the possibilities for innovation.
2. The MVM has an obvious interest in promoting the existing structure which is easily controlled, both technically and economically, by this distributor.
3. The chosen scenario planning model is pro-active with regard to new investments (which it prescribes), and the composition of the fuel mix, which is a political priority. It is re-active to most other inputs (such as electricity demand, fuel costs, etc.), but these parameters are 'institutionalised' through their incorporation in the plan, in the way that they are altered from mere assumptions to references for the planning process.
4. It is worth noticing that the strategic planning department comprises the same planners who prepared the investment plans before the introduction of the unbundled structure (largely by use of the same tools). Therefore, the image of a proper sector development looks much like the preferred structure of the former energy conglomerate.

Most of the technological change in the sector (on the structural or 'macro' level) is prescribed by the least cost investment scenario. But this is seen to work contrary to market competition by excluding the effect of innovation, excluding competition between different supply concepts, promoting a structure beneficial to the transmission company, institutionalising assumptions (such as the demand curve) and basing itself on the mind-set of a limited number of planners, rather than a large number of (potentially) innovative competitors.

The arguments for planning the electricity supply sector development rather than leaving this development to the market are legion, and largely fall within the categories of National security and market imperfection. These will not be debated here. Relating to the issues at hand, it must only be noted that the chosen 'least cost' planning method pretends to 'emulate' the performance of a perfect market, but does so with a number of limitations as listed above.

As was the case in the previous example (the privatisation discourse), there is a discrepancy between the real use of the market concept, and the imagery generated by the mention of the market as decisive for the choice of technology.

In the real decision process, the market mechanism plays an insignificant role, and 'modernisation' is a simple question of replacing technology with more up-to-date hardware. Yet because certain elements of the market rationale are built into the process, and the market is at play at certain stages, it seem possible to relate the choice of technology to the concept of a market based development. A practice which differs from central planning only in detail has been linked to the image of Modernisation which is intrinsic in the implementation of the market rationality.

One of the real motives for continuing this planning seems to be that it allows the MVM to maintain considerable control over the sector, and at the same time conserve the original power supply structure. This is demonstrated by examples of strong resistance to the idea of opening the field to uncontrolled entry of small generators, or the introduction of de-centralised power production, as expressed by MVM planners (interviews). The control of power development is exercised without offending the interests of the other strong players in the field, and without threatening the image of rational development.

3. Environmental modernisation

In market economic theory, the role of environmental regulation is to correct those market failures (externalities) relating to the fact that the costs induced by pollution are not afflicted on the polluter, but on his environment. However, this line of argument is not used in its radical form in Hungary (as it is in few places in Europe), and thus demands that the external costs of pollution should be calculated and paid by the polluter are not a concern.

The discourse gains much of its momentum from Hungary's aspirations to be included in the European Union. Legislation has been adjusted to meet European standards and is likely to be reinforced because of European pressure. Environmental concerns are not the first priority among the Hungarian population, according to decision makers as well as environmentalists (interviews).

As described previously, environmental regulations are a driving factor in the reform of the Hungarian power sector. Emission limits render much of the generation capacity obsolete, and retrofitting is technically or economically unfeasible.

Environmental regulations are not coupled with a direct concern for the power sector. Regulatory principles, mostly emission standards, are general, relating, for example, allowable emission levels to plant size. Regulations are introduced gradually, with the highest pace for large generators.

Focus of the regulations is on the plant (re-active). There has been no systematic attempt from environmental regulators to calculate the effects of regulations on the power sector, or to optimise the effort. The pace of the introduction of new standards is negotiated with the actors, mainly the MVM.

The regulatory principle is that pollution must be reduced to a certain minimum standard; otherwise the polluter will be fined or will not be allowed an operational license. In a market economic sense, the argument is to ensure that conditions are the same for all polluters. However, this argument is only valid if the pollution is reduced to a negligible level. If the issue is to reduce the total amount of, for example, CO_2 emissions, a pollution fee or similar would be necessary to introduce competition between clean technologies (if this is deemed unacceptable or insufficient, similar results can be obtained by emulation of effects of alternative technologies and the according, pro-active planning measures. This, however, would introduce the same faults as mentioned in the section on least-cost planning).

To summarise, the introduction of new environmental standards is a driving force in the renovation of the sector. But it is the aspiration to membership in the European Union which has given the environmentalists the power to implement these standards, and the scope of reforms reaches only so far as to fulfil the needs for accession (to be in the market economic league), and not to ensure an economical form of pollution abatement.

As in the previous examples, this can be related to the two concepts of modernisation. In this case it is evident that modernisation in the sense of 'bringing up to date' is the applied interpretation, as the main driver is to bring environmental standards up to EU level and to meet the expectations of a population likely to become more environmentally conscious if experience from the West can be extrapolated.

This is not controversial, however, as the modernisation of environmental regulation has never been claimed to be 'Modern' or rational in a more universal sense. What is interesting to our analysis is that this discourse generates the framework under which the two other discourses (and hence choice of technology) must take place, and is indeed the main driver for the replacement of most of the power plant park. The inputs to these discourses are completely arbitrary, if assessed from the perspective of the 'perfect market' which lends legitimacy to the two discourses debated previously.

Environmental standards are here an example of social constructions which become so strongly institutionalised that they appear in other contexts as if they were of primary nature, outside the control of human rationality. This once again points to the limited scope of the 'universal' market mechanism, which in its own vision can only be valid if it is allowed to transcend all spheres of human economic activity.

Discussion: technology as a central institution

The modernisation of Hungary's electricity sector is largely driven by three dis-courses. Each contains elements of the principles of the market economy, but this is far from the central element:

- The market is applied only to a limited part of the selection process, which is pre-defined by institutions, and;

- The main driver in the process is not the promotion of the market economy, but the promotion of other interests with a more limited scope.

These discourses have little overlap and few elements of co-ordination. However, their accumulated effect is to effectively promote the renovation of Hungary's power sector. At first glance, the process looks as if it is a turn towards the market economy, and the choice of technology as if it is guided by market forces. With a closer look, the result can rather be described as arbitrary. The three discourses, their elements of market orientation, and their main driving forces are presented in the table.

Reference to the market principle has two elements: The one is a subscription to the rational elements of the theory of the market mechanism, which establishes a symbolic link between market principles and the ideas of Enlightenment and the Modern. This helps to establish decisions which are made by 'the market' (that is, by actors operating in a competitive environment) as 'natural' or 'unavoidable', and therefore legitimate. The other is a more practical approach, which introduces elements of the market in order to obtain specific objectives. This relates to the concept of modernisation as simple 'updating', and is far more controversial as it permits the decision makers (planners, politicians and others who can influence the process) to shape the development. This chapter has argued that despite the emphasis which has been put on the theoretical 'perfect' market in the discourse on transition economies, this concept has played an insignificant role in the reform of Hungary's power sector, where the market is only allowed to work locally and incoherently. However, the transformation of the sector may have been impossible if it had not taken place under the guise of introducing the 'transcendental market', and thus linking reform to the universalist ideas of Modernisation and Progress.

Table 4.4 The theoretical reference to market economy, compared with direct incentives of active carriers of institutional reform in the Hungarian power sector

Discourse	Main carrier	Theoretical scope	Actual scope
Privatisation	Privatisation minister	Corporate control via external ownership Competition between suppliers	Improve central budget Secure investments and know-how
Technical modernisation	MVM	Least cost investment planning/balance market and strategic considerations	Maintain control/ maintain structure
Environmental protection	Ministry of environment	Correct market failure: externalities	EU accession

The analysis has demonstrated how the market economic discourse has been able to link lines of action and interests which were otherwise likely to be incompatible. The market economic concept is used incoherently, and the outcome of the process is far from an economic optimum. However, the apparent harmony between strong interests allows for an effective renovation of Hungary's electricity sector.

One of the costs of this 'consensus' is the lack of potential for technological development in the sector. It appears that existing technology is a much more influential force than the market mechanism in formating the sector development, which is strongly conservative of the existing technology. It is suggested that this extra-proportional role of existing technology can be explained by at least two factors, one related to the real economy, and the other to the conceptual sphere.

Existing agents relate to existing technology. Therefore, discourses centred around this technological structure are well established, and the agents are powerful in economic and political terms. This is the case, for instance, of the National power transmission company, MVM Rt. (the former National Electricity Trust) and the foreign power utilities which are reconstructing

Hungarian companies. Carriers of alternative technologies are not well established (nor consolidated), which is a particular constraint in the transition economy, where capital is scarce, the demand for new investments is massive, and uncertainties are important.

Uncertainty also seems to create a need for technology as a provider of a common conceptual reference: It is impossible to implement abstract ideas (such as the market principle) without a fixed reference. This is particularly so in areas such as power generation, which demand complex regulatory practices. In the transition process, where uncertainty is substantial, 'society', 'the economy' or 'the market' do not provide useful references, as they are themselves changing rapidly. Here, existing technological structures lend themselves as a refe-rence for the individual elements of reform, such as corporate ownership structures, tariff and licensing regulation, development schemes and environmental regulation, which are implemented in the otherwise changing environment.

In this way, existing structures become a reference for the transition, and institutional reform is designed to accommodate these structures rather than to cause them to change.

Notes

[1] 'Regime' designates the detailed organisation of the economy (forms of ownership, transactions, regulation and enforcement, division of labour, etc.). It is related with the mode of production, but emphasises the level of concrete transactions.

[2] In very brief terms, Coase argues that the existence of firms (systems where the market economic principle is not valid internally, as resources are allocated by the management) proves that the market mechanism is not always the optimal allocation mechanism. Simon argues that the data collection and processing capacity of real individuals is a far cry from the perfect knowledge demanded by neo-classical theory. The neo-institutionalists argue that the actions of economic agents are largely guided by habit rather than calculation, and that this ensures a stable environment which is a precondition to transactions. Further, the 'new micro-economy' shows that the optimisation of individual gains does not always lead to the most economic choices (the game theoretic argument).

[3] The Pareto optimum is the optimally productive allocation of scarce resources at any time, and is, according to neo-classical theory, ensured by the perfect market.

[4] Efficiency of a power plant is indicated as the ratio of the energy content of the fuel, which is converted into electricity. It follows from the laws of thermodynamics that a significant proportion of the energy used in the power generation process must be given off in the form of heat. As fuel is by far the main operation cost in power generation, a significant R and D effort has been made to improve this parameter. An improvement of the fuel efficiency of a few per cent can justify substantial investment.

5   In combined cycle technology the heat given off from a gas turbine (first cycle) is utilised for further electricity production in a steam turbine (second cycle). This reduces the amount of heat which is unused in the process, hence the relatively high total efficiency.

6   These are gas turbines designed to be started up at short notice to supply electricity when the load is highest ('peaks') or in the event of failure in other generation plants.

7   A co-generation plant is a unit where the unused heat from the electricity generation process is used for other purposes such as heat supply to a district heating network or industrial processes. The heat is extracted from the exhaust gas or from steam condensation at relatively low temperatures. The utilisation of this heat makes it possible to achieve a high total efficiency (high total degree of fuel utilisation).

8   This is sometimes referred to as the 'fence definition': Power and heat production takes place behind the same fence, and the heat is considered as co-generated, though it is in reality produced in heat only boilers. A high thermal efficiency is, of course, only obtained when heat is extracted from a physical electricity generator (turbine or other).

9   Also the computerised WASP tool, developed by the International Energy Agency (IEA) of the OECD, has become an institution, as it is seen by foreign lenders as a guarantee that thorough least cost planning has been carried out. But the computerised model pre-selects those technologies which it is programmed to handle, and does not, for example, handle co-generation well.

10   Two examples might illustrate that the costs of the programmed development are higher than necessary: In England and Wales, the introduction of competition led to remarkable changes in the choice of technology; higly efficient combined cycle plants constructed by independent power producers have partly displaced 'base load' units in the base load period (proving them economically obsolete). Scenario analyses point to de-centralised co-generation as far more efficient than centralised plants in areas with existing district heating schemes, to the extent that the OECD refers to co-generation as 'the technology of transition' with a view to the well developed district heating schemes in Eastern Europe (Knudsen, forthcoming). Investment in energy efficiency is usually cheaper than investment in new plants.

References

Berger, Peter, and Thomas Luckman (1966), *The Social Construction of Reality: A Treatise on the Sociology of Knowledge.* Garden City: Doubleday.

Cahuc, Pierre, 1992: *La nouvelle microéconomie.* Paris: La Découverte.

Chatelus, Michel, and Jacques Fontanel (eds) (1993), *Dix grands problèmes économiques contemporains.* Grenoble, PUG

Coase, R. (1937), *The Nature of the Firm.* Economica, vol. 4, No 3.

CO-GEN Europe (1996), *An assessment of the impact of liberalisation of the European electricity and gas markets on cogeneration, energy efficiency and the environment.* Brussels, Co-gen Europe.

Dilley, Roy, (ed.) (1992), *Contesting Markets.* Edinburgh, Edinburgh University Press.

DiMaggio, Paul J. and Walter W. Powell (eds) (1990), *The New Institutionalism in Organisational Analysis*. Chicago, University of Chicago Press.

Frydman, Roman, and Andrezej Rapazanski (1994), *Privatisation in Eastern Europe: Is the state withering away?* London, New York, Central European University Press.

IEA (1995), *Energy policies of Hungary: 1995 Survey*. Paris: OECD/IEA.

Jameson, Frederic (1990), *Postmodernism, or, the cultural logic of late capitalism*. London, Verso.

Knudsen, Niels, forthcoming: *CHP expansion in Hungary: a wasted opportunity?* Aalborg, Aalborg University, Department for Development and Planning – Series.

Latour, Bruno (1993), *Aramis ou l'amour des techniques*. Paris, Editions de la Découverte.

Latour, Bruno (1994), *Nous n'avons jamais été modernes. Essai d'anthropologie symétrique*. Paris: Editions de la Découverte.

MVM (1995a), *Power system expansion strategy of the Hungarian Power Companies Ltd*. Budapest, MVM RT.

MVM (1995b), *Statistical Data*. Budapest, MVM Rt.

MVM (1995c), *Charts about the Hungarian power system*. Budapest: MVM Rt.

North, Douglas (1990), *Institutions, Institutional change and economic performance*. New York, Cambridge University Press.

Ruthland, Peter (1985), *The myth of the plan*. La Salle, Illinois: Open Court.

Samson, Ivan (1993), *La transition au marché des économies post-socialistes*. In: Chatelus et al. (eds).

Simon, Herbert A. (1957), *Models of Man Social and Rational*. New York, Wiley.

Valentiny, Pál (1994), *Energy regulation in Hungary*. Edinburgh, Heriot-Watt University, Centre for Economic Reform and Transformation.

5 Energy Planning and the Ability to Change

The East German example

FREDE HVELPLUND AND HENRIK LUND

Societal goals, and the necessary technical changes

By March 1997, EU had decided to reduce CO_2 emissions by 10 per cent in 2010 (compared to 1990). According to this decision both Germany and Denmark have to reduce CO_2 emission by 25 per cent. In addition, further future reductions are needed to respond to the global environmental threat from the greenhouse effect.

In the former DDR extensive investments since 1990 can be characterised as rebuilding without restructuring the energy system, investing heavily in renovating old and building new brown coal fired power plants, combined with very low levels of energy conservation, renewable energy and cogeneration activities.

We define societal path-dependency as the inability to establish and realise parliamentary defined and declared goals, due to institutional bindings from organisations, investments, interests, and knowledge from the past ('past dependency'). Any development contains and develops institutional paths, which more or less closely favour the development of specific clusters of techniques. This turns into path-dependency when the institutional paths result in almost insurmountable difficulties in developing and implementing new technical clusters, which better than the old techniques realise goals defined in a well functioning parliamentary process.

The aim of this article is to examine the types of path-dependencies that cause difficulties in the ability to restructure energy systems with a particular focus on East Germany 1990-1998.

The general path-dependency at the energy scene

To get a more exact understanding of the change in institutional path required by the needed restructuring of the technical energy system, it is useful to describe how the new energy efficient techniques differ from the old

Table 5.1 Characteristics of the old and new technologies and their institutional paths

OLD TECHNIQUES	OLD INSTITUTIONAL PATH
1) Based upon a high level of fossil fuel and uranium consumption.	Interests and institutional conditions linked to fossil fuel. Publicly paid infrastructure linked to transportation of fossil fuel and uranium. Pollution costs are not systematically included in prices.
2) Technical solutions the same from place to place.	Tax supported universities and technical schools teach the necessary general knowledge.
3) Implementation in *single purpose* organisations.	Already well established energy supply companies linked to the single-purpose of supplying energy within a specific sector.
4) Sectorized energy systems.	
5) Historically strong from a capital point of view	In general no problems linked to financing new supply systems. Often very favourable taxation and capital accumulation conditions.
6) Historically strong from a political point of view.	In general often economic as well as personal links to the political system.
7) Mostly using basically known techniques.	High level of public research money available just to continue technical refinement within a well-known technical path.
8) Often linked to *existing* knowledge.	
9) Often based on existing organisations.	Strong organisations already exist.
NEW TECHNIQUES	NEW INSTITUTIONAL PATHS
1) Based upon energy conservation, renewable energy and integrated efficient energy supply systems.	Establish a capability to cross the boundary between: - supply systems and end-user systems. - heat and power production - fossil fuel and renewable energy systems. and to act strategically with a long time horizon
2) Technical solutions differ from place to place.	Establishment of a network of decentralised energy offices, which can advise organisations with non-energy main goals in establishing energy efficient solutions tailored to their specific conditions.
3) Implementation in *multi-purpose* organisations.	
4) Integrated energy systems.	
5) Historically weak from a capital point of view.	Establish a new tariff and financing system with, for instance, public security for loans, etc.
6) Historically weak from a political point of view.	Improve the political processes making new solutions increasingly independent of the lobbyism of the old technologies.
7) Often requires *new* techniques.	Establish systematic research within these areas, so they have public research subsidies which equivalents the public research.
8) Often requires *new* knowledge.	Subsidies given to the fossil fuel and uranium technologies.
9) Often requires *new* organisations.	Removing the barriers to entry, which the old technologies have established against establishment of new organisations.

supply-oriented techniques. What these differences mean for the discussion of path-dependency and public regulation are also outlined. This information is presented in table 5.1.

Denmark and many other countries are restructuring their energy systems away from undifferentiated fossil fuel and uranium based supply system solutions, which are typically implemented by few single-purpose[1] organisations, to differentiated technological solutions implemented by many multi-purpose[2] organisations (Hvelplund, 1995). This change of technological path is a historic[3] challenge to public regulation, which must establish new institutional paths for the new technologies.

Analytical framework and path-dependency of the electricity scene

Our analysis of the East German energy sector takes its point of departure in figure 5.1 and in items a) to f) below.

Figure 5.1 illustrates the system categories which we find relevant to include when describing path dependencies or ability to perform radical technological changes within the energy area.

The three main system categories are (I) the democratic process and (II)+ (III)+ (IV)+ (V), the electricity service supply system (ESS), and (VI) the dyna-mics of the concern.

The Electricity service system consists of:

The indirect electricity supply system (II) producing the capital equipment for the electricity system and the *direct electricity supply system* (III) including fuel extraction, power production, transmission and distribution and,

(IV) *The direct electricity receiver system (ERS)*, consisting of equipment which receives the electricity and transforms it to energy services, and (V) *the indirect electricity receiver system* producing the capital for the direct electricity receiver system.

This system structure can be divided into the following dynamics influencing path-dependency:

a) The dynamics within existing energy companies. The question is here to what extent existing energy companies are motivated – and able – to break away from their existing development paths.

b) The dynamics of the concern that influence the behaviour of the energy company.

c) The dynamics of corporate propaganda, which is the way corporate propa-ganda is used to influence the parliamentary processes.

Figure 5.1 The direct and indirect electricity service supply system

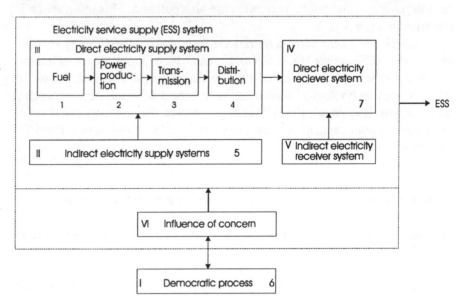

d) The dynamics *within the existing parliamentary process*. The question here is to what extent the constructions of the parliamentary processes have such a character that they support the development of new institutional paths.

e) The relationship *between energy companies, the parliamentary process and public regulation*. This is a major focal point of this chapter, the question being to what extent the parliamentary process is institutionalised in such a way that it is able to establish public regulation procedures which establish new institutional paths.

f) Relationships between *new energy-related organisations, the parliamentary process and public regulation*. This will be developed as a major perspective in the conclusion where the question is to what extent new grassroots and business organisations evolve such strength that they can influence the parliamentary processes to establish new institutional paths.

The East German Case

The socio-economic situation in East Germany

In the nineties the socio-economic situation in East Germany can be characterised as a process of deindustrialisation. Around 50 per cent of the work places
were closed down during the period 1989 to 1992. This was partly compensated
by public employment arrangements, but unemployment in East Germany is
still around 20 per cent of the workforce, and much higher in small towns in the
countryside. From 1991 to 1992, 46 per cent of the workplaces in the brown
coal industry were closed down. In the same period, 53 per cent of the
workplaces in the machinery industry, and 72 per cent in the textile industry
were closed down. Traditionally a very high share of the workforce in the Lausitz
area south of Berlin was employed in the mining sector. In Cottbus, a city 200
km south of Berlin with 200,000 inhabitants, 46 per cent of the workforce was
employed in the mining and energy sector as late as in November 1990. The
above-mentioned deindustrialisation process has established a very difficult
social situation with unem-ployment and an unstable political situation with
increased possibilities for extreme right wing parties.

The DDR energy system

The organisation of energy production was based upon large state owned energy
companies which via state ownership were closely linked to the brown coal
mining companies. Nevertheless there were separate companies for mining, power
production, transmission and distribution. The energy system was mainly based
upon the use of brown coal for electricity and heat production. In 1989, 300
million tons of brown coal were mined and total brown coal mining was reduced
to 150 million tons in 1995. This reduction was caused by a combination of
negative industrial growth, reducing electricity consumption with 30 per cent
from 1989 to 1995, and a process of replacing brown coal briquettes in heat
generation with oil and natural gas (Prognos 1992).[4]

As a consequence employment dropped from 160,000 in 1989 to 56,000 in
1992, and by 2005 only around 20,000 people will be employed in brown coal
(Stoll 1993).[5]

The transportation costs for coal were high thus large power plants were
placed close to the brown coal mines. High transportation costs were due to the
low energy content of brown coal of 8.6 MJ pr. ton compared to hard coal which
has an energy content of around 29 MJ pr. ton.

The emissions of the DDR system were extremely high compared to the emission in West Germany (in brackets). The emission per inhabitant per year in 1989 was: CO_2 20,3 tons (11,2), SO_2 315 kg (17,2), dust 119 kg (2,6) (Prognos 1992). The high emissions were due to inefficient energy plants and an inefficient production structure[6] in combination with no filters in the chimneys. These very high emissions made it necessary to make considerable investments in order to reach the EU and German pollution standards.

Privatisation of the DDR energy system

The process of privatisation started already the 22nd August 1990, before the reunification of the two German states, when the West German power companies, the 'Treuhandanstalt' (West German state organisation handling the privatisation process) and the DDR government signed the 'Stromvertrag' agreement. With 'Stromvertrag' the DDR government, 'Treuhandanstalt', and the West German power companies established a vertically integrated monopoly structure parallel to the principles practised in the West German power sector.

In short the agreement had the following contents:
- The DDR transmission company and the DDR power companies were merged into one company named VEAG (Vereinigte Energiewerke AG).
- The establishment of 15 contracts with the 15 DDR electricity distribution companies. In these contracts the distribution companies were obliged to buy at least 70 per cent of their electricity from VEAG.
- Furthermore it was agreed upon that VEAG and the 15 distribution companies would be administered by a consortium consisting of the West German power companies from 1990 until the companies were privatised.

All this was decided without the parliamentary influence of the East German population, and it is noteworthy that the power of control over the new monopolic structure was transferred to the West German power companies already in 1990, which was four years before they bought VEAG.

Altogether the above process has resulted in an East German electricity system where brown coal mining, power production and electricity distribution are vertically integrated under the same West German power companies. This system has a sales monopoly on at least 70 per cent of the electricity market.

The rebuilding of the East German energy system

We find it interesting to analyse to which extent the structure now represents an institutional path placing limitation upon technical development possibilities. The East German energy system is in a process of complete rebuilding due to the low efficiency and high emission characteristics of the old power plants. In a period of approximately 10 years it is planned that 60,000 million DM will be spent (Hvelplund, 1993) on the energy system. Such an extensive investment within ten years is probably historically unique. East Germany was and still is to some extent placed at a turning point of history, and the strategy chosen is of paramount importance when investment is made.

In principle the strategy, possibilities and consequences of the investment can be described as two extremes:

a) You can keep the 'old techniques', see table 5.1, and simply rebuild the system based upon brown coal, without restructuring it. This will create the worst of all situations, namely the situation in which one will have a new but outmoded energy system, i.e., an energy system that cannot be expected to fulfil the future environmental requirements. Many energy installations have a lifetime of 20 to 40 years. In this case East Germany will be placed in a worse situation than most other countries.

b) One can take the opportunity of shifting to 'new techniques', see table 5.1, with energy efficiency strategies and a restructuring of the energy system while rebuilding it, by investing in energy conservation, renewable energy and cogeneration. Implementing this strategy means investing in the most appropriate and most highly developed technologies wherever possible.

The most important of all factors is to implement the necessary institutional changes in the whole organisation of energy generation and consumption. This could create a situation in which East Germany would serve as a model for other Eastern European countries in need of the same development. Several export possibilities could emerge from such a position. This opportunity is particularly relevant now because all of the Western countries are faced with calls for action due to the global environmental threat from the greenhouse effect.

Unfortunately, mainly strategy a) is being implemented now. By using this strategy it will be possible to reduce the CO_2 emissions in East Germany from 20 tons/inhabitant in 1990 to 13 tons/inhabitant in the year 2010. Since the EU average is now 8 tons/inhabitant and the world average is below 4 tons/inhabitant the East German pollution will remain comparatively high. This means that the present strategy does not meet the environmental demands of the future.

The contemporary strategy is to expand the electricity capacity by building new brown coal fired power stations and by rebuilding the best of the old ones. In the Lausitz region it is planned and partly implemented to invest 15,000 DM in building or rebuilding a total capacity of 7,200 MW. All the power stations are placed next to brown coal mines making it impossible to benefit from cogeneration. Therefore, the planned use of cogeneration only comprises a minor district heating capacity of 200 MW for the city of Cottbus at the Jänschwalde power plant, and heat production capacity of Boxberg/Schwarzepumpe for a plasterboard production. Only 5 per cent of the cogeneration potential is used at Jänschwalde and only 11 per cent will be used at Boxberg/Schwarzepumpe.

Due to the lack of cogeneration it is necessary to use large amounts of oil and natural gas for house heating. An analysis of the situation shows two characteristics of the present strategy: first, within the house heating sector East Germany will become dependent on a large import of foreign fuels, i.e., natural gas and oil. The argument for using brown coal for electricity production to avoid supply failures does not involve the entire energy sector. Second, one must assume that most of the house heating boilers in the former DDR are old and must be replaced by new gas- and oil-fired boilers. The strategy will therefore lead to major investments not only in big power stations, but also in central heating systems and gas- and oil-fired boilers in detached houses, apartment buildings and district heating plants. For the whole East German area these investments can be calculated at approximately 35,000 million DM before 2010 (Hvelplund and Lund, 1998).

In this system electricity production is separated from heat production. Therefore, this strategy cannot benefit from fuel savings due to cogeneration.

Energy efficiency scenarios for the Lausitz region

In 1993 we made a set of energy scenarios for the Lausitz region. Berlin is situated in this region which accounts for around 40 per cent of the energy consumption and 40 per cent of the population in East Germany (Hvelplund, 1993). By means of such analyses it is possible to discuss whether other technical scenarios existed, which better fulfilled the goals of the parliamentary process with regard to supply security, environment, employment and economic development. We therefore elaborated and described a set of alternative energy efficiency scenarios, including systematic use of energy conservation, cogeneration and renewable energy.

The scenarios were compared with the reference scenario, which is close to the contemporary strategy. They were published in Hvelplund (1993) and were used by 'Grüne Liga',[7] and 'Bundnis 90',[8] among others, in the energy debate in Brandenburg.

The alternative scenario

The alternative scenario includes a reduction in heat demand of 20 per cent and in electricity demand of 15 per cent compared with the reference, i.e. the contemporary strategy. The necessary investments in achieving these targets are of course included in the cost analysis.

The marginal fuel consumption for electric heating is twice the fuel consumption used in gas- and oil-fired boilers and 5 to 10 times the marginal fuel consumption in cogeneration. Therefore the alternative is put together with the purpose of avoiding electric heating and promoting district heating based on cogeneration. All electric heating is substituted by central heating systems. Additionally district heating systems and cogeneration are proposed in all residential areas.

Extensive use of renewable energy should be an important part of a strategy which aims at meeting the future environmental demands. This alternative strategy is based on using 50 per cent of these possible resources by the year 2010 in the following way: wind turbines produce electricity for the grid; straw substitutes coal in the cogeneration units; wood substitutes oil in individual boilers; biogas substitutes natural gas in cogeneration units.

Added to this is the possibility of using sun collectors for residential heating. The alternative strategy proposes utilisation of sun collectors for production of hot water in detached houses which are not supplied with district heating. It will lead to a 20 per cent decrease in the fuel consumption of these houses.

Comparison between the alternative and the reference

A cost analysis of the two strategies has been made by comparing the total costs during a period of 20 years. Based on world market prices, one of the alternatives, the hard coal energy efficiency alternative, is slightly cheaper than the reference but has two disadvantages. It results in fewer jobs and a higher import of fuels than the reference, due to replacement of indigenous brown coal with imported hard coal. But the higher energy efficiency in the alternative can also be implemented on the basis of other fuels than imported hard coal. Therefore two other energy efficiency alternatives have been analysed: one in which the hard coal is substituted by brown coal, processed into 'brown coal dust' with a low content of water, and another in which the hard coal is substituted by natural gas and extensive use of biomass resources. The main results of the reference as well as all three variants of the alternative are shown in Table 5.2 (Hvelplund and Lund, 1998).

Electricity and heat consumption

The reference and the three variants of the alternative produce or save exactly the same amounts of electricity and heat.

Fuels

The three variants of the alternative cut the fuel amounts by 50 per cent compared with the reference. This is due to 1) demand-side efficiency, 2) cogeneration, and 3) substitution of electric heating.

CO_2-emission

In the alternative the CO_2 emission is cut down to an emission between 20 per cent and 40 per cent of the reference emission. This is partly due to low fuel consumption and partly due to the use of renewable energy.

Economy

In a calculation based on today's fuel prices the alternatives have more or less the same total costs as the reference. The variant based on hard coal is 8 per cent cheaper, the brown coal variant 5 per cent, while the variant based on natural gas and biomass is 12 per cent more expensive. It may be surprising that the very large investment in district heating and cogeneration in all the variants of the alternative does not make them much more expensive than the reference. But this is due to the fact that also the reference has made huge investments in changing the house heating system, i.e. natural gas boilers, central heating and natural gas pipe systems.[9]

Employment

The employment effects of the reference can be calculated to 55,000 jobs on the average over a 20-year period. The brown coal and the biomass variants of the

Table 5.2 Comparison between the alternative and the present strate

Main Results	Ref.	Alternative		
	Brown coal / oil	Hard coal	Brown coal	Biomass / natural gas
Electricity (TWh/year)10				
Savings	-	5,8	5,8	5,8
Reduction in heating	-	4,0	4,0	4,0
Production	42,4	32,6	32,6	32,6
Sum	42,4	42,4	42,4	42,4
House heating (TJ/year)11				
Savings	-	40,0	40,0	40,0
Production	199,9	159,9	159,9	159,9
Sum	199,9	199,9	199,9	199,9
Fuels (TJ/year)				
Brown coal	485,1	-	208,6	-
Hard coal	16,8	189,6	-	-
Natural gas	99,3	99,3	99,3	209,2
Oil	72,2	14,3	14,3	14,3
Biomass	4,3	19,5	19,5	102,3
Sun/Wind	-	23,8	23,8	23,8
Sum	677,7	346,5	365,5	349,6
Environment (Million t/year)				
CO_2-emission	68,7	24,6	28,4	12,7
Economy (1,000 million DM)				
Construction works	28,6	47,2	47,2	48,2
Maintenance	18,9	8,9	8,9	9,3
Fuels	46,0	29,9	31,9	46,8
Sum	93,5	86,0	88,0	104,3
Economy (1,000 million DM)				
Incl.. EU tax	116,8	95,2	97,8	110,1
Employment (jobs)				
Construction (1/20)	14.000	29.000	29.000	29.000
Maintenance	23.000	10.000	10.000	11.000
Fuels	18.000	7.000	15.000	13.000
Sum	55.000	46.000	54.000	53.000

Source: Hvelplund and Lund, 1998, page 541.

alternative have more or less the same employment effects, while the hard coal variant has 46,000 jobs. This is caused by importing hard coal. None of these figures included any export effects. In the alternative the construction works account for many of the jobs. Therefore the alternative strategy will result in increase in employment during the construction period, while employment in the reference due to brown coal mining and maintenance will be higher over the longer period.

Supply failure safety

The reference strategy will depend on 72 PJ[12]/year imported oil, while the alternative strategy uses only 14 PJ/year. Again this is due to taking advantage of the cogeneration possibility in the alternative strategy, while the reference strategy results in heating the houses with oil. Moreover the reference uses the storage of the domestic resource brown coal in a rate of 485 PJ/year contrary to the alternative which uses between 0 and 209 PJ/year. The alternative strategy is then superior to the reference in terms of leaving brown coal resources for future demand.

Meanwhile, the hard coal variant of the alternative is dependent on imported hard coal of 190 PJ/year. But in case of future supply failures hard coal can be substituted by brown coal being processed to 'brown coal dust' with a low water content. The brown coal variant as well as the hard coal variant is therefore better than the reference for securing against future supply failures.

The natural gas and biomass variant results in a dependence on imported natural gas of 209 PJ/year versus the other variants and the reference using only 99 PJ/year. Coal or an even more extensive use of biomass can substitute the use of natural gas. This substitution will, however, cost a number of new investments.

We therefore conclude that a change in energy structure by means of accelerated energy conservation, cogeneration and renewable energy is better than the reference in relation to a set of environmental goals. But it is not this restructuring of the energy system which is being undertaken. On the contrary the East German energy system is being rebuilt, but not restructured according to energy efficiency principles. Following the present (reference) strategy the energy system will be totally renewed, but unfortunately not restructured. More specifically the system will be changed from being totally based on brown coal into a system in which electricity production is still based on brown coal, and residential heating is based on oil and natural gas. Only a very small percentage of the house heating will be based on combined heat power production. This system will not meet the future environmental demands. The rebuilding activities will reduce the CO_2 emission from 20 ton/inhabitant in 1989 to 13 ton/inhabitant in the year 2010, which is still much higher than the EU average of 8 ton/inhabitant.

The Parliamentary goal of decreasing the CO_2-emission by 25 per cent from 1990 to 2010 faces serious difficulties in Germany.

In the following we will briefly mention examples of what should be done in order to introduce the energy efficiency alternatives.

Necessary institutional reforms

The implementation of the above-mentioned energy efficiency alternative requires that the Parliament introduce an array of institutional reforms. One of the methods used in Denmark since 1987, is to introduce a set of reforms to support the implementation of decentralised cogeneration.[13] In comparison the German system completely lacks such reforms within the area of decentralised cogeneration. At present cogeneration is obstructed on the market by means of unfavourable payments for sale of electricity to the public grid, unfavourable rules regarding payment of reserve capacity, the 'Stromvertrag', compelling the regional electricity distribution companies to buy at least 70 per cent of their sales from the large East German power company VEAG, and the cross subsidisation mechanisms established in 'Stromkonsensrunde Ost'.[14] One may conclude that the institutional preconditions for an energy efficient energy system are, so far, very poor.

In order to understand the roots of these unfavourable institutional conditions, it is essential to study the institutional dynamics of the *new owners* of the East German power system, the West German power companies, and the interaction between these dynamics and public regulation processes. Here we will mainly look at the second largest West German power company, PreussenElectra, its parent company VEBA, and its subsidiary companies, VEAG and the brown coal mining company LAUBAG. Preussen Electra has the majority ownership in 5 of the East German distribution companies, owns 26,25 per cent of VEAG and 30 per cent of LAUBAG.

West German institutions of path-dependency

In the following we will describe a set of institutions which hamper the introduction of energy efficient energy systems in Germany. We are using the analytical framework illustrated by figure 5.1.

Dynamics within existing energy companies

Vertical integration. Preussen Electra is owned by the VEBA group, which is owned by private shareholders. The activities of the VEBA group are divided into the areas of power production and distribution, petrol exploration and sales, trade and service, chemical production, etc. In 1996 the VEBA group had 124,000 employees. The organisation of the VEBA group is shown in figure 5.2. The VEBA group both has a power production and distribution company, and a company selling gas and light fuel oil for heating purposes.

This ownership structure ties the East German direct electricity supply system to continued use of brown coal at the 1994 consumption level. The West German power companies have a majority ownership in East German brown coal mining, power production and distribution. Power production and transmission are organised in VEAG but owned by the West German power companies. Brown coal mining is organised by the LAUBAG corporation owned directly and indirectly by the same West German power companies. Furthermore electricity distribution is organised in East German power distribution compa-nies in which West German power companies have the majority ownership. In 'Stromvertrag' from 1990, the East German power distribution companies became, as already mentioned, bound to buy at least 70 per cent of their sales from VEAG. The VEBA company has economic interests in both a large power market and a power market based upon centralised power plants. In the event that a development based on cogeneration is furthered, the relative competitiveness of Preussen Electra against independent power production in the cities would weaken. The VEBA group would therefore lose markets related to sales of brown coal, electricity and oil for heating purposes. The RWE group would meet similar economic difficulties in these energy efficiency scenarios.

Returning to figure 5.1, we can conclude that the East German electricity system has a very high degree of vertical integration, having the same owners organising fuel extraction, power production, transmission and distribution, the levels 1+2+3+4 in figure 5.1. With such an ownership structure, the energy system will, naturally, run into great economic difficulties, if the technical systems are made more energy efficient by the introduction of cogeneration and electricity and heat conservation measures. Even the scenario with brown coal based cogeneration leads to difficulties for these organisations, as the brown coal consumption would be decreased by more than 57 per cent (See table 5.2) . The common ownership of coal and power production companies would result in decreased economic surpluses in the energy efficiency scenarios, leading to a dependency linked to the reference scenario characterised by a comparatively high consumption of brown coal.

Figure 5.2 Ownership structure in the East German Energy System

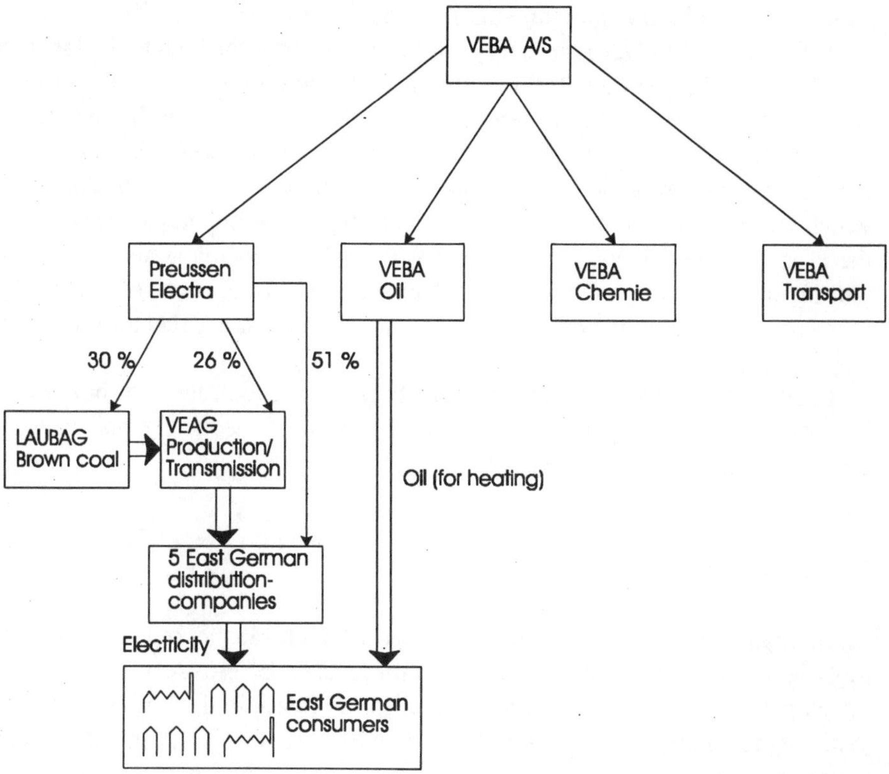

Horizontal integration

The RWE energy company, the largest German power company, has its own construction company which has renovated the East German brown coal power station Jänschwalde for around 6 billion DM. In Germany some ownership integration exists between the indirect electricity supply system linked to the building of large coal based power plants and the direct electricity supply system linked to power production, transmission and distribution. As this integration is linked to the construction of large brown coal based power plants, there is a relative path-dependency for this power production technology compared with decentralised cogeneration plants, windpower plants and energy conservation technologies. Looking at figure 5.1 it appears that the vertical and the horizontal integration include the levels 1+2+3+4+5, which can be estimated to more than

60 to 70 per cent of the value added in the production process including brown coal, power production and transmission and electricity distribution.

In the above *East German* energy efficiency scenarios the light fuel oil market is reduced by 75 per cent and the brown coal mining by at least 57 per cent compared with the reference scenario. This reduction will naturally reduce the economic surpluses in companies selling oil for the heat market. An example is the VEBA company, which owns Preussen-Electra and also VEBA Oil Company, which sells oil to the heat market. The proposed energy efficiency scenarios may therefore, induce losses in the VEBA oil company. In that sense there is a win-or-lose situation, where the VEBA concern will lose, if one of the energy efficiency alternatives is implemented, and win if the reference scenario is carried out.

In sum, the German system is characterised by a high level of horizontal integration supporting the traditional separation of electricity and heat as practised in the reference scenario.

Economic motivation

In Germany, the electricity sector acts as a 'stock rate locomotive'. When looking at the annual profit development, Preussen Electra seems to act as a 'stock rate locomotive' and a profit stabilisation factor in the VEBA concern. Without the relatively high profit of Preussen Electra, the VEBA concern might have serious difficulties in competing on the stock exchange market, as the profit of Preussen Electra constitutes 58 per cent of the total profit of the VEBA concern. This should be seen in relation to the fact that Preussen Electra only constitutes, with regard to turnover and number of employees, one fifth of the VEBA concern.[15] In the past ten-year period, the profit of Preussen Electra has amounted to between 50 per cent and 66 per cent of the total VEBA concern profit. This profit is linked to a situation in which German electricity prices are by far the highest in the EU. For instance the German average electricity kWh price for a 160,000 kWh/year consumer is 150 per cent higher than the Danish kWh price for the same consumer group (Eurostat 1997).[16]

Preussen Electra also acts as a profit stabilisation factor. In the above-mentioned period the Preussen Electra profit is balanced in such a way that the VEBA concern profit is kept rather stable from year to year.

The large degree of vertical and horizontal integration in the German power system results in a system with very low short-term marginal costs. If at the same time a surplus capacity exists in the brown coal mines, at the power plants, and in the transmission and distribution grids, then the short term marginal costs of electricity production will only be the short-term labour and maintenance costs in the whole vertical production and distribution system. The short-term marginal cost will, in such a highly vertical integrated system, appear far lower than in a system where the different levels of production are embedded in different organisations.

In times with spare capacity, this high degree of vertical integration causes a high degree of economic incentive for establishing economic 'barriers to entry' against technological newcomers. Preussen Electra, for instance, has achieved a lower short-term marginal cost through a higher degree of verticle integration. Brown coal can only be sold to VEAG's power production plants, as brown coal has lost the heat market. The short-term marginal costs in the brown coal mines are between 0.25 and 0.75 Pf/kWh power production. If the short-term marginal costs at the power plants are added, the short-term marginal costs of power production in such a technological system with common ownership from brown coal to customer, are between 0.75-1.25Pf/kWh (Højgaard, 1994).

The short-term marginal costs linked to power production based on imported hard coal are between 2Pf/kWh and 3.2 Pf/kWh and between 3.75Pf/kWh and 5Pf/kWh when dealing with power production based on natural gas. In times of spare capacity, due to its very low short-term marginal costs, a brown coal based power production system with the German degree of vertical integration of ownership will be willing to reduce its prices below the prices of almost all other technologies. But this will result in bad economic results, as the long-term marginal costs are not included in the prices. Therefore companies with this cost structure also have a comparatively strong tendency to try to establish strong 'barriers to entry' against potential technological competitors in specific market segments. In its annual report of 1995 VEAG mentions that the high level of fixed costs and low running costs (short-term marginal costs) in the brown coal mines, in combination with spare capacity, makes it economical to reduce the average costs by conquering new markets through reducing prices in large border areas of the market.

This tendency is enforced by the role of the power companies to be 'stock rate locomotives' for their parent companies.

In a conclusion we can say that the German power companies are extremely path-dependent, because of their being strongly linked to technologies based on fossil fuel. They do not seem to have any ability to change paths themselves.

The dynamics of corporate propaganda

In Germany a very high economic motivation exists in the power companies for trying to control parliamentary processes. Democracy is a risky 'business' seen from the established power companies' point of view. Democratic processes, which decide on legislation supporting energy conservation, renewable energy and cogeneration may imply economic risks for fossil fuel based energy companies. Alex Carey describes how the large companies cope with such risks in the US by corporate propaganda (Carey, 1997). When analysing publications from the German power companies it therefore is not surprising that a considerable propaganda activity can be found. As the political process is dependent upon what the actors in the public political processes perceive as possible and advantageous from a technological and societal point of view, the corporate propaganda works especially at this level of perception. Corporate propaganda of the VEBA concern, therefore tries to influence the political perception processes in correspondence with the interests of the concern. As one demonstrated example, it is in the economic interest of the VEBA concern to maintain a separated production of heat and electricity. This influence is exerted through press releases, publications elaborated in co-operation with connected research institutes to weaken the trustworthiness of new competing technologies.

The VEBA concern publishes an array of information materials regarding future technological possibilities, one of which is 'Zukunftenergien-Fakten und Argumente' (VEBA, 1989), from the time before the discussion regarding cogeneration in Germany became intensive. In this publication VEBA mentions a number of coming energy technologies, among others renewable energy tech-nologies, nuclear power and energy conservation technologies. The cogeneration technology is not mentioned, and is in that way kept off the agenda.

In 1994 cogeneration nevertheless had forced its way into the German energy agenda. This meant that Preussen Electra and VEBA no longer could ignore this technology. At the same time Preussen Electra hired the Pestel Institute (Pestel, 1994) to analyse and compare the economic and environmental effects of cogeneration and separated production of heat and power. The Institute concluded that a system with separate production of heat and power was cheapest – even though it concludes that a decentralised cogeneration system uses around 15 per cent less fuel than a system with coal based power production and oil/-gas-based heat production.

In the Danish newsletter ELSAMposten (ELSAMposten, 1995) the Administrative Director of Preussen Electra, Dieter Harig is quoted as saying:

'there are large advantages with regard to economy and energy economy related to large coal fired cogeneration plants. But decentralised natural gas fired cogeneration plants, as proposed by many municipalities, are a bad solution both with regard to resource economy and money economy. PreussenElectra used an independent consultant namely the Pestel Institute for system research in Hannover to examine these questions.'

Later in the same newsletter, he puts forward the results of the Pestel Institute examination with the following remarks: 'It is easier to solve environmental problems with centralised, than with decentralised solutions. It can simply be said that the cheapest solutions are also the best from an ecological point of view.'

The dynamics within the existing parliamentary process

The German parliamentary process has not yet been examined thoroughly here. In the present context it is important to know to what extent the parliamentary system has characteristics enabling it to introduce path-changing policies. From the Danish case we know[17] (Hvelplund, 1995) that the following features should be built into the parliamentary process to establish parliamentary innovativeness:

- Openness in the administrative processes, giving new actors the possibility to participate in the parliamentary processes in a qualified way.
- Research resources allocated to organisations independent of the established fossil fuel technologies, establishing well functioning prototypes of the new technologies.
- Participation in governmental committies regarding the establishment of a long-term energy strategy.

During our research in East Germany we did not find any systematic description of alternative energy scenarios. This indicates that the resources to establish well-described alternatives to the above-described reference were not given to the groups in opposition to the extensive use of brown coal. The Parliament was therefore not in a position to select between different strategies, because the German authorities did not elaborate such strategies.[18]

The relationship between energy companies, parliamentary process and public regulation

As mentioned previously, the German power companies are economically motivated to act against a restructuring of the power and heat system with energy conservation, renewable energy and cogeneration. It is not surprising that the power companies are following their own interest on the energy scene. But to what extent is public regulation able to control and direct the activities of the power companies in accordance with parliamentarily defined common interests?

The German municipalities receive a concession fee from the electricity distribution companies, which is important for their economy. It gives them a considerable degree of common interests with the established electricity com-panies. The trade unions linked to the coal mines have an interest in the jobs related to the existing structure of the energy system, and at the same time they have strong connections to the political parties. Their political influence is used extensively in the present situation with its high level of unemployment in Germany and especially in East Germany.

As shown, a restructuring strategy would be against the economic interests of the existing power companies. When this fact is combined with public regulation processes which are strongly interlinked with the existing energy structure, a very strong path-dependency linked to the brown coal based technologies is present in the German electricity supply system. If we look at figure 5.1, we see integration at the levels 1+2+3+4+5+6, where 6 is the political system.

The German electricity system is interconnected with the political system through personal and economic links. Generally mayors, county mayors, and higher public officials are members of the boards of power companies. A member of such a board receives a fee of around 15,000 to 20,000 DM/year (Hennicke et. al., 1985). The board of Preussen Electra has around 30 members; including the Minister for the Environment of Niedersacksen, the Minister of Finance of Schleswig-Holstein, the Mayor of Frankfurt/Main, etc. In the Preussen Electra owned distribution company MEVAG, the board consists of 14 members; including a minister from Brandenburg, the Mayor of the town Brandenburg, and the Head of the central administration in Potsdam. Preussen Electra has an advisory committee called 'der Beirat'. In this committee the Minister for Industry and Technology in the state of Brandenburg was, for instance, a member in 1994.

The relationship between new energy related organisations, the parliamentary process, and public regulation

We have not thoroughly examined this question in Germany. But from the last 20 years' development in Denmark we know (Hvelplund, 1995) that initial stages of the development of new technologies do not come from the old fossil fuel companies, but from independent grass-roots groups and firms outside these companies. Without active and resource strong[19] groups outside the old fossil fuel companies, it does not seem possible to generate radical technological changes within energy conservation, renewable energy and cogeneration. At present there are in Germany rather strong organisations linked to the promotion of windpower, which to some extent are able to defend the political position of windpower.[20] An opposition also exists among industrialists against the comparatively very high German electricity prices. Furthermore, some German towns want electricity independence and are establishing their own cogeneration plants. It cannot be estimated here to what extent these groups will in the future be able to cope with the prevalent political force of the established newer companies.

Danish institutions of path-dependency in comparison

When looking for alternative institutional constructions, it is worthwhile to compare the institutional settings of different countries. We have studied the Danish institutions on the energy scene for two decades, and an analysis of the institutional ability to change in the Danish electricity system can be seen in Hvelplund (1997). Here we will give a brief summary of the results of this analysis.

In some areas the Danish system has demonstrated a high ability to establish technological changes on the energy scene. In the fifties and sixties centralised cogeneration was introduced in all major cities, and expanded systematically in the seventies and eighties. In the nineties decentralised cogeneration based on natural gas and biomass fuels was successfully introduced. The proportion of electricity from decentralised cogeneration grew from 1 per cent in 1989 to around 20 per cent in 1997. Windpower was reinvented and adapted to actual technical conditions in the late seventies. In the eighties and nineties windpower was systematically implemented, and in 1998 a production of 8 per cent of the total electricity production is expected. Biogas based power and heat production has been developed and implemented in various cities. These developments are all caused by, among other things, a systematic governmental energy policy introduced as a result of a parliamentary process where independent grass-roots groups have played a major role. At the same time there were power companies that had based their technology on fossil fuels, but had no ownership links to fossil fuel mining. Furthermore the power companies are consumer and municipality owned within a legislation, not allowing any profit to be transferred to other than energy purposes. Therefore the Danish electricity companies do not have a strong economic dependence related to coal, nor are they under pressure to give profit to shareholders on a stock market.

Conclusion

From totalitarian state to corporate state path-dependency

We have defined path-dependency as the inability to establish and realise parliamentarically defined and declared goals, due to institutional bindings from organisations, investments, interests, and knowledge from the past. This means that path-dependency is unfavourable for the wishes and goals established in a parliamentary process.

For the Lausitz area we have analysed alternative energy efficiency scenarios, and seen that they fulfil declared parliamentary goals better than the technical reference, which is being implemented. Lausitz alternatives which are better from an economic, innovation and ecological viewpoint are not discussed, developed or implemented.

Before 1990 the DDR system represented an extreme version of path-dependency, where it was almost impossible to establish and realise any technological developments that were against the established path, as the communist party defined it.

The transition to the West German institutions only represented a change from one set of path-dependency institutions to another. The West German institutions, which took over from the DDR institutions represented an insti-tutional path which supported almost the same type of supply oriented fossil fuel technology which was supported and developed in the DDR.[21] Naturally the West German power companies must have been well aware of this fact when in 1990, in corporate negotiations with the DDR government and the West German administration they replaced the totalitarian DDR path with the West German 'corporate state'[22] type of path-dependency by way of the 'Stromvertrag'. Consequently the character of this transition was decided upon before the introduction of democratic institutions in East Germany. The population was not asked, as they had no access to any parliament, when the 'Stromvertrag' was designed and decided upon.

Possibilities for change

The analysis shows that it is not to be expected that a change away from the fossil fuel path-dependency will arise within the German power sector system. This sector simply seems to be in an economic situation where it does not have the economic freedom to change direction, even if the board of directors and a majority of the employees should want such changes.

Furthermore the parliamentary processes and public administration appear to be so closely linked to the economic interests of the power sector that public regulation would not be able to induce any changes away from fossil fuel path-dependency. Although this question has not been sufficiently analysed here, our preliminary analyses indicate that the corporate links between the parliamentary system and the power companies are very strong. In fact they are so strong that a change away from extensive use of coal is difficult to imagine, without considerable political reforms freeing the parliament from its corporate links to the power sector. Consequently the German energy system seems very difficult to change. But the same conclusion could have been made with regard to the DDR path-dependency institutions in 1987, and yet the DDR system changed a couple of years later. Therefore short-term history indicates that things which look unchangeable can nevertheless change very quickly. Consequently any innovative development on the energy scene can be expected to come from the involvement and strengthening of new organisations at the grass-roots level, which are independent of the corporate state organisations. But such organisations are only sufficiently constructive if they are given public financial support to be able to describe well-documented alternatives and establish well-organised prototypes of new techniques. We therefore believe that if a government wants constructive changes, programs should already now be initiated to increase the support to grass-roots groups wanting to develop new technological possibilities. The establishment of financial support to such groups and programs might be within the limited political possibilities of politicians in a state with very strong corporate state tendencies. By financially supporting such activities, an array of constructive solutions could be developed, which could initiate an innovative development on the energy scene.

Notes

1 Organisations which have one main purpose for instance to sell heat and/or electricity. Such organisations have energy questions as the totally dominant activity area.
2 Organisations which have many purposes such as households, production and service firms, etc. Such organisations usually have energy as a less important area of activity.
3 We name it historic, as we see this change as general for the development conflicts on the energy scene all over the world since the 1970s and ongoing after the year 2000.
4 Prognos 92. Energiereport 2010, Konrad Eckerle/Peter L./Klaus P. Masuhr, Prognos, Schäffer-Ooeschel Verlag Stuttgart. 1992.
5 Tagebauentwicklung in der Lausietz. R.D. Stoll, Institut für Bergbaukunde der RWRH Aachen. 1993.
6 With almost no cogeneration of heat and power.
7 Green grass-roots organisation in East Germany.
8 Green political party, which was represented in the Parliament of Brandenburg in 1993.
9 A number of sensitivity analyses have been conducted, among others an analysis in which the mixture between detached houses and apartment buildings have been changed. These sensitivity analyses have not changed the main results described here. But another sensitivity analysis is worth mentioning. A situation in which the European Community introduces a tax on energy and environment has been analysed. As an exemple an energy tax of 41 DM per ton SKE (SKE is a German abbreviation of 1 ton hard coal equivalent/29,3 MJ) and a CO_2 tax of 18 DM per ton CO_2 chosen (Shiffer, 1992). As expected, the reference in particular is sensitive to such taxes. In fact such taxes will make the alternative between 5 per cent (natural gas and biomass) and 20 per cent cheaper (hard coal).
10 Abbreviation of TeraWatthour= 10^9 kWh
11 Abbreviation of TeraJoule= 10^{12}
12 Abbreviation of PetaJoule. 1 PJ = 23,900 tons oil equivalents.
13 For example, cogeneration units have the right to sell electricity to the public grid at a price based upon the long-term marginal cost of a large coal fired power plant. Also clear rules regarding payment for grid connection have been introduced, and a carbon dioxide subsidy of 1,4 UScent per kWh on electricity from natural gas based cogeneration plants has been implemented. Furthermore the municipalities are obliged by law to give guaranties for the needed loans. Consequently, in Denmark, there has been built around 2000 MW of decentralised cogeneration capacity since 1990, and electricity production from these plants now amounts to around 20 per cent of the total Danish electricity consumption.
14 Agreement from January 1996 between VEAG and the German government allowing VEAG to subsidise market expansion outside the 70 per cent monopoly share, achieved in the 'Stromvertrag' agreement.
15 The turnover of Preussen Electra was, for instance in 1997, 19.5 per cent of the turnover of the VEBA concern, its number of employees 17 per cent of the employees in the VEBA concern. The same year, the profit of Preussen Electra was 58 per cent of the total profit in the VEBA concern.
16 Statistics in Focus nr. 28. Eurostat 1997.
17 'Demokrati og forandring', Frede Hvelplund, Henrik Lund, Karl E. Serup og Henning Mæng, Aalborg University Press 1995.
18 Our publication (Hvelplund, 1993) was, nevertheless vigorously attacked by the brown coal firm LAUBAG, which elaborated a 20 page report, 'Zu einer Studie des Aalborg Universitets-Centers', where they argued against the conclusions in the study. This report was made in colour on high quality paper, and distributed to the press and politicians.

19 With regard to organisational and intellectual capacity and financial support from the Government.
20 Bundesverbandes Windenergie e.V.
21 Regarding the changes in 'communication' between the energy supply system and the energy receiver system it should be emphasised that this has not been the focus of this study. Nevertheless it should be mentioned that probably the most important institutional change from the DDR system to the West German system is within this area. In the DDR time, houses were owned by the state, and therefore by the same organisation as owned the supply system. The DDR system therefore was developed in a direction in which it was difficult for the consumer to influence the heat bill, as it was paid as a part of the house rent in general. There were no meters, and electricity was extremely cheap. In the West German system this has been changed in such a way that apartments and houses are to an increasingly degree privately owned, and supplied with heat and electricity meters.
22 A type of path-dependency, where state institutions, politicans and power cooperations work closely together.

References

Carey, Alex (1997), *Taking the risk out of Democracy- Corporate Propaganda versus freedom and liberty*. Illini books edition.

ELSAMposten (1995), 'PreussenElectra: Jeg tror, man overdriver betydningen af det åbne marked' interview with Dieter Harig, in *ELSAMposten, February 1995*.

Hennicke, P, Johnson, J P, Kohler, S and Seifried, D. (1985), *Die Energiewende ist möglich* Fischer Verlag Frankfurt am Main.

Hvelplund F., Lund H., Serup K. E., Mæng H. (1995), *Demokrati og Forandring, energihandlingsplan 96* (Democracy and Change, Energy Action Plan 1996) Aalborg University Press.

Højgaard, A., Larsen, K. (1995), *Elmarked i forandring*. Master Thesis. Department of Development and Planning Aalborg University.

Pestel (1994), *Vergleich der Strom- und Heizenergieerzeugung in gekoppelten und ungekoppelten Anlagen vor dem Hintergrund der Einsparmöglichkeiten durch Wärmedämmung*, ISP Eduard Pestel Institut für Systemforschung e.V. Hannover im Auftrag der PreussenElectra AG.

Prognos (1992), *ENERGIEREPORT 2010, Die energiewirtschaftliche Entwicklung in Deutschland Prognos AG*, Schäffer-Poeschel Verlag, Stuttgart.

Schiffer, H W (1992), Der Richtlinien Vorschlag der EG-Commission zur Einführung einer CO_2-Energiesteuer in *Braunkohle Volume 11*.

VEBA (1989), *Zukunftenergien-fakten und Argumente* VEBA AG Düsseldorf.

6 Institutional Change and Electricity Sector Reform in Transition Economies

JUNIOR R. DAVIS

Introduction

This article focuses on the interrelated institutional, regulatory and financial reform issues that are essential in improving electricity sector performance in the transition economies.

Most transition economies remain hampered by relatively low levels of economic growth and tight fiscal budgets to control both money supply and to provide a stable macroeconomic environment. They still have problems both widening their tax base and improving their relatively low tariff collection rates. Thus, most of these countries do not have the financial resources to fund electricity capacity expansion to meet future demand. To some extent, reform of the electricity sector is not solely a function of the transition process and the demand for cleaner sources of energy (less coal fired power stations), but also a result of the 'dash for gas'.[1] The structure of the energy sectors of both East and Western Europe are changing. Competition is increasing, and the EU is encouraging greater diversification and co-operation in electricity supply.

The electricity industry is very important to transition economies because economic growth depends upon it. However in most formerly centrally planned economies the electricity industries have taken the form of government monopolies which are capital intensive, and have generally performed badly. Thus, in the transition economies of Central and Eastern Europe (CEE) and the Commonwealth of Independent States (CIS)[2] the drive to privatise and radically reform the sector has been based on concerns about planning, operational inefficiencies and high national debt [EBRD, 1997, Stern and Davis, 1998].

Our point of departure is couched in mainstream economics but relates the analysis to elements of political economy and institutional economics. The article is written within the framework of the guiding principles for World

Bank support of power sector restructuring programmes. The main components of the World Bank's power sector lending strategy and economic reform agenda is summarised in Table 6.1 and based on the following five principles: (i) transparent regulation;[3] (ii) importation of services; (iii) commercialisation/corporatisation; (iv) commitment lending; and (v) investment guarantees [World Bank, 1993].

Table 6.1 Summary of power sector goals, approaches to achieve the goals, and resulting actions for the bank

Goals	Sequential approaches to achieving goals	
Where justified expand the provision of power in transition economies	Put in place mechanisms tht allow greater autonomy for and accountability of sector managers	Independent board of directors
Greater efficincy in the generation and end use of power		A more transparent regulatory framework
Reduction in the financial and debt burden of the power sector on public finances	Provide some form of clearly defined and transparent buffer between government, with its legitimate political and policy concerns, and power enterprise managers	- Tariffs - Service standards - Service targets - Issues of entry & exit - Supply side integration of end use options - Environmental impacts, siting, emissions, fuels, and disposal issues
Where cost-effective, identify and incorporate options (including fuel substitution) to mitigate negative environmental impacts of electricity supply and end use		
Guiding principles	1. Transparent regulation	
	2. Importation of Services	
	3. Commercialization/corporatization	
	4. Commitment lending	
	5. Investment guarantees	

Source: World Bank (1993)

In this paper, we take the World Bank framework outlined in Table 6.1 and attempt to analyse some of the more detailed aspects of institutional change in the CEEs (and where possible CIS) electricity industries by concentrating on the aforementioned priorities and trading structure. The World Bank framework is critically assessed in the light of the changing power sector circumstances in transition economies. We will make reference to the political economy of electricity reform, the development of the regulatory framework, competition policy and EU-wide issues involved in this institutional change. Section 1 of this paper introduces and discusses the dominant forms of trading and electricity industry structures emerging in the transition economies. Section 2 considers electricity price developments and price setting mechanisms introduced. Section 3 of the paper considers the emerging forms of economic regulation of the electricity industry in the transition economies and section 4 reviews the progress made to date.

Changes in the Electricity Industry Structure of Transition Economies

In Central and Eastern Europe the electricity industry structures and companies may be placed on a continuum where at one end there is no separation between distribution and generation (usually involving substantive state ownership) and at the other end substantial distribution, generation and private involvement in running or owning these industries. Lithuania may be said to illustrate the former, Czech Republic the latter and Hungary an intermediary position, namely a monopoly-monopsony model of electricity supply. Thus, it should be stressed that each of the three models presented has two dimensions: a) separation between distribution and generation; and b) private and public ownership. Figures 6.1 to 6.3 graphically illustrate the respective elements of institutional and industrial development in the transition economies.

Figure 6.1 shows the traditional organisational structure, the physical flows of electricity and the pattern of customer relations of a typical electricity utility under nationalisation. Everything inside the dotted lines depicts state control or no competition and is fully integrated. Figure 6.1 presents a structure that is basically an extension of what currently exists and fits within the existing economic and institutional environment. There is no separation between the distribution and generation of electricity. Thus, there is no individual accounting (as cost centres) or competition between each company or stage of the process of delivering electricity to consumers. The advantages of this model, which maintains the status quo with minor improvements, are usually that it is relatively less disruptive and more easily implemented than the following models outlined in figures 6.2 and 6.3. Lower transitional costs are incurred and the stability of the existing structure may encourage some investment in independent power pro-ducers and provide a more commercial orientation. However, the disadvantages of the model are extensive, it does not provide any of the benefits of competition and the existing utility may limit independent power producers' participation and engage in discriminatory behaviour. There has been some evidence of the latter in the Baltic States and Romania [Davis, 1998]. Furthermore this model is susceptible to ineffective regulation mainly because governments often use the utility as an instrument of public policy. Also, the ministerial supervision of performance contracts may not be very effective.

Figure 6.1 Vertically Integrated Electricity Utilities
(Ed.F, France; RENEL, Romania)

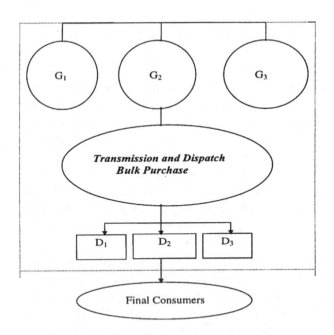

Key to the figures 6.1-6.3:
DC   Distribution Company
GC   Generation Company
LIC Large Industrial Consumer (> 2MW)

The traditional vertically integrated structure of Figure 6.1 is often criticised for providing the worst incentives for efficiency. This is because it inhibits competition and is usually accompanied by some form of cost of service regulation. The combination of these two forces tends to reduce incentives to good performance.Moreover, typically the owners of these new property rights in transition economies expect reasonable compensation if there is any significant government mandated restructuring, e.g. privatisation. Since most transition economy governments are unable to provide such compensation, it may find itself both politically and practically unable (as in Romania) to restructure the power sector beyond what has since 1990 been envisioned as a temporary industry structure. On the other hand, this does not necessarily mean that well-managed firms are never found under this structure. Indeed, there are many well-motivated firms (i.e. Electricite de France) that appear to be well run; but most of these are not found among transition economies. This does not however negate the basic point that the structure does not provide sufficient efficiency incentives. Moreover, it does seem unlikely that for most transition economies, after years of state ownership and control, that the utility will transform itself into an efficient, innovative organisation in the absence of competitive pressure.

Figure 6.2 shows how the industry might change with the introduction of competition between the generation companies. This is often termed the 'Open Access Model' which further exposes the power sector to market forces, but retains the characteristics of a vertically integrated monopoly. A key feature of this model is the introduction of open access with common carriage. A common carrier is an entity required to transmit electricity for buyers and sellers on a non discriminatory basis and, if necessary, to construct additional transmission capacity if the existing capacity is not adequate to meet all needs. Competition in this option tends to result from fair and open access to the transmission and distribution grids for large industrial customers.

The physical flows of electricity remain as in Figure 6.1 because the generation still flows across the national transmission system and across the wires of local distribution companies. In the UK both the National Grid Company and 12 regional distribution companies were required to offer terms for the use of their services. However, only generation, transmission and dispatch remain outside the scope of competition. Generation companies sell into the pool and distribution companies buy from the pool. Generation companies and distribution companies may also sign bilateral contracts for differences, which act as a hedge against fluctuations in the pool price. Most importantly, the generator can sell to any large industrial consumer and any large industrial consumer can buy from any distribution company, generation company or directly from the pool. Whether or not there are separate distribution companies may at first glance seem a fairly trivial issue. However, in practice it is important because it greatly increases the degree to which the power industry is commercially driven by giving focus to customer needs. Furthermore, for some governments (and certainly the World Bank) as a desired structural goal, it is much easier to develop wholesale competition and open access to the transmission and distribution networks if there are separate and independent distribution companies.

Figure 6.2 Vertically Semi-Integrated Electricity Utilities
(CEGB, England and Wales pre- 1989; Czech Republic, Ukraine)

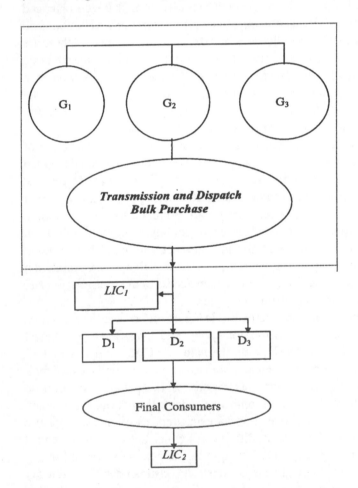

Figure 6.3 Monopoly - Monopsony
(Northern Ireland; Hungary; Poland)

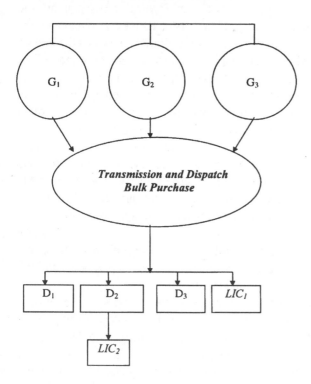

Figure 6.3 illustrates the structure of the electricity industry in the dominant transition economies. Here the transmission company retains full control of the wires and dispatch, whilst retaining a monopsony position over bulk purchases from generation companies and a monopoly of sales to distribution companies (as in Northern Ireland, Poland and Hungary). Although many transition economies have begun the process of unbundling, the trading (or contract) structure remains largely unchanged (see Figure 6.1). There has been comparatively limited competition *in* the market, as there is virtually no competition in generation, supply or transmission services [Stern and Davis, 1998].

With regard to Figure 6.1, RENEL (the Romanian State electricity utility) is probably the most obvious example of this fully integrated unreformed electricity industrial structure in CEE. RENEL produces and transmits electricity and dispatches it through the 'national energy system'. It imports and exports electricity, whilst importing fuel and machinery for operation and maintenance. RENEL produces electricity and heat through its own plants using the capacity necessary to meet the load curve, administers the hydroelectricity plants and manages the Cernavoda nuclear plant [Chisiu, 1997]. RENEL also manages the national dispatching grid system through its subsidiaries, oversees the energy activities of end-users, reviews and validates its production costs and energy supply tariff setting with both the Ministries of Industry and Finance.

In Romania, the advantages of the model outlined in Figure 6.1 have failed to materialise for the following reasons: a) because of a lack of competition in generation (over 70 per cent of RENEL's costs are associated with this function); b) the viability of management contracts which is the principal mechanism for promoting transparency and commercial behaviour. In the current institutional environment it would be difficult to put in place effective and enforceable contracts, particularly as RENEL knows its costs and operations better than any ministry and can therefore negotiate from an advantageous position when setting performance targets; and c) the maintenance of government energy sector policies which allow cross subsidisation that create economic distortions and inefficiencies which make the attraction of independent power producers difficult if they limit payments without economic justification.

Poland and Hungary are good illustrations of the monopoly – monopsony situation (see figure 6.3), as they have not yet moved to wholesale competition despite going the furthest in terms of industry restructuring. In both countries the transmission company retains full control of the wires and dispatch, whilst retaining a monopsony position over bulk purchases from generation companies and a monopoly of sales to distribution companies. In neither Hungary nor Poland is it possible for large industrial consumers or distribution companies to purchase power directly from generation companies. Distribution companies must purchase power from the transmission companies, and the large industrial consumers can only buy from distribution companies. Moreover no third party access is as yet possible in Hungary or Poland.

Figures 6.1 to 6.3 graphically illustrate the present situation and recent changes in the electricity industry structure for transition economies. For example: the Lithuanian Energy is a vertically integrated electricity company with 91 per cent state ownership and 9 per cent of the equity privately owned. Lithuanian Energy provides 50 per cent of Lithuania's generating capacity covering, all fossil fuel generation, transmission, distribution and supply of electricity. Lithuanian Energy owns the majority of district heating assets and combined-heat-and-power plants. Municipalities own some of the distribution infrastructure and boiler houses. One area of current debate concerns the desirability of transferring these assets from Lithuanian Energy to the municipalities.

Hungary's electricity sector is in the most advanced state of privatisation in CEE, with the most vertically disintegrated structure. In 1992 the former Hungarian Electrical Works Trust was transformed into a joint stock company MVM; organised as a holding company with 15 subsidiaries: 8 for power generation, 6 for distribution, and one National Transmission Company. The 1962 Electricity Act was modified to encourage privatisation, by ending the requirement of a State monopoly of electricity production and distribution. Since December 1995 strategic stakes in all 6 distribution companies and 2 thermal power stations have been sold to private bidders. MVM still organises most electricity power generation.

In the Czech Republic there is one main electricity utility the Czech Power Company (CEZ) which owns and controls over 80 per cent of the power generating plants and high voltage transmission networks of 440-kV and 220-kV. CEZ provides the bulk of electric power to the Czech Republic. A small proportion of generation capacity belongs to industries producing electricity for their own consumption and selling the surplus to the system. There are 8 regional power distribution company monopolies, with state majority control. Interconnection prices between CEZ and the regional power distribution companies are created by negotiations between both parties under the supervision of the Ministry of Industry and Trade.

Ukraine's electrical power supply is produced by 44 thermal power plants, 7 hydro power plants and 6 nuclear plants. The main generating capacity is provided by nuclear stations, and mostly old and quite unreliable thermal stations which are either gas or coal fired. There is very little flexibility in operation as stations are currently dispatched according to fuel and plant availability, with load shedding being the major method of balancing supply and demand. Ryding (1998) has argued that although the unbundling of the Ukrainian power industry into separate businesses requiring income and expenditure to be properly allocated to the separate businesses was economically rational, this could not be achieved without an improved accounting system, the knowledge and training to manage accounting in this way and without the removal of the current directions of the Ministry of Energy and Electrification (Minenergo).

Latvia, Slovakia, Slovenia and the Ukraine have made some progress in creating both separate distribution companies and generation separate from transmission in the electricity industry. However, this is a little misleading because these enterprises although formally disintegrated, or transformed into joint stock companies (as in Slovakia) to some extent remain state owned enterprises either under the supervision of a ministry or National Privatisation Agency. Moreover, in most of the CIS the degree of vertical integration has remained largely unchanged since 1989. However, there are signs of growing private sector interest and involvement in the development of independent power producers throughout the region.

Electricity Price Developments in the Transition Economies

During the centrally planned economy era electricity prices bore little relation to the economic cost of providing power to both households and industry. In general turnover taxes were used to subsidise various groups, especially households. Energy pricing was based on the recovery of average financial costs (which included operating costs but excluded large elements of the capital costs). The state financed the electricity utilities investment programmes and consequently at the start of transition (1989) most had little debt. Since 1989, CEE have been trying with varying degrees of success to move from a system of generally subsidised low energy prices (in absolute terms below international levels), where low household prices were sustained by relatively high prices charged to industry (the revenues of which were used to cross-subsidise household prices). Distorted electricity prices and the soft budget constraints for industry have contributed to comparatively high-energy use (see Table 6.2). The high numbers imply low energy intensity, so that the energy intensity of Bulgaria in 1994 is 4 times that of Hungary.

The privatisation of the power industry and accompanied rationalisation of tariff structures along long-run marginal cost (LRMC) lines (see Stern and Davis; 1998) would result in a long-term decline in energy intensity in transition economies from their high levels. However, it may not satisfy energy needs in the medium term of those transition economies able to accelerate economic growth.

Electricity price regulation

In the EU and the USA, industrial electricity tariff rates are between 45 per cent and 55 per cent of those for households in industrialised market economies. Stern & Davis (1998) found that in most transition economies with the exception of Hungary and Poland, tariff charges are inverted, in the sense that charges to households are below those to industrial users, or as in the case of Latvia very close to parity. In the Czech Republic there are signs of the gradual deregulation of different consumers and different types of consumption. Electricity prices will rise soon due to changes in VAT for energy increasing from 5 per cent to 22 per cent. However, the main area of cross subsidisation remains between large industrial customers to householders (see Stern and Davis, 1998).

Table 6.2 Energy Use (oil equivalent)
GDP per Kg ($) in Transition Economies (PPP)

	1980	1994
Czech Republic	1	0.9
Hungary	0.8	1.6
Poland	0.5	0.9
Slovak Republic	N/A	N/A
Bulgaria	0.7	0.4
Romania	N/A	0.8
Estonia	N/A	0.9
Latvia	N/A	1.3
Lithuania	N/A	0.6
Slovenia	N/A	4.7
Russian Federation	N/A	N/A
Kazakhstan	N/A	0.3
Ukraine	N/A	0.5
High Income Countries (OECD)	N/A	4.7
Upper Middle Income Countries	N/A	2.8
Lower Middle Income Countries*	N/A	1.1

Source: World Development Report 1996

* All the transition economies (with the exception of the Czech Republic, Hungary and Slovenia) fall within the Lower Middle-Income Country group.

What we found was that the prices to industrial consumers were around 50 per cent of LRMC in Estonia; 60-65 per cent in Poland and Latvia; 70 per cent in Hungary. However, for household consumer prices, the EBRD methodology suggests that only in Poland is the household price approaching even 50 per cent of LRMC; in Hungary, Latvia and Estonia its around 30 per cent of LRMC; in Romania, Slovakia and CIS around 15-20 per cent of LRMC.

This is important because as households are usually more expensive to supply than industrial consumers per unit of electrical energy (due to the higher dis-tribution costs to households and the fact that they contribute much of the peak-load demand, which is normally supplied by generation capacity with the highest marginal costs), it is doubtful whether electricity tariffs in transition economies reflect the true economic costs of supply. For most state owned power utilities controlling prices for household consumers may be achieved by a combination of: a) restraining average prices (e.g. by financing new investment directly or indirectly from the State budget); and b) cross-subsidises from large industrial consumers to households. This might well be described as an implicit form of taxation, as utilities are being used to redistribute income in favour of household consumers. However, Freund and Wallich (1995) in their study of Poland show that the bulk of the benefits received do not benefit low-income householders, rather they are primarily accrued by middle and high income households which consume the most power. This type of pricing policy may also unnecessarily raise the production costs of large industrial consumers.

Current tariff structures do not reflect the long run marginal cost methods based on economic theory, prevalent in the EU, as presently the cost structures and financial systems of the electricity companies are difficult to analyse. This is further complicated by the prevalence of arbitrary utility pricing policies by governments and municipal authorities, which do not liberalise tariffs to world market or economically (cost coverage) viable levels.

In contrast, most western economies have tended to implement utility pricing policies based on either *RPI-X* or *rate of return* (RoR) regulation. The *RPI-X* approach was introduced to overcome incentive problems associated with cost of service regulation (also termed *rate of return* regulation because of the inclusion of what is termed a 'fair' rate of return on capital). Under the RoR approach, price controls are reset each period to reflect changes in the cost to the utility of providing the regulated service. As a result, the regulated utility has little incentive to reduce costs; for if it were able to reduce costs by say 5 per cent, it would expect regulators to step in relatively quickly to reduce its allowable prices by an equivalent amount. The reward in terms of higher profits, for reducing cost efficiency would therefore be relatively limited. In contrast, under *RPI-X* regulation, allowable prices are predetermined for a period, during which the benefits of cost reduction will feed through fully into higher profits, thereby giving the firm greater incentives to reduce costs.

The most common forms of price regulation in the transition economies are administrative price setting and cost-based regulation. This has been administratively easier to implement and estimate as electricity utilities of most transition economies generally are incapable of providing the accuracy of cost analysis and level of financial reporting necessary to support cost of service regulatory structures such as RoR on capital employed. However, Hungary has moved the fastest of the transition economies in the direction of greater RoR price regulation. In Hungary, increases in electricity prices were introduced in three stages from September 1st 1995;[4] under the Electricity Act, charges for electricity since 1997 has contained justified costs and allow for an 8 per cent return on equity. Charges for district heating (including hot water and steam to industrial consumers), following a 1995 amendment to the Pricing Act, are determined by the Ministry for Industry and Trade in consultation with MVM (in the case of power stations owned by MVM), on the basis of actual costs, and by the Municipalities in the case of district heating companies (comprehensive legislation and regulation of heat supply is pending). It is important that all the transition economies phase out energy subsidies and more closely align domestic prices with world prices, despite the payments difficulties incurred following periodic large increases in energy prices. Effectively targeted social welfare support measures or the use of super-lifeline household tariff structures could provide some protection for the poor, particularly where social safety nets are weak.[5]

The Development of Electricity Regulation in the Transition Economies

Table 6.3 shows the differing degrees (and proliferation) of regulatory structures and mechanisms in the transition economies. The most contentious issues regarding the effective regulation and privatisation of electricity utilities in CEE and the former Soviet Union concern: (i) the appropriate ownership of the utilities; (ii) the nature of the regulatory structure, in particular whether regulation should be conducted by an independent agency, a branch of the Ministry of Economy, Finance or Transport, or the enterprise itself; (iii) the desirability of allowing entry and competition; and (iv) how to choose procedures for the control and setting of prices. The main elements of the regulatory structures and bodies in the CEEs and the former Soviet Union are presented in Table 6.3.

As previously noted, Hungary has developed the most extensive and established regulatory framework of the CEE. Thus the following will describe the regulatory mechanism as set out in legal documents and with reference to the practical experience gained in three different countries at different stages of developing the necessary regulatory framework: Hungary, the Czech Republic and Latvia.

In Hungary, the most important pieces of legislation as regards regulation of the energy sector are the Act on Gas Supply and the Act on the Generation and Distribution of Electrical Energy (Acts Nos. XLI and XLVIII of 1994), whose scope includes not only regulation of the transmission, supply and sale of gas and electricity, and the obligation to meet reasonable demand for a supply, but also safety provisions and provision for environmental and consumer protection. The Gas Act also makes provision for establishing the Hungarian Energy Office (MEH), a government agency under the supervision of the Ministry of Industry and Trade, and defines its regulatory functions, which include the issue of licences, e.g. for the supply of gas.[6] MEH also has the power (both under the Act and in the terms of the operating licences) to inspect installations (including consumer appliances) and their operation and maintenance, and may require licensed supply companies to seek authorisation in the case of certain commercial decisions which could affect their ability to supply (e.g. mergers, demergers, reduction of equity and 'sale of a significant stake') (Canning and Hare, 1996).

The regulatory system in Hungary is undoubtedly still in its infancy, and analysts are quick to point to actual or potential shortcomings. While legal loopholes may present problems of interpretation, however, and it may yet be some time before the institutions monitoring the operations of the regulated utilities develop the mechanisms for smooth and clear communication between the various groups whose interests they are designed to protect, such problems do not necessarily represent an insurmountable risk to investors in the utilities, while consumers in Hungary and other CEEs have yet to develop adequate representative mechanisms. A far more important question, certainly as far as the investors (and the companies themselves) are concerned, is the credibility of the government's commitment to maintaining an Aarm's-length' relationship with the regulatory framework it has put in place.

By comparison, the process of establishing an effective and independent regulatory framework in the Czech Republic has been subject to political constraints and ineffective institutional developments. The Czech energy public utilities operate under a mixture of general and specific energy sector legislation. The sector's regulation, in terms of anti-trust law is based on the 'CSFR Competition Act of 1991' which prohibits unfair business practice that restricts or excludes competition and aims to prevent abuses of dominant market positions and to review mergers. The Amendments to the 'Competition Act' (1993) provide additional enforcement powers to Czech competition authorities, however in practice these institutions have limited power. The Ministry of Industry and Trade is responsible for overall energy policy, including the electricity sector. The Czech Energy Agency (promoting energy conservation) and the Czech Inspectorate of Energy (undertakes public sector and subsidised enterprise energy audits are supervised by the Ministry of Industry and Trade). The Ministry of Finance administers general energy price legislation and approves regulated prices. The Ministry of Environment formulates environmental policy and regulations. The Office of Economic Competition is responsible for the development of competition policy. In practice the Office has been obliged to take a passive approach to the effect of privatisation on competition. The prohibition of monopoly abuse is a relatively low government priority as compared to the rapid privatisation of some of the largest Czech companies so as to raise capital and promote investment.

In Latvia, energy sector competition and regulation legislation are controlled by the State Anti-Monopoly Committee (SAMC), which is supervised by the Ministry of Economy. The SAMC and its chairperson were nominated by the 'Resolution of the Council of Ministers' in November 1992. The new 'Draft Law' provides for the re-organisation of the existing SAMC to the State Committee of Competition Protection, within which the Competition Board will act. The Competition Board will make all decisions regarding the violation of the competition law. The 'Draft Law' also provides that the members of the Competition Board be nominated by the *Saeima* (Latvian Parliament) for five year terms. Competition Board decisions may only be overruled by the Appeal Court [Davis, 1998]. What each of these case studies illustrate and have in common is that their regulatory authorities are not fully independent and have relatively limited, mainly advisory powers in electricity utility regulation [see Stern, 1997].

Table 6.3 shows that most CEEs are introducing legislation to encourage competition within the electricity sector. The Czech government is a good illustration of the broad direction in which most CEEs are moving. The Czech Republic is currently considering options for the structural reform of the sector towards increased competition. The main options under discussion include the entry of independent power producers, Third Party Access and dividing the CEZ into several generating companies and a separate transmission company. The management of the electricity sector in most CEEs is still characterised by

Table 6.3 Electricity Competition and Price Regulatory Bodies in Transition Economies

	Regulatory bodies	Competition regulation	Price regulation
Czech Republic	MIT; MoF	Some competition in generation	Cost oriented but politically influenced
Hungary	Hungarian Energy Office *(HEO)*	Competitive whole-sale market intended	MIT. Price Cap 01/97
Poland	Antimonopoly Office, MoF MIT, Regulatory Agency	Competitive market being developed	MoF and price adjust-ment path
Slovak Republic	MoF, MoE, Energy Inspection Office	Monopoly for T&D, some TPA	Administrative prices
Estonia	Energy Market Inspectorate; MoE.	Market based system envisaged	Regulation No.7 (1996) of MoE.
Latvia	Energy Council, Anti-Monopoly Committee	Monopoly	Average Cost-based C/S
Lithuania	Energy Agency	Some competition	Energy Pricing Council Cost based
Romania	MoF	Debating competitive restructuring	MoF and RENEL Administrative prices
Slovenia	MoE	Limited TPA due to shortage of capacity	Administrative prices
Russian Federation	Federal Energy Commission, MoE, Regional Energy Commission	No competition	Cost based
Kazakhstan	MoE, State Energy Supervisory Commit-tee, State Commission on Pricing, Coal Ind.	Restructuring	Conversion approach (gradual adjustment to cost covering prices)
Ukraine	National Electricity Regulatory Commis-sion, Minenergo, MoE	Developing compe-titive pool system	Cost based

Notes:

C/S: Cross subsidisation   MoE: Ministry of Economy (or Economic Affairs)
MoF: Ministry of Finance   MIT: Ministry of Industry and Trade
TPA: Third Party Access   T&D: Transmission and Distribution

the dual role of the State i.e., the responsibility of the Ministry of Industry and Trade as both owner and regulator of the sector. Both these responsibilities reside with the ministry and there is no independent regulatory authority or clear competition legislation in the sector.

The Latvian Privatisation Agency is also considering plans to divide the state-run Latvenergo electricity and gas energy company into two enterprises on privatisation. Latvenergo could be divided into a generating and supplies company, and an administrative enterprise. The agency also envisages a similar ownership structure as that introduced for Latvia Gas, where the state retains e.g. 75 per cent of the interest, whilst 25 per cent would be sold to private companies.

In the CIS, there are some embryonic electricity regulatory institutions in Russia, Ukraine and Kazakhstan (e.g. the Federal Energy Commission in Russia and the National Energy Regulatory Commission in the Ukraine). However, none of them seems yet to have achieved any real degree of autonomy de facto and none has as yet been assigned powers and duties by parliamentary statute. Political influences appear still to be dominant viz. the 1997 price and trading structure interventions by Deputy Prime Minister Nemstov. Nonetheless, Table 6.3 shows that there is still much to be done if the CEEs are to join the EU and successfully adapt to the European Union (EU) Electricity Directive introduced in 1997 (see Stern and Davis, 1998).

While competition depends on access to monopoly network facilities, economic regulation is required to ensure that network access and pricing support competition. This can clearly be very difficult where transmission and generation are combined, but remains a significant issue even when they are separate - and similarly for distribution and supply. Indeed, the need for and difficulty of regulation can increase as competition over networks is increased. The nature of regulation changes considerably but the need for it does not. For electricity, there is as yet no sign of competing high voltage transmission or low voltage transmission networks. This is in contrast to telecommunications, where radiotelephony and internet telephony offer competition and it can be economic to build competing fixed link networks. Even in gas, given sufficient demand growth, it can be economic to build competing high-pressure pipeline networks. That is not the case in electricity.

Political Economy Aspects of Electricity Regulation

Many economists have argued that the unbundling of the transition economies power industries into separate businesses is essential for improved economic performance. Where economists differ is as to whether the current unbundled structures as in the UK or being planned in the EU is politically or economically appropriate for transition economies. We attempt to address some of these issues by initially highlighting the main political and institutional constraints underlying electricity sector regulation and reform in the transition economies as follows: (i) economic nationalism, (ii) subsidisation and (iii) bureaucratic co-ordination.

Economic nationalism, by this we mean that some governments seek to control the destiny, structure and planning of the electricity industry because it is seen as being central to the economic infrastructure. In the CEEs there has been much evidence of this where the state has either retained complete control of the electricity industry or privatised a minority of its shares, thus retaining a signifi-cant influence over enterprise affairs.[7] Of all the transition economies, only Hungary has made any substantial progress in privatising its electricity industry. However, the political economy implications of economic nationalism with regard to the power sector increasingly extend beyond the domestic sphere and have geo-political implications.

For example, since 1996 Kazakhstan has allowed six of its northern regions to enter into barter agreements with Russia for the supply of electricity in exchange for industrial goods and agricultural produce. These are predominantly Russian areas and this expansion in their ties with the Russian Federation may reinforce the views of many residents there and in Moscow that these areas should be part of Russia.[8] Certainly, this concession has allowed the Russian government to have a greater say in the economic and political affairs of Kazakhstan. To some extent this highlights the increasing links between energy flows and political ones in the CIS.

Kazakhstan owed Russia more than US$ 400 million, and in mid-August Russia turned off the supply of electricity to Kazakhstan. As a result, many regions of that country do not have power, many of its factories are operating at reduced capacity, and Kazakhstan's economic difficulties have been compounded, leaving it with even less cash to pay its bills. However, at another level, the forced decision of the Kazakhstan government on this point has a political meaning far broader than this economic one. Like a number of the other newly independent states, it has tried to raise money to pay energy debts by selling off its energy infrastructure.

Foreign companies now own more than 60 per cent of the country's power plants. In most cases, this foreign ownership is Russian, a pattern that gives Russian firms and often the Russian government enormous political influence. Moreover, this pattern of Russian acquisition of the energy infrastructures in former Soviet republics is not restricted to Kazakhstan; it has also occurred in the Ukraine, and Latvia.

At the political and social level, it could be argued that the influence of nationalism in the context of 'nation-building' and 'Russo-phobia' have been important factors in the Estonian and Latvian privatisation process, particularly in Latvia with the privatisation of Latvenergo (the state-owned power utility) [Davis, 1998]. The Latvian government was widely criticised in Parliament and through the press for seeking to privatise the government oil enterprise Ventspils Nafta, and the power utility Latvenergo, because they were seen as being vital to national security and economic independence (Davis, 1998).[9] There remain restrictions in many transition economies on the amount of foreign ownership allowed in the power sector. The amount of permitted foreign ownership tends to depend on three factors: (i) the utilities need for foreign direct investment in the sector (typically for new plant or generation); (ii) the capacity of the power industry to satisfy the level of demand for electricity. As there has generally been excess capacity, although inefficiently produced many countries have opted to restrict foreign ownership; and (iii) the aforementioned political economy factors.

Subsidisation, here we emphasise the control of consumer prices and the politically sensitive issues surrounding the elimination of these subsidies. Even in developed western economies cross-subsidies between different consumer groups and subsidies to other industries such as fuel suppliers (e.g. coal mining), may delay the restructuring of the power industry. This issue is extensively discussed in Stern and Davis (1998). However, Freund and Wallich (1997) in their study of raising household energy prices in Poland found that they were able to rule out the oft-used social welfare argument for delaying household energy price increases. They maintained that raising prices, while targeting relief to the poor through a social assistance program is the first-best response. This is far more efficient than the present go-slow price adjustment policies, which imply energy subsidies that provide across-the-board relief to all consumers. However, if governments want to provide some relief for consumers during the transition to ease the adjustment, several options are open to them: in-kind transfers to the poor, vouchers, in-cash transfers and lifeline pricing for a small block of electricity (the latter is strongly supported in Stern and Davis, 1998); accompanied by significant price increases, are all possible approaches. Freund and Wallich's (1997) simulations show that, if raising prices to efficient levels for all Polish consumers is not politically feasible at present, it may be socially better to use lifeline pricing and a large price increase than an overall, but smaller, price increase. Lifeline pricing for electricity in combination with an 80 per cent price increase has better distributional effects than a smaller, 50 per cent across-the-board price rise. Ideally the public utility would be compensated for any reduced-price sales from the budget, rather than having to finance this through internal cross-subsidies. In-kind transfers to poor households are also effective from an efficiency perspective, but may be harder to administer in some countries than lifeline pricing.

Bureaucratic opposition from government utility managers, trades unions or employees with a variety of agendas ranging from trades unions aiming to maintain existing wage and employment levels, to managers seeking 'insider' privatisation opportunities may delay the restructuring of the power industry. This is all the more important in transition economies where utility managers are a politically powerful force; Russia is a good case in point.

After quitting his post as deputy Prime Minister in March, Anatoly Chubais was appointed in late April to take over as chief executive of Russia's giant electricity company Unified Energy Systems (UES), which owns a controlling stake in Komienergo and almost all of the country's regional utilities, known as energos. The appointment came after months of behind-the-scenes wrangling and intense opposition from the State Duma, which balked at Chubais running a company that allows him to wield political influence over the regions in the run-up to parliamentary elections.

The state-controlled energy system is at the centre of the biggest structural problem facing Russia: non-payments. The energy system is at the centre of a vicious circle of unpaid bills worth an estimated US$ 96 billion which is choking the economy and putting a break on investments. The energy system and its subsidiaries are owed roughly US$ 21 billion, including massive unpaid bills by government-funded organisations. It in turn has built up unwieldy debts to state budgets and suppliers, such as the gas monopoly Gazprom.

The power sector is blamed for holding back economic growth by over-charging industry in order to subsidise Russian households, which pay just a fraction of their income for electricity. One of the greatest challenges facing Chubais will be to reduce tariffs for industry and encourage market-based competition among energy suppliers. UES currently owns the national electricity grid, operates 34 power plants and holds controlling stakes in 70 regional utilities, which have a monopoly on local distribution. Under reforms outlined in a presidential decree, Russia's power generating facilities will be separated from transmission, over the next two to three years.

Competition is currently limited because instead of independent power stations competing to supply power on a national grid, local regulators set prices. While a wholesale market for power exists at the national level, regional utilities often block industries from seeking other cheaper sources of electricity by charging high transmission fees. Moreover, a web of opaque financial deals carried out in barter and unregulated promissory notes, known as *veksels* is widespread [Bagratian et.al, 1997]. Thus, one of the main priorities should be to improve the firm's finances and to make its transactions more transparent.

The company's Soviet-era directors sacked Anatoly Chubais' predecessor Boris Brevnov, after less than a year on the job. Their reform programmes for the Unified Energy System are almost identical, however, unlike Brevnov, Chubais has the political muscle to push through reforms, such as raising electricity tariffs for households, breaking up regional monopolies and turning off non-paying customers. This will bring Chubais into direct conflict with a number of vested interests e.g. electricity sector investors, managers and regional leaders. The success of the reforms will rely heavily on his political ability to retain the support of most of the managers and politicians involved in the Unified Energy System activities. Chubais has said he will force the federal government to pay its bills to local energos that agree to implement tough reforms and he has the political credibility to make these promises [OMRI, 1998].

In transition economies, competition law, institutions and utility reform and regulation may not operate in practice as anticipated. The political and legal culture may not support it sufficiently. As previously noted, in Hungary there is now the issue of how to re-establish the credibility of the Hungarian Energy Office and to ensure the new electricity and gas laws operate in a way which sustains effective regulation. It is very difficult to sustain independent utility regulation where: contract and commercial law is under-developed; competition policy is absent; the legal process is insecure and or corrupt; and there is little or no separation of political powers, which dominate economic and commercial factors. Clearly, under these circumstances the political constraints that transition economies face regarding the reform of their power sectors restrain the opportunities for independent utility regulation. Stern (1997) correctly (in my view) argues that where political economy pressures dominate, as they clearly do in all transition economies (particularly regarding winter energy prices for households), an independent regulator following standard principles of regulation is likely to be unfeasible. In practice, the political risks for policymakers are too great and neither they nor their voters would allow it; irrespective of what the World Bank might think or propose.

Conclusion

In Table 6.1 we outlined the main components of the World Bank's power lending strategy and economic reform agenda for the electricity industries of the transition economies during the early 1990s, which encompassed:

1. raising prices to long-run marginal cost (LRMC) levels and re-balancing them between industry and households;
2. achieving commercialised power companies, with management autonomy and freed from the tutelage of sponsoring Ministries;
3. the establishment of independent economic regulation;
4. privatisation; and
5. the introduction of competition in generation and, where appropriate, wholesale competition.

Regarding the first point, in no transition economy is there yet any transmission prices for access to transmission networks. In this paper we have argued that one of the main reasons for the lack of progress in this area is the unwillingness of transition economy governments to raise household electricity prices for logical political reasons. This unwillingness has been economically sustainable because, currently, the unavoidable investment needs in transition economies power industries are not particularly great, given the volume of spare capacity. However, in the medium to long-term realistic LRMC prices need to be established in the transition economies power industries for the following reasons: (i) to improve economic efficiency and the quality of service to its customers; (ii) to meet the requirements of environmental legislation; and (iii) for the CEE countries seeking accession to the EU, to meet the requirements of its Electricity Directive (see Stern and Davis, 1998). However, in the short term, where political economy pressures dominate, as they clearly do in all transition economies (particularly regarding winter energy prices for households), if governments want to provide some relief for consumers during transition to ease the adjustment, they should utilize less incentive distorting measures such as: in-kind transfers to the poor, vouchers, in-cash transfers and lifeline pricing for a small block of electricity.

The transition economy power sector also needs to develop complementary policies to improve collection rates (in Albania 70 per cent of households do not pay their bills, in Russia and the Ukraine large state owned enterprises have failed to pay their bills and been cut-off) to increase investment in the industry and to mitigate the adverse effects of economic reform on the poorest members of society.

Secondly, in terms of achieving commercialised power companies, with management autonomy freed from the 'tutelage' of sponsoring Ministries progress here has been slow. In some transition economies the strategy appeared to be to implement the market first and then worry about corporatisation later, with little emphasis placed on developing the technical and managerial infrastructure to implement the market. We have shown that where significant political pressure is brought to bear on a utility, that effective independence in either management or regulation is very difficult to achieve. Thus, the latter together with the prevalence of politically influential vested interests have slowed down the possibility of privatisation in the sector, which might have made the World Bank's objective more achievable. Ryding (1998) has emphasised that to achieve this, adequate managerial training, improved corporate governance, new accounting procedures and legal measures are required as well as reformed tariff structures. Indeed, the major problem appears to be the scale of the changes required and the lack of both political will and institutional capacity (legal, economic and technical) to deal with these forces.

On independent economic regulation, clearly foreign investors and the World Bank are likely to see an effective regulatory agency independent of government as critical to protecting their interests. For the World Bank (and other foreign investors) an effective regulatory agency with the appropriate powers provides both: a) credibility for the economic viability of their long-term investments; and b) low-cost monitoring and enforcement institutions. Only Hungary and (since 1998) Poland have statutorily established independent regulators, although their powers are limited, particularly on prices. However, as previously noted the sector is subject to tremendous political economy constraints. Thus, it could be argued, that even if a formally independent regulator existed in transition economies, they might be considered as too great a political threat from all politicians if they balanced the interest between the utilities, large industrial consumers and their investors against those of household consumers and the government in the prevailing climate.

Regarding the last two points, only Hungary has made any substantial progress on privatisation and no transition economy has yet introduced competition in generation or any liberalisation of bulk power markets. In particular, the trading structure still operates in the electricity industries of all the dominant transition economies as if they were vertically integrated.

We would argue that the particular political, economic and institutional conditions such as non-payment, disconnection or a lack of legislation, were inappropriate for the successful reform of the power industry in most transition economies.[10] The economic consequences of transition have placed great financial stress on the power industry and its customers. Nonetheless, electricity markets world-wide are unbundling and different structures, as we have seen, are emerging. The transition economies are not immune to these pressures. The 'appropriate' model for any particular country is a function of its cultural, historical and economic circumstances.

Notes

1 The term transition economies is used to describe the new political geography of the former CMEA, comprised of the CEE states (the Czech Republic, Hungary, Poland, Slovakia,), the Balkans (Albania, Bulgaria Romania) the Baltic States (Estonia, Latvia and Lithuania), the former Yugoslavia, and the Commonwealth of Independent States (Russia, Ukraine, Armenia, Azerbaijan, Belarus, Georgia, Kazakhstan, Kyrgyzstan, Moldova, Tajikistan, Turkmenistan, Uzbekistan).

2 Since the early 1980s, the world-wide development of cheap natural gas reserves has encouraged innovation in small-scale gas-fired technologies. These new technologies and greater environmental regulation have encouraged power companies and independent power produceres to adopt gas as a cleaner and cheaper source of energy, rather than e.g. coal or nuclear power to generate electricity, which have higher costs; thus the co-called 'dash for gas'.

3 In this article, we treat transparent regulation as being synonymous with independent regulation as in both cases for the World Bank (and other foreign investors). An effective regulatory agency with the appropriate powers provides both: a) credibility for the economic viability of their long-term investments; b) transparent and clear justification and methodologies for the decisions reached, which are open to public debate and discussion; and c) low-cost monitoring and enforcement institutions.

4 In the case of electricity, average consumer prices of end-1994 were estimated to cover only 50 per cent of costs.

5 See Stern & Davis (1998) for a fuller discussion of super-lifeline tariffs.

6 In the case of the regional gas companies, which previously enjoyed exclusive rights to supply in their respective geographical areas, the new licensing rules allow for competition to take place between suppliers applying for a licence to operate in areas not already served by a gas supply; MEH issues licences for such areas to the company offering the highest standard of service at the lowest cost.

7 For example, in Latvia during 1997, the Russian Gas company *Gazprom* and German consortium *Ruhrgas*, and *Preusen Electra* were successful in their bid for the rights to acquire shares (each being allowed to purchase up to 16.25 per cent of the shares) in Latvian Gas. However, the Latvian State still retains a 66 per cent stake in the enterprise [Davis, 1998].

8 By removing part of the Kazakhstan economy from the monetary system of that country, this latest move will have the effect of reducing Kazakhstan's ability to raise the new revenues that it will need to escape its current economic crisis. Furthermore, it may have the effect of increasing, rather than reducing, economic differences between the

predominantly ethnic Russian north of Kazakhstan and its predominantly ethnic Kazakh south [OMRI, 1997].
9   The Latvian Privatisation Agency plans to sell privatisation vouchers in at least 10 large and medium-sized state enterprises this year. Those companies include: the gas supplier Latvijas Gaze, and the shipping company Latvijas Kugnieciba. The third issuance of stocks in the oil concern Ventspils Nafta is also slated to take place in 1998. Janis Naglis, director-general of the Latvian Privatisation Agency, said Ventspils Nafta stocks could be sold on foreign exchanges by the fall.
10 It is also questionable whether loans to power industries that already face tremendous liquidity problems (as in Romania and Ukraine) is a help or a hindrance [Ryding, 1998].

References

Bagratian, H and Gurgen, E. (1997), Payments arrears in the Gas and Electric power Sectors of the Russian Federation and Ukraine, *IMF Working Paper* WP/97/162, December 1997.

CEZ (1996) CEZ Annual Report 1996.

Canning, A. and Hare, P.G. (1996), *Political Economy of Privatization in Hungary*: A Progress Report. CERT Discussion Paper No. 96/13, Department of Economics, Heriot-Watt University UK.

Chisiu, D. (1997), Romania: Utility Regulation and Privatization, pp. 265-271, in Lewington, I. (ed.) (1997) *Utility Regulation 1997*, Published by CRI Privatisation International Ltd, London.

Davis, J.R. (1997), Latvia: Utility Regulation and Privatization, pp.235-242, in Lewington, I. (ed.) (1997) *Utility Regulation 1997*, Published by CRI Privatisation International Ltd, London.

Davis, J.R. (1998), Privatization and Regulation of Public Utilities in Latvia, in Batt, J., Cave, M., Estrin, S., and Hare, P. (eds) (1998) *Reconstituting the market: The political economy of microeconomic transformation*, Publishers IAP gmbh.

EBRD (1997), *Transition Report*, The EBRD, London.

Freund, C. and Wallich, C. (1995), *Raising Household Energy Prices in Poland: Who Gains? Who Loses?* World Bank Policy Research Discussion Paper, No. 1495.

OMRI (1996, 1997 and 1998), various issues.

Ryding, H. (1998), Electricity restructuring in Ukraine: Illusions of Power in the power industry? Forthcoming *CERT, Department of Economics*, Heriot-Watt University UK, Discussion Paper.

Stern, J. (1997), What Makes an Independent regulator Independent? *Business Strategy Review*, London Business School, Vol. 8, Issue 2, summer 1997.

Stern, J. and Davis, J.R. (1998), *Economic Reform of the Electricity Industries of Central and Eastern Europe.* Economics of Transition, vol. 6, No. 2.

World Bank (1993), *The World Bank's role in the electric power sector: Policies for effective institutional, regulatory and financial reform.* A World Bank policy paper, IBRD, ISSN 1014-8124.

World Bank, 1996, *World Development Report.* Washington D.C.

Section 3:
Science, Technology and Innovation in Industry

Introduction

ANNE LORENTZEN, BRIGITTA WIDMAIER, MIHÁLY LAKI

Whereas the question of innovation in CEE is seen more from the enterprise level in part one, the three following chapters inquire into conditions for and recent developments of the conditions for innovation in the context of more general aspects. The main focus is how past, present and future institutional settings and structures together can lead to new innovative patterns in industry, part 3 concentrating on linkages between science and technology and industry.

Patterns of industrial innovation are widely discussed not only in CEE countries but also in the advanced industrial societies because innovation is seen as the main vehicle for economic growth and competitiveness of national economies. The circumstances under which innovation takes place occupies social sciences as a whole. In economic theory the factor 'knowledge' as embodied in 'social capital' has recently been introduced. New concepts of innovation, today seen as a complex of mutually reinforcing variables in socio-economic research, led to closer attention being paid to the factors and processes which are conducive to the successful introduction of new products and services into new markets.

The loss of markets followed by a serious decline of production characterized the situation of CEE in 1989. During the coming years many CEE enterprises fought for survival and tried to compete with the cheap and simple products from the world market which very quickly gained free access to the newly opened markets. Such strategies envisaged no return for investment in the type of innovative activities that would be necessary to access higher value markets. Due to this development one of the biggest problems since 1989 has been the observable decline of technological sophistication of products in most of the new market economies. In order to be competitive on worldwide markets and in global production chains, high quality, technologically advanced products are required. For this, efficient innovation systems are necessary but if they ever existed, they have at best been heavily disturbed by the transformation in CEE countries.

The three contributions in this part of the book examine the chances for and prospects of newly developed institutions to facilitate new links and networks being established in order to turn economically relevant knowledge into innovation. This is not only a task of single enterprises, though they are the ones that must develop their ability to 'manage' knowledge. It is also a matter of co-operation among old and new institutions to find new ways to enrich their inherited 'paths' in order to meet the new demands that are emerging from the new socio-economic order. In this context, questions are raised as to how politics can provide the proper conditions within which innovative activities can prosper. It often seems as if this is mainly a question of available money. Upon taking a closer look, however, it becomes obvious that the state should not only provide the means in terms of investment in research, etc., but also must consider possible synergies in defining more long-term and more integrated innovation strategies. All three contributions make it clear that this is a problem of inherited institutions and their inertia.

The contribution of *Brigitta Widmaier* looks at the chances for the emergence of new innovation systems. It argues that, in order to integrate in a European and global economic environment, it is necessary for CEE countries to renew their production by innovating. Even though developments in the production of technologically more sophisticated goods and services look different between a number of CEE countries, it is argued that there is still a substantial 'knowledge gap' in these countries which has to be overcome by new systems of innovation that link together the (still) existing potentials. The paper starts out by arguing that knowledge-based development is not only a matter of pushing forward high-tech industries, but rather one of incorporating new knowledge in as many industries as possible. This is probably even more important for CEE economies because, even if they have had advantages in advanced industries, they have almost everywhere lost them after 1989. In order to develop new innovative capacities it is of utmost importance that enterprises demand new knowledge and combine it with their own resources into new processes, products and services. For this, a powerful infrastructure in science and technology is just as necessary as co-operative links and intermediary institutions. In the chapter, science systems, enterprises and markets are looked at to get a view of how far they can contribute to new innovation systems. It is concluded that the starting position for new innovation systems is not very encouraging because old structures have not yet been transcended and new institutions are, on the one hand not sufficiently developed and, on the other, not sufficiently empowered in order to work.

Maureen Lankhuizen outlines in her contribution that the economic system of the socialist countries with its centralised production and trade patterns isolated these countries from the reality of the world markets. This had consequences not only for the quality of products, but also for the scope of new developments in that they were directed towards very limited areas like military purposes or promising foreign markets.

Lankhuizen analyses the situation of the Baltic countries with respect to their recent trade structures and comes to the conclusion that the export structure has changed substantially from technology-intensive goods to technologically simple, raw material based products. Many studies investigating the scientific potential in a country only look at the amount of expenditures or the level of human capital. For successful innovation, however, organisation is the essential variable. By looking at the organisation of human capital and the structures of science and technology in the Baltic countries, she infers that the ability to catch up in terms of 'future, technology- induced competitiveness' is not very promising. In particular the lack of communication between research organisations and the separation of R and D from production are much more serious impediments for future competitiveness.

Attila Havas adds the political aspects of innovation in Hungary to this section. By outlining the recent theoretical discussion, his main thesis is that the 'missing link' between the scientific basis, which is on a high level in Hungary, and it is employment in new products and services is the main problem politics are confronted with.

In analysing past developments he concludes that central planning has left behind a fragmented S and T system which the political and economic changes of the recent years have not been able to alter considerably because of lacking systematic policies.

Havas shows with recent data that, even though the government supports R and D infrastructure projects as well as applied research, a commensurate support in terms of financial means and number of R and D personnel is lacking. The positive effects of a number of institutional changes can not be denied. However, insufficient continuity through changing political majorities and lacking evaluation of single initiatives diminish the positive effects of the newly established institutions. He concludes his chapter by arguing that governments should indeed play a vital role in shaping the national system of innovation. He suggests a number of policy measures for changes in the science and education infrastructure and discusses their probable impact on diffusion of new technologies.

7 Knowledge and Innovation in Industry in Central and Eastern Europe

BRIGITTA WIDMAIER

Introduction

When talking about industrial development in Central and Eastern European (CEE)[1] countries, there are two main sets of issues to be mentioned as precondition for their internal development and their integration process into the European and global economic environment. The first one refers to institution-building in order to facilitate the working of a modern industrialized economy and to enhance the conditions of the stability of the transition process. The second one refers to knowledge, learning and innovation in these economies in order to overcome the 'technology gap' and - as is argued in the paper - also a 'knowledge-gap' which so far hinders an integration in global trade and production chains as precondition for growth and development.

Based upon own research in 6 CEE countries[2] during 1994-1996 and more recent literature, this chapter deals with problems of innovative developments in industrial transformation in CEE. It starts out with aspects of the economic situation during the last 6-8 years in comparison with other European countries. Its main focus is on institutional aspects and social and political conditions which can contribute to re-organizing the web in which a market economy has to be imbedded in order to be innovative.

Innovative potentials in CEE industry

It is a well known fact today that transformation of industry in the former socialist countries is not only a matter of the replacement of central planning by market principles but also concerns the conditions under which reconstruction of the political systems takes place and the social changes which follow from this.

One of the main results of the mentioned research project which aimed towards an assessment of future potentials of CEE industries was that due to the enormous disruptions and radical changes, the innovative potentials in these economies which are urgently needed for their ability to join global trade-production- and supply-chains, are endangered. It also turned out that, even if they exist, these potentials are not challenged and mobilized, because there is little demand for innovation. Finally, even if there were demand, the social mechanisms which underlie the processes of integrating knowledge in order to successfully introduce novelties in the markets are not well developed yet.

These results agree with other studies that deal with the role of innovative potentials in industrial development in CEE. Radosevic (1997b) in a recent paper remarks that the CEE countries 'inherited a large stock of research and development (R and D) and technology capital from the socialist period' and comes to the conclusion that the main shortages do not lie in the capacities but in demand for R and D and the quality and mechanisms of R and D supply. The findings of OECD, in its Reviews of National Science and Technology Policy in several countries (OECD 1992b, 1993, 1994a, 1994b, 1996) point in the same direction.

When measuring innovative activities on an aggregate level with quantitative indicators data do not show discouraging results. Expenditures for R and D per gross domestic product (GDP), for instance, were always on a very high level during the socialist period. Though the subsequent downsizing was considerable, today in many of the CEE economies the level of variables like gross expenditures for R and D and R and D personnel is quite comparable at least to less developed European economies. The same general picture holds for R and D output, measured in patenting activities (Radosevic 1997b; CEU 1994). The question is, how these potentials are and will be deployed in order to establish new innovation systems under conditions of ongoing transformation.

Problems of industrial development in a larger Europe

A considerable recovery of the CEE economies has taken place in the past seven years. Still there are important differences compared with the average of the EU countries and it has to be asked how these gaps can be closed in due time. Some of the CEE countries are preparing to join the European Union, and the rules and conditions are defined by the advanced Western industrialized economies. In this chapter it is claimed that Central and Eastern Europe will only succeed in this process, if it mobilizes its endogenous potentials and enlarges the stock of knowledge which leads to innovation in industry. This necessity not only emerges from transformation and its consequences but also from worldwide developments.

If we look at Europe as a whole, industrial regions in East *and* West are confronted with structural problems that find their expression in lagging growth and high unemployment. The analysis of such phenomena indicates (Lehner 1993; Gordon 1994; Hilpert 1996) that these problems are linked with globalization processes and the shifting of production capacities away from the old industrialized countries to new locations. They shape a new pattern of international division of labor and can be tackled by the development of new products and new markets in the old industrialized countries. The reorganization of the global division of labour and of international trade and production linkages requires an active and flexible approach to new entrepreneurial and political concepts for innovation. The World Bank came to the conclusion in 1991 that 'it is intangible investment in knowledge accumulation which is decisive rather than physical capital investment' (cited after Freeman 1995, 5). Successful innovation is based on this kind of investment. The existing scientific, technological and social resources together form the knowledge-base of a country. For CEE countries and Western nations alike this is an important device for integration into European and global production chains.

In the following, after a look at the present situation in CEE, we discuss different notions of 'knowledge' and 'innovation'. Past and present conditions which influence the emergence of new innovation systems in CEE countries show some of the main problems. Accessing them by new research might bring some light into a situation which, even after seven years is still in flux and often hard to assess.

Some empirical observations

To give a general picture of the current status of CEE economies in the study mentioned above we employ a comparison of their GDP with that of other European countries and USA. This table indicates that the differences between the peripheral EU-countries and CEE countries have practically evened out. However, there is still a large gap in comparison with e.g. Austria and the United States.

Table 7.1 GDP per capita European Union (12) average = 100

	1990	1991	1992	1993	1994	199	2000
Czech Republic	61	52	49	50	51	54	62
Hungary	38	35	34	35	37	38	44
Poland	28	25	26	28	29	31	36
Slovak	41	34	36	36	38	41	47
Slovenia	61	54	52	54	57	60	69
Bulgaria	31	27	25	25	26	27	31
Romania	27	23	21	22	23	25	29
Russia	37	35	30	28	25	24	28
Ukraine	29	25	21	19	15	13	15
Austria	109	109	109	112	112	112	112
Germany	103	106	109	108	108	108	108
Greece	49	49	50	51	51	51	51
Portugal	61	65	67	70	69	69	69
Spain	77	80	77	78	77	77	77
USA	144	140	135	142	144	144	144

Notes: Projection (2000) assumes no population growth. 5 per cent GDP growth in Eastern Europe and 2 per cent growth in the European Union and USA.
Source: Knell 1996.

Table 7.1 conveys the impression that a remarkable consolidation has taken place. However, there are still many doubts left, as to whether this development can be considered sustainable (Knell 1996; EBRD 1996; UN - Economic Survey of Europe 1996-97).

In order to get a more differentiated picture, it is worthwhile to consider two observations of the last seven years and their consequences for the comparative performance of industry in East and West. The first one is that at the beginning of the transformation process the most prominent comparative advantages of CEE economies seemed to be their low wages and the relatively well qualified workforce. What followed from this was a strong emphasis on labour-intensive production which slowed down increases in productivity and improvement of production processes. The second observation refers to the breakdown and complete re-orientation of markets after the demise of the Council for Mutual

Economic Assistance (CMEA). For quite some time this entailed a steady decline of quality and technological sophistication of production since market pressures and technology gaps were joined in a vicious circle. This can be shown with the development of the revealed comparative advantages (RCA-values),[3] i.e. the changing patterns of specialisation over time.

Figure 7.1   Changing significance of Revealed Comparative Advantages (RCA-value) of selected CEE countries 1988-1993

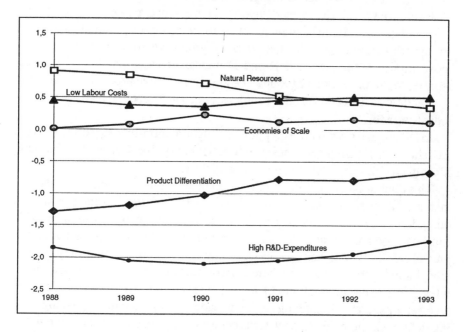

Source: Trabold and Berke 1996 (translation by the author)

Figure 7.1 shows the development in the comparative advantages in exported goods during the years 1989 to 1993 with a still rising tendency in labor-intensive production.

Recent data, however, show 1) that the picture is getting more differentiated and 2) that there are indications that the downward movement is at least halted, if not reversed. Carlin and Landesmann (1997) employ four indicators to measure the quality of change in the comparative performance of CEE industries in Europe: quality of traded goods, quality gaps, factor intensity of products and intra-industry trade.

Their indicators for the quality of traded goods and quality gaps are based on a quantitative analysis of trade statistics of the EU markets.[4] As an example, the results for the engineering and the clothing and footwear branches are given. They show that the high-quality segment in both branches is underrepresented and that there exist considerable quality gaps. Looking at the indicators over time, however, makes evident that there are considerable improvements in the 'Western' CEEs[5] and much less improvement or even deterioration in 'Eastern' CEE countries.[6] This divergent development in essence remains constant for the other indicators. The measurement of factor intensity of products points to a stronger differentiation within the 'Western' group: whereas Hungary shows the most important turn towards R and D-intensiveness, Poland is still underrepresented in the exports of R and D and skill-intensive products. Along with the trend towards R and D and skill-intensive products goes an increase in intra-industry trade.[7]

In all countries, with the exception of Bulgaria, intra-industry trade with the EU shows increasing tendencies, where Hungary, the Czech Republic and Slovenia reach values which come close to the EU-average.

This qualitative re-orientation was, among other things, a reaction to the fact that soon after trade had been liberalized, CEE countries felt the pressure of other low-wage economies, i.e. the East-Asian countries (which provide finished products mainly). It soon became obvious that trade, based upon the prevailing relative advantages in labor and raw materials could only lead to inter-industry trade patterns whereas intra-industry trade is necessary for an integration in the production-chains of advanced industrial countries. As the data demonstrates, a beginning has been made, but, in order to keep strengthening their position in this respect, CEE countries have to close a gap through the permanent improvement and development of new products and processes and related reactions to organizational and market requirements. To achieve this all the available knowledge and its synthesizing into new innovation systems is necessary.

Figure 7.2 Grubel-Lloyd indices of CEE countries in trade with the EU

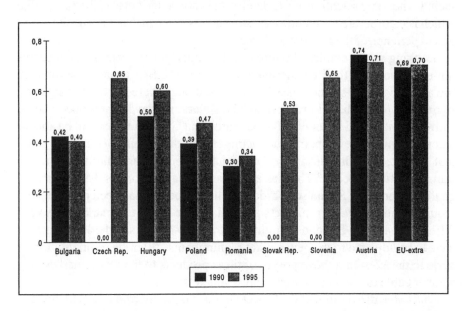

Source: Wiener Institut für Internationale Wirtschaftsvergleiche (WIIW): calculations from Cronos trade statistics; the GL-indices were calculated from export and import data by 108 NACE 3-digit industries, 1993. The Standard-Grubel Lloyd Index runs from 0 to 1, where the value of 0 indicates complete *inter*-industrial and the value of 1 complete *intra-industrial* specialization (see e.g. Greenaway and Milner, 1986).

Knowledge based industrial development in CEE countries

During the last decades the concept of knowledge and its consequences for growth and employment not only has found entrance into the economic theory (Romer 1990; 1993; Lucas 1988), but is more and more taken into consideration as a crucial factor in the discussion of economic, social and political research on the future of industry in a globalising world. For the purpose of the present paper, i.e. to show that innovation in CEE industry is not a problem of availability of 'knowledge' per se, but of the combination and application of different kinds of knowledge,[8] it is important to emphasize that knowledge is not to be confined to technological or scientific knowledge and 'high-tech'. The concept of 'knowledge', therefore, here is understood in a more encompassing sense. It includes not only scientific and technological knowledge but also the knowledge which is incorporated in enterprises and markets and which is rooted in learning and experience of the entire workforce.

Looking at our empirical reference, the transformation countries, it seems quite obvious that their development can not in the first instance be directed towards advanced, science-based industries, though there has been excellency in military research and production. The situation today, as presented above, shows that it would be an illusion to assume that CEE countries will be able to enter the worldwide economic race at this end. Rather, results of our study show that 'high-tech' industries in most cases have been hit particularly hard in the transformation process.[9] This has a number of reasons: one is the question of quality. Even if, by Soviet standards, excellent products had been produced the requirements of Western markets are still higher and these markets are very difficult to access. Beyond that, different technological standards and norms have to be adjusted to the new market requirements. After the re-orientation of trade to the West and the exposure of these products to the world market they were not able to compete in high quality markets.

Due to the dissolution of the Soviet Union and the enormous cuts in military spending, demand for advanced, science-based products within the area of the CMEA declined considerably and, together with products, considerable parts of R and D have vanished. Consequently these industries suffer particularly from the break-up of scientific and technological 'supply chains'. If they still exist, many of the enterprises have turned to the production of other, more simple goods.

A long-term strategy which is based on the readily available comparative advantages, cheap labor and raw materials, however, will not be sustainable. It can only lead to competition over prices with simple, low quality goods. What seems essential for these countries is to sustain the ability to produce and sell products which fit into world-wide production chains and which can be based on and developed from their own knowledge potentials. To focus on areas where present strengths are becoming visible and to supplement them with long term-political strategies which pay attention to the emergence of new industrial clusters will be one of the main tasks for innovation policy.

There is no doubt that CEE-economies have a technology gap. This can, at least partly, be overcome by buying advanced, science-based machinery and licenses and by the 'side effects' of foreign direct investment. What is even more important, however, is to fill the knowledge gap which will be described in the following.

From knowledge to innovation systems

This notion of knowledge is closely related to the notion of innovation systems. If we define 'innovation systems' in the sense of Lundvall as 'the elements and relationships which interact in the production, diffusion and use of new and economically useful knowledge' it becomes obvious from this definition[10] that innovation must be looked upon and analyzed as a complex social process which - if we again follow Lundvall, 'must be rooted in the prevailing economic structure' (Lundvall 1992, 9). The problem for CEE economies is that these roots are not very deep and, to remain in the picture, have been transplanted several times within the last decades.

For analytical reasons and presentation purposes we refer in the following to three elements in the innovation process: Science, enterprises and markets. This differentiation, of course, does not imply that these three levels are considered disconnected from each other or from the framework conditions in economy and society. And, it equally does not imply that innovation is considered as a one-way-road. Too often, and also in recent developments in CEE in political planning the same error is repeated: policies start out from a 'technology-push' perspective instead of asking what the demands of the enterprises and the markets are. So also Chaball concludes in his paper: 'At both firm and government level, the innovation process requires a much broader perspective than that of research' (Chaball 1995, 105).

Elements of new innovation systems

As we have just argued, innovation is no longer seen as merely technology driven nor as a sequence of several independent stages, but as a social process which involves elements and relationships in a dynamic process (Lundvall, 1994). This change in the approach to innovation to a certain degree also delineates the core problem of the economies in CEE: they have to change from a linear, strictly hierarchical system of innovation for which the 'Soviet model' was an excellent example, *to a dynamic model*, composed of 'private organizations and public institutions, which interact in the production and distribution of economically relevant knowledge throughout the economy' (OECD 1995a,16).

If we look at the situation in CEE countries, the conclusion must be that an interactive system of this kind is still in a very nascent stage. In order to shed some light on the present situation the following section addresses three topics more closely:

- the science system and the R and D infrastructure which has the explicit task to produce new basic (scientific, technological) knowledge and provide education;

- the enterprises which, as far as they do their own R and D, also provide technological knowledge. Essentially, however, their task is to absorb new knowledge and turn it into products and services.

- the markets which define the demand for new products and services and thus should provide the feedback-loop to enterprises and the science system. This feedback is ideally provided by close connections between customers and producers.

The science system

Generally speaking, all of the countries in the CMEA area have commanded a considerable potential of scientific research and education institutions. They have either a century long tradition, like in former Czechoslovakia and Poland, where some of the world's oldest universities are located, or these institutions have been developed during and together with the establishment of an industrial structure by the Soviet Union (as in the Baltics). In spite of these traditions, which, of course, had their impact on the transformation process, the Soviet-type science and technology (S and T) system was what the countries were left with at the beginning of the transformation process, or rather with its ruins, because this highly developed and supported system of scientific and technological infrastructure was seriously damaged after the demise of the system of central planning. Because of its centralised structure there were no sectoral or regional differentiation which could serve as basis for new developments.

The traditional science system consisted of several more or less isolated elements. Roughly speaking, Academies of Science provided basic research, branch institutes did applied research and R and D departments in enterprises transformed blueprints into products. The whole system was controlled by the state and its ministries and was structured in a strictly hierarchical way.[11] Research was in many cases focused on subjects defined by external factors and in the form of long-term projects, but without direct mechanisms for interaction with enterprises and markets. Its erosion after 1989 was accelerated by the fact that institutions were spread all over the Former Soviet Union and the emergence of new national states split up the whole system. It left countries with highly qualified research institutes which had no links to local industry (Lithuania) or, as in the case of Ukraine, the 'design shops' responsible for new products, were totally isolated from their scientific basis. Along with this organizational break-up of the old innovation system went a disruption of established networks between institutions and researchers within and between the countries.

In an analysis of the developments in CEE scientific institutions since the early 1990s Schimank and Lange (1998) come to the conclusion that essentially three problems had to be solved after the changes in 1989. Scientific institutions steered towards, and had to cope with, autonomy from the state. This, on the one hand, freed research from the ever-present political control, on the other hand it entailed a certain neglect of research by the state, at least in the most difficult early times of transformation. This goes along with the second problem, the enormous decline of resources[12] which hit all research institutions, but in particular branch research which was closest to industry. The third problem was, under all these difficult circumstances, to newly define and even increase capacities and achievements of the surviving institutions. Taken together, according to Schimank and Lange this has led to two different development paths: First, an institutional renewal headed by the research community itself (e.g. the case of the Czech Republic) or guided by the state (e.g. the case of Hungary); second, institutional rigidity and inertia because of the lack of such driving forces (mainly Russia, Belorussia and Ukraine). Though the latter has some advantages in continuity, it can be expected sooner or later to fall behind the requirements of research and development in a globalising economy. Institutional renewal can be expected not only to break up 'path dependence' in the science system but will also facilitate access to the global scientific community.

Recent research also comes to the conclusion that there is no very clear picture yet about the future shape and capacities of the scientific basis for innovation. Rather, different forms of organizational transformation like diversification, spin-offs and spontaneous privatization have led to an atomization of the R and D landscape in most of the CEE countries.[13] Differences in administrative capacities to manage change, together with lack of resources and vested interests from the past render the transformation of science and technology a cumbersome process.

It sounds promising when it is reported for the case of the Czech Republic that there are many diversified bottom-up activities, niches of action and networking, the diffusion and growth of which may have impact on the re-institutionalization of a national innovation system (Müller 1996). This, however, will not work without the institutions for a basic infrastructure of science and education which is appropriate to the emerging new industrial structures or without the (re-)establishment of networks.

This admittedly very rough picture of the reorganization of science and technology certainly also leaves the open question of how the links between science and industry can be re-established. It remains doubtful whether the widespread establishment of science parks and incubators is useful if there is no coordination of demand from the enterprises and supply by research, since ... 'their success depends on the flow of knowledge rather than necessarily technical products from academia to industry' (Webster, p. 5). Also, as Balazs concludes of the Hungarian situation: '..the market has not played a positive role yet in the evaluation of the R and D sector, but has caused losses in professional standards and research capacity' (Balazs in Webster, p. 61).

The general political tendency in the restructuring processes of the science and technology institutions is that there is an inclination to promote the technology-push model and to put too little emphasis on the processes emerging from the micro-level, i.e. from enterprises and markets. However, with a view to the technology-gap on the one hand and to overcoming the organizational segmentation of science, research, education and training on the other, the re-organization of an effective infrastructure is certainly crucial. It is also important because, unlike in developed market economies, industry itself has not been engaged in doing much of its own research so far.

The enterprises

The essential function of the enterprises in the innovation process is to create a demand for and to absorb new technological, organizational and social knowledge, turn it into new products and sell them. In CEE countries, as already mentioned before, enterprises did not play previously a significant role in defining demands for new technology. As a rule they were specialized in a limited number of products (and were monopolists in these fields) whose technology was provided to them in the form of blueprints by the corresponding branch institutes. The production and distribution of new products and processes was centrally steered; enterprise R and D accounted for less than 10 per cent of R and D expenditures (Radosevic 1997b), and thus enterprises in general had never been prepared to develop and market products on their own. There was little need to be innovative except in incremental improvements of products and production processes. Being exclusively focused on production, enterprises, however, commanded a well qualified workforce, and management was trained in technical disciplines, but not in stimulating innovative processes.

In the beginning of the transformation process, therefore, one of the most serious deficiencies was that enterprises had to fulfill business functions which they had never been involved in before. Due to their technological qualifications managers suffered from a complete absence of knowledge about markets and market behavior. On the other hand there was the qualification of the workforce as an asset for future innovation systems which, in the meantime, if not deployed adequately, might be devaluated.

Whereas the demand for education in commerce and business administration has exploded after 1989, statistical evidence shows a sharp decline of techno-logical education. Furthermore, both the decline in technology content of products and some of the foreign direct investment activities[14] imply a danger of the de-qualification of the workforce. Therefore it is important, as Hilpert puts it, that .. 'enterprises need to find more appropriate and more efficient ways to ...derive benefit from the knowledge accumulated in their human resources' (Hilpert, 1996, 144). One should add: and vice versa, enterprises should invest in the development of their workforce and keep this stock of knowledge alive.

A lot of newly acquired business-related knowledge has been applied in the newly emerging private sector (trade, services). There are many hints that this is where more demand for innovation could emerge over time. So far, many of these new business activities (often combined with joint ventures or foreign direct investment), rather make use of imported technology and knowledge. On the one hand this carries the danger that domestic R and D potentials do not get involved sufficiently in the newly-emerging networks and might vanish. On the other hand it has a very important impact on the 'technology gap', because many countries cannot rely on domestic sources yet. Sometimes imported technology is the only available new 'input'. New relationships with business partners and customers from abroad offer the chance to establish new (innovative) networks which also might have positive impacts on the 'knowledge gap'.

Demand for new knowledge and innovations is also influenced by the emerging new enterprise structure in CEE (Stark 1997; Radosevic 1997a). Privatization processes lead to new types of enterprises which might have different implications for the organization of innovation processes. Important variables are the availability of capital and the ability to co-operate in horizontal relationships. Generally the consequences for innovative capacities are difficult to assess. Our research indicated that ownership structure does not necessarily prove to be the crucial variable for the selection of strategies for progress and innovation in a firm. Where qualified managers have the necessary competence and freedom for decision-making, they have opened new markets and developed links to new customers. In other cases state owned enterprises more or less have not changed. Due to the tenacity (and the inability to learn) of the old management they continue 'business as usual' and there is no organizational or technological restructuring.

Pressure from the markets, diffuse property relations and lack of investment in new developments lead to the conclusion that enterprises are not very well prepared yet to become a central force in new innovation systems. Though positive developments are under way, there remains the question how these scattered elements can be organized in new production networks. There is not much empirical evidence as to what the central organizing principles will be. It is left to further research to discover new regional or sectoral clusters in CEE.

The markets

After the disbanding of the CMEA in 1991, the majority of countries employed economic strategies based on neo-liberal theories which overemphasized the macro-economic stabilization and did not pay much attention to the micro-transformation. There was too little attention given to the fact that the emerging market forces have to be imbedded in the appropriate set of institutions and non-market relations (Jessop 1993).

One of the main components of the macro-economic transformation strategy was the sudden opening of the markets. Enterprises were confronted with the situation that not only the formerly secure markets of the CMEA had vanished, but also domestic markets were not available any more because they were flooded with cheap products from abroad. This breakdown of markets was followed by a breakdown in production. Enterprises were confronted with a sheer fight for survival, which turned investment in S and T into an unaffordable 'luxury' and a very risky undertaking.

Though the re-orientation of trade towards the West happened within a surprisingly short time, the quality of traded goods steadily declined. Many enterprises produced for readily available markets, and often concentrated now on former 'side products' which neither corresponded to their technological standards nor the abilities of their workforce. In many cases it turned out that simple, raw-material and labor intensive products could be sold with the best profits. Therefore the demand for new knowledge decreased. Since cheap labor became one of the main competitive advantages, investment in new technology was rare. As mentioned above, a general reduction of products with higher or high technological standards is observable in all countries. As a consequence not only the chances to establish the necessary feedback between technology, products and markets are diminished, but there is the particular danger of losing touch with and access to high value-added markets.

The efforts to compete on international markets by means of low-cost strategies lead to a vicious circle: Lack of innovation in products causes low rentability, which in turn means lack of resources for innovation. This tendency is opposed to the requirements of global markets and therefore these countries might face the danger of missing their connections with global trade and production chains. So far, CEE countries are still more successful in the export of labor intensive and the import of technology intensive goods, but as we have seen before, recent analyses show tendencies towards changes in the trade structure and increases in inter-industry trade.

Conclusions and outlook

This chapter started out with the assumption that institution-building and innovation are the crucial elements for industrial development and the EU integration of CEE countries. Empirical evidence has been given in order to demonstrate that some of the countries have escaped the downward slope and slowly start to become potent partners in trade and supply relationships with developed market economies. Still this development is hindered by a 'knowledge gap' which keeps enterprises from demanding new knowledge.

The chapter also claims that knowledge, defined in a wider sense, exists in CEE economies. Due to the former organization of production (industry) and the disruptions the transformation process has brought along, these knowledge potentials, however, are difficult to activate in new innovation systems because institutional and social links are missing.

Of course, there is no ready-to-use blueprint to construct a new system of innovation in CEE countries. The research about these processes in Western developed economies tells us clearly enough that even under relatively stable conditions innovation systems do not work perfectly. Even more, it is a nearly insoluble project in a situation where not only economic, but also social and political transformation processes are still full speed ahead.

Certainly a lot has been done from the side of governments to supply economy and society with the most 'basic needs' in terms of legislation, creating of new institutions and, within narrow limits, with capital for support. So far long-range strategies for a knowledge-based development have played a minor role vis á vis conventional subsidy policy. This, of course, is sometimes unavoidable for social reasons.

The most difficult part in this process is the establishment of mediating structures between the formal and informal areas. This takes time and includes co-operation and interplay between private, intermediary (association, chambers) and public institutions. The coming integration of some of the CEE countries into the European Union could be used as a device for faster integration into networks and environments conducive to innovation.

Notes

[1] It becomes more and more difficult to speak about 'Central and Eastern Europe' because differentiation between countries and regions becomes more and more prominent. The empirical reference in this paper is generally based upon the six countries and study in the research project 'Future of Industry in CEE', i.e. Bulgaria, Czech Republic, Hungary, Lithuania, Poland and Ukraine.

[2] The project was carried out under the COPERNICUS scheme of the European Union.

[3] For a discussion of the Revealed Comparative Advantages (RCA) indicator see Trabold and Berke, 1996. Positive RCA-values (vertical axis) indicate comparative advantages.

[4] For a detailed description of the indicators see Carlin and Landesmann, 1997.

[5] Czech Republic, Hungary, Poland and Slovenia.

[6] Bulgaria, Romania, Russia and Slovakia.

[7] For a more detailed discussion of the significance of intra-industry trade see Döhrn (1998).

[8] Lundvall (1996) explains this illustratively by describing different kind of knowledge as : know-how, know-why, know-how and know-who.

[9] e.g. the Lithuanian electronics industry (Juvenicius 1996).

[10] As Lundvall says himself, innovation systems are social systems and dynamic systems (Lundvall 1992, 2).

[11] For a more elaborate description see e.g. CEU, 1994.

[12] e.g. for the Czech Republic it is reported that 'in the period 1990-93 state funding declined by 62 per cent, enterprise funding by 54 per cent (in current prices)'. (Muller 1996)

[13] See Radosevic, 1997b.

[14] Which, at least in the first years, was often directed towards the mere exploitation of wage advantages.

References

Balazs, Katalin (1996), Transition Crisis in Hungary's R and D Sector. In: Webster, A. (ed.), *Building New Bases for Innovation. The Transformation of the R and D System in Post-Socialist States.* Cambridge.

Carlin, W. and Landesmann, M. (1997), *From Theory into Practice? Corporate Restructuring and Economic Dynamism in Transition Economies.* Wiener Institut für Internationale Wirtschaftsvergleiche, Forschungsbericht 240, August.

Chaball, R. (1995), Characteristics of Innovation Policies, Namely for SMEs. In: OECD: *Science, Technology, Industry Review No. 16*, Paris.

Commission of the European Union (EU) (1994), *The European Report on Science and Technology Indicators 1994*. Report EUR 158897 EN, Brussels/ Luxembourg.

Commission of the European Union (EU) (1994), *Eastern and Central Europe 2000*. Final Report, Luxembourg.

Döhrn (1998), The New Trade Structure Between East and West. Is Integration already a matter of fact? In: Potratz, Wolfgang, Widmaier, Brigitta (eds) 1998: *East European Integration and New Division of Labour in Europe*. Workshop Documentation. Graue Reihe des Instituts Arbeit und Technik 1998-09. Gelsenkirchen

Economic Commission for Europe (1997), *Economic Survey of Europe in 1996-1997*. United Nations, New York and Geneva.

European Bank for Reconstruction and Development (EBRD) (1996), *Transition Report 1996: Infrastructure and Savings*. London.

Freeman, C., (1995), The "National System of Innovation" in historical perspective. In: *Cambridge Journal of Economics, 1995*. 19. 5-24.

Greenaway, D. and Milner, C. (1986), *The Economics of Intra-industry Trade*. Oxford.

Hilpert, U. (1996), The Role of the Social Partners in Designing Learning Organisations. In: OECD 1996: *Employment and Growth in the Knowledge-based Economy*, Paris.

Jessop, Bob (1993), International Competitiveness, Regional Economic Strategies and the Post-Socialist Economies: Constraints, Dilemmas, and Prospects. Conference on: *Transforming Post-Socialist Societies: Theoretical Perspectives and Future Prospects for Economic and Political Change in Europe*, Krakow, October 21-23.

Junevicius, Vytenis, (1996), *Knowledge-Based Industrial Development in the Baltic States. Technologiju Valdymo Centras Kaunas/IAT Gelsenkirchen*, unpublished manuscript.

Knell, M., (ed.) (1996), *Economics of Transition. Structural Adjustments and Growth Prospects in Eastern Europe*. The Vienna Institute For Comparative Economic Studies Series; Edward Elgar, Cheltenham,UK/Brookfield, Vermont, US.

Lehner, F. et al. (1993), *The Future of Industry in Europe: New Markets*, New Structures, New Strategies. FAST Occasional Papers 365, Vol. 1, Brussels.

Lundvall, B.A. (ed.) (1992), *National Systems of Innovation*. London.

Lundvall, B.A. (1996), *The Social Dimension of the Learning Economy*. DRUID Working Paper No.: 96-1. Danish Research Unit for Industrial Dynamics, Aalborg.

Lucas, Robert E. (1988), *On The Mechanics Of Economic Development*. Journal of Monetary Economics 22, 3-42.

Müller, K. (1996), Academic-Industry Relations and Economic Reform in the Czech Republic. In: Webster, A. (ed.), *Building new Bases for Innovation. The Transformation of the R and D System in Post-Socialist States*. Cambridge

OECD (1992a), Technology and the Economy. The Key Relationship, Paris.

OECD (1992b), *Reviews of National Science and Technology Policy: Czech and Slovak Federal Republic*. Paris.

OECD (1993), *Science, Technology and Innovation Policies: Hungary*. Paris.

OECD (1994a), *Science, Technology and Innovation Policies: Federation of Russia, Volume I* Evaluation Report. Paris.

OECD (1994b), *Science, Technology and Innovation Policies: Federation of Russia*, Volume II Background Report. Paris.

OECD (1995a), *Science, Technology, Industry Review No. 16*, Paris.

OECD (1995b), *Science, Technology, Industry Review No. 18*, Paris.

OECD (1996), *Reviews of National Science and Technology Policy*. Poland. Paris.

Radosevic, S. (1997a), *Transformation of Science and Technology Systems Into Systems of Innovation in Central and Eastern Europe*. Paper prepared for the "European. Association for Evolutionary Political Economy" conference, Athens, November 1997.

Radosevic, S. (1997b), *Restructuring of RTD in Countries of Central and Eastern Europe*. Paper, International Conference on Technology Transfer: The Polish Perspective. September.

Romer, Paul M. (1993), *Implementing a National Technology Strategy with Self-Organizing Industry Investment Boards*. Brookings Papers on Economic Activity. Microeconomics 2. Washington DC.

Romer, Paul M. (1990), *Endogenous Technological Change*. Journal of Political Economics, vol. 98, no.5, 71-102.

Schimank, U./Lange, S. (1998), *Wissenschaft in Mittel-und Osteuropa*. In: Leviathan. Zeitschrift für Sozialwissenschaften 1/1998.

Stark, D./Kemeny, S. (1997), *Postsocialist Portfolios: Network Strategies in the Shadow of the State*. Manuscript.

Trabold, H./Berke, C. (1996), Die Veränderung der komparativen Vorteile Mittel- und Osteuropas im Transformationsprozeß. In: *Deutsches Institut für Wirtschaftsforschung, Schwerpunktheft Systemtransformation; Vier-teljahreshefte zur Wirtschaftsforschung Heft 1*, 65. Jahrgang, Berlin.

United Nations (UN) (1997), *Economic Survey of Europe 1996-97*. New York and Geneva.

Webster, A. (ed.) (1996), *Building New Bases for Innnovation. The Transformation of the R and D System in Post-Socialist States*. Cambridge.

8 Competitiveness and Technological Capabilities in Baltic Industry

Future potentials in a historical perspective[1]

MAUREEN LANKHUIZEN[2]

Introduction

Exports are an important source of economic growth. Countries with above average competitiveness in a given sector will have a growing export share in the world market for this sector. There are several sources of competitiveness on world export markets. Technological progress is considered to be an important source of competitiveness. Technological progress is defined as the improvement of production technologies; it either raises productivity (in the case of process innovations) or increases product quality and variety (product innovations). For our present purpose, we will concentrate on the impact of technological progress on product quality and variety.

In this paper we will first try to assess the competitiveness of exports from the Baltic states, i.e. Estonia, Latvia and Lithuania. That is, we will evaluate in what sectors the Baltics have improved their export position since the beginning of transition. We find competitiveness of the Baltics in sectors with little technology-intensity. We argue that the reason is the inferiority of production technology in the Baltics in comparison with their trading partners. We find that, as yet, there is little indication that production technology is improving relative to their trade partners. This brings us to the second issue in this paper: one may wonder whether the Baltics have the potential to reduce the existing technology gaps in the future. The Baltics have a relatively well developed stock of human capital, but when it comes to the organisation of human capital, in particular the organisation of R and D personnel, and the communication of

195

knowledge between the different research organisations involved in technological progress, the prospects are less promising. Developing technology-induced competitiveness might take longer than generally assumed in studies that look only at the stock of human capital. The paper is organised as follows.

In the second part we analyse changes in exports from the Baltic states. The analysis is split up in two parts: if one wants to evaluate the evolution of export shares of formerly centrally planned economies, one cannot omit an analysis of the Council for Mutual Economic Assistance (CMEA), since it has heavily influenced contemporary trade patterns in these economies. So first we look at trade patterns until 1991. The CMEA was dissolved in January 1991 after which date substantial liberalisation and stabilisation measures have been taken. The second part of the analysis of changes in exports involves changes from 1992 onwards. In the third part we assess whether competitiveness in the Baltics is due to technological progress. Part four deals with the analysis of catching up. First we will assess the prerequisites for catching up, and then apply these to the Baltic countries. From this we will derive implications about what needs to be done to improve technology-induced competitiveness. We end the paper with concluding remarks in part five.

The evolution of trade patterns

The CMEA

Contemporary trade patterns in all Central and Eastern European countries and the successor states of the former Soviet Union have been influenced heavily by their past. So if one attempts to make a proper assessment of the changes in former socialist countries' trade with Western Europe since 1989, one has to pay explicit attention to the role of the Council for Mutual Economic Assistance (CMEA).[3]

Established in 1949, the CMEA was intended to serve 'the purpose of co-operation to achieve the objective of balanced industrialisation' (Hillman and Schnytzer (1992), p. 521) across its members.[4] In other words, the benefits of 'international' division of labour were also recognised in socialist economies. Patterns of specialisation were negotiated bilaterally.[5] Trade was based on physical volumes, rather than on values. External relative prices used in CMEA trade were negotiated *ex ante* to ensure that trade would be balanced bilaterally, and were therefore devoid of any proper signalling function.[6] Moreover, external relative prices did not feed through upon prices for domestic producers.

In each CMEA country the right to conduct actual trade, once negotiations had been concluded, was given exclusively to a small number of Foreign Trade Organisations (FTOs) for respective ranges of products. As such, FTOs were the sole intermediary between domestic firms and international markets (both CMEA and non-CMEA). Trade flows were denominated in transferable rubles.[7] However, FTOs and domestic enterprises dealt with each other in domestic currency exclusively. The result was that domestic enterprises were completely isolated from international prices. Moreover, prices for traded goods in domestic currency were highly distorted as they were set so as to ensure balanced trade in domestic currency.[8] So international prices played only a very limited role – to say the least – in conveying information to enterprises in the CMEA arrangement. Consequently, patterns of specialisation within the CMEA framework did not reflect comparative advantage or relative prices.

Another significant feature of the CMEA arrangement is its creation of a duality in trade within the CMEA on the one hand, and trade with market economies on the other. Supply in socialist economies was determined by the central plan. The inputs deemed necessary to fulfil the output targets were allocated to the various industries via a system of administrative planning. Prices for producers were fixed by the government and they reflected government priorities in the sense that inputs for some industries were heavily subsidised.[9] Consumer prices were not entirely fixed. However, demand was regulated through the use of taxes and subsidies. For example, prices of cars and electric appliances were heavily taxed so as to discourage demand (Lavigne 1995). By applying different pricing rules for the production sector on the one hand and the consumer on the other, producer and consumer markets were effectively separated. The socialist economy was a supply-restricted economy: whatever was supplied was determined by the central plan, eliminating every kind of consumer sovereignty. So consumer preferences were effectively eliminated. The result of this was that producers did not have to worry about quality and product variety, not to mention innovation. 'More of the same' became the motto.

This motto dictated trade throughout the CMEA framework: the products that were traded were generally of low quality and the extent of product and process innovation was low. This distinguished trade within the CMEA framework from trade on Western markets where competitiveness in price or quality were the rules played by. Products traded within the CMEA are referred to as 'soft', as opposed to 'hard' products which are sold against hard currency on Western markets. The softness of products traded within the CMEA made such products highly context-specific, in the sense that these products could not be (easily) redirected to world markets.[10] This created a duality in trade, with low-quality trade within the CMEA on the one hand, and trade conforming to international quality standards on world markets on the other.

In summary, the CMEA has had a major impact on trade patterns in Central and Eastern Europe and the USSR by (i) centralising trade and isolating enterprises from world market prices, thereby preventing trade from being determined by comparative advantage or relative prices, and (ii) creating a duality in trade, with commodities traded within the CMEA largely unmarketable in Western markets because of their low quality.

The Baltics' commodity pattern of interrepublic and extrarepublic trade is shown in Tables 8.1 and 8.2, respectively.[11] Machinery (more specifically electrical machinery and electronics), light industry products, food products and, to a lesser extent, chemicals were the main categories of trade in all three countries in 1990. In all three countries, trade in machinery was dominated by interrepublic trade. This implies that traded technology was mainly of low quality and outdated. In the light industry, all countries ran surpluses in interrepublic trade and deficits in extrarepublic trade. In other words, the surpluses in light industry trade were generated in soft markets, whereas trade on hard markets yielded deficits. The surpluses in soft markets dominated so that overall trade in light industry was in surplus. As a result, the 'competitive strength' in the light industry was in low-quality products. The fact that exports in the main export categories (e.g. machinery, light industry and chemicals) were almost totally dependent on interrepublic markets (over 90 per cent of total exports in these categories was interrepublic) implies that Baltic exports were generally of low quality and capital intensive, and practically unmarketable in world markets.

When the CMEA collapsed in January 1991, followed by the disintegration of the USSR two months later, enterprises throughout the CMEA were suddenly exposed to world market prices, which in most cases meant coping with deteriorating terms of trade as prices of fuels rose and prices of machinery dropped, and were faced with the challenge of having to redirect their exports to the West. The next part analyses how the Baltic states have adjusted their trade patterns in the aftermath of the above-mentioned events.

Changes in exports after trade liberalisation

As of 1992-1993 (CEECs and the Baltics, respectively), macroeconomic stabilisation policies and foreign trade liberalisation implemented at the beginning of the transition process have taken effect. Strict monetary and interest rate policies have been implemented to bring down inflation rates, which soared after price liberalisation in 1991-1992. Estonia and Lithuania adopted a currency board[12] to provide an anchor for prices. Moreover, extensive currency reforms have been undertaken, with the introduction of national currencies in all three countries in the course of 1992-1994. The Baltic states have virtually eliminated all export controls and state trading (Kaminski, Wang and Winters (1996)), so that firms can engage in foreign trade themselves and are exposed to foreign competition. Moreover, as a result of currency convertibility domestic produ-cers are no longer isolated from international price signals.

Let us analyse how trade patterns in the Baltic states changed during and after these reforms. We will focus on trade with the European Union (EU) as the emerging major trade partner, as opposed to the formerly centrally planned economies, mainly the Commonwealth of Independent States (CIS). Ideally we would have liked to use export shares of the Baltics in the EU market as a measure of competitiveness, but as the statistical yearbooks of Estonia, Latvia and Lithuania do not classify trade in standard international trade classification (SITC), this has not been possible. Therefore, we use exports from the Baltic states to the EU as an indicator of competitiveness (with the exception of Latvia for which total exports are used), and compare export performance to imports. The results are shown in Tables 8.3 to 8.5.

Trade between Estonia and the EU has increased across the board from very low base levels in 1992. Both with respect to imports and exports the EU has become the main trading partner as of 1995. This trade has not replaced trade with the CIS, though: with the exception of exports of 'footwear, head-gear, umbrellas, ...' and imports of 'miscellaneous manufactured articles', trade with the CIS on the one hand, and with the EU on the other hand has increased over 1992-95 (Statistical Yearbook of Estonia 1996). The recovery of real out-put during 1993, after a cumulative decline of 30 per cent in 1991-93 (IMF (1994b)), accounts to a large extent for this increase. The fastest growing export categories are (in declining order) 'wood and articles of wood', 'mechanical and electrical machinery', 'optical instruments and apparatus', 'footwear, headgear, umbrellas, and 'textile and textile articles'. However, only in 'wood and articles of wood' Estonia has an export surplus in trade with the EU. Notwithstanding a growth rate of 8,377 per cent over 1992-95 in 'mechanical and electrical machinery' exports, there is a substantial trade deficit in this category.

In Lithuania there appears to be trade reorientation from the CIS to the EU in some categories, although the fact that figures for 1995 only cover January-September (Department of Statistics to the Government of the Republic of Lithuania, 1995-96).[13] In 'footwear, headgear, umbrellas, ...', 'mechanical and electrical machinery', 'optical instruments and apparatus, ...' and 'miscellaneous manufactured articles' CIS is still the main export destination, but the volumes are decreasing whereas exports to the EU in these categories have increased in the period 1994-95 (until September). However, imports from the EU in these four categories exceed exports by far. Export surpluses in trade with the EU are obtained in 'wood and articles of wood', 'textiles and textile articles', and 'base metals and articles of base metal'. Though not a fast growing category, 'products of chemical and allied industries' stands out as an important export category and one in which there is a trade surplus.

Exports in Latvia decline between 1993 and 1995 in such categories as 'footwear, headgear, umbrellas, ...', 'transport vehicles' and 'optical instruments and apparatus', but increase otherwise. Total exports increase in 1993-95. The strongest export growth rates are found in 'wood and articles of wood', 'plastics and articles thereof; rubber', and 'pulp of wood; paper and paperboard', but the last two categories start from low initial volumes. Main export categories, i.e. categories with export surpluses, are 'raw hides, leather, furskin and articles','wood and articles of wood', 'textiles and textile articles', and 'base metals and articles of base metal'. An important export category is 'products of chemical and allied industries', but there is an increasing trade deficit between 1993 and 1995.

It appears from these tables that the Baltics are competitive in such categories as 'wood and articles of wood', 'textiles and textile articles' and 'base metals and articles of base metal'. In Latvia and particularly in Lithuania, 'products of chemical and allied industries' is the only category among the former main export categories in which a reasonably strong export position is sustained.

Technological progress as a source of competitiveness

Is present competitiveness in the Baltics technology-induced? From an analysis of 'unit values' we can gauge the comparative level of technology. The unit values of exports and imports are calculated by dividing the respective dollar values by the corresponding physical weights. The UN Economic Commission for Europe describes how, by comparing the unit values of exports and imports in the same categories, one can assess the difference in technology: '[a] higher export 'unit value' than that of imports for a given category may either reflect a quality advantage of exported goods over imported ones, which in turn may arise from more advanced production technology or higher skills, or it can be the result of the exported goods being technologically different from the imported ones, ...' (UNECE (1990), p. 48). Comparing unit values over several years one can assess whether there has been technological progress. The exercise of calculating unit values has been carried out. Due to data limitations, we have only been able to do so for Latvia. The results in Table 8.6 show unit value ratios, i.e. unit values of exports divided by the corresponding unit values of imports. A ratio of more (less) than one, indicates that the technology content of exports is higher (lower) than that of imports.

It can easily be seen that the level of technology in Latvia is below that of its trading partners (the majority of which are OECD-Europe countries) in most categories. Moreover, there is little indication that the level of technology is increasing between 1993 and 1995. The low level of technology explains why competitiveness has shifted to industries like 'wood and articles of wood' and 'base metals and articles of base metal': these are products of little technological intensity, i.e. products for which quality and variety, and consequently technological progress, are of relatively little relevance. Exceptions to the low level of technology are 'products of chemical and allied industries', 'plastics and articles thereof; rubber', 'raw hides, leather, furskin and articles', and 'articles of stone, plaster, cement, ...'. Sustained competitiveness in 'pro-ducts of chemical and allied industries' may thus be due to a relatively advanced level of technology. But the unit value ratio is decreasing over the period 1993-1996. This implies that overall Latvia is at risk of losing ground in this pro-duct category. The analysis of unit values also explains why exports in 'transport vehicles' decline: the level of production technology is too low to produce high-quality transport vehicles that are competitive in international markets. In general, the issue of technological disadvantage is particularly critical in the case of high-tech products such as aerospace, computer and office machinery, electronics, instruments, electrical machinery, and engines: these are products in which technological progress is the main source of competitiveness. Yet, machinery and instruments are categories in which the Baltics lag behind substantially. Innovation and quality were given low priority under socialism.[14] The result of this is that former 'high-tech' industries like electronics have become largely unviable in an open market environment and that, while machinery and instruments are still important overall for the domestic industry and international trade, production and exports shift to the lower end of technology spectrum.

Summarising the first part of this paper, we can say that there has been a general shift from technology-intensive products that were important under socialism (e.g. electronics) towards export of products with little technology-intensity that can be redirected fairly easy from soft markets to hard markets.

This pattern was to be expected after the collapse of the CMEA. Only the chemical industry appears to be technologically relatively well advanced and consequently competitive, albeit decreasingly so.[15] There is little indication that production technology has improved relative to their trade partners. The question that is important to answer in order to make an assesment of future developments is: is there any potential in Estonia, Latvia and Lithuania to increase the level of technology with respect to their trade partners (mainly OECD-Europe) and thus improve their international competitive position? And if so what sectors should they focus on? We will deal with these important questions in the next part.

Catching up and future competitiveness

Prerequisites for catching up

From a new growth perspective, catching up with the technology frontier by laggards is relatively easy. Technological progress is generated by developing and diffusing new knowledge or new combinations of existing knowledge. One of the characteristics attributed to knowledge in new growth theory (see e.g. Romer (1990)), is that it is a non-rival good. In other words, once knowledge has been produced it can be reproduced at little or no additional cost. This implies that countries that lag behind technological leaders can capitalise on spill-overs from knowledge developed at the technological frontier. Thus, whereas technological progress in leader countries is dependent on the production of new knowledge and relatively small leaps of progress are consequently made, laggard countries can assimilate knowledge developed by the leaders and achieve a higher rate of technological progress. In this manner, catching up is relatively easy.

However, we argue that catching up is more complex. A lagging country may not be able to absorb kowledge if it does not have sufficient capacity to absorb knowledge spill-overs. Below we will argue that in order to catch up with the technological frontier a lagging country needs sufficient human capital, it needs to organise the co-ordination and integration of various types of knowledge, but foremost, it needs to organise this human capital properly.

Absorbing knowledge from the technological frontier, first of all requires a well developed stock of researchers who are able to interpret external knowledge spill-overs and recognise their value in operation. In other words, a lagging country needs a strong human capital base with an emphasis on scientific, engineering and technical skills.

Technological progress requires the mobilisation, co-ordination and integration of many different types of knowledge, and thus involves different types of knowledge producing organisations like firms, research institutes, and universities.[16] This illustrates the strong link that exists between science and technology. Nelson and Rosenberg (1993) provide examples of the link between science and technology to show that the interaction is complex and varies between industries and technologies. For instance, technological progress in electrical equipment industries and the chemical industry is largely the result of advances in scientific disciplines as physics and chemistry. On the other hand, technology can also trigger off progress in science. The flying machine built by the Wright Brothers lead to new scientific fields like aerodynamics and aeronautical engineering, and progress in chemical industries gave way to chemical engineering. Yet, knowledge does not diffuse automatically between the various types of organisations involved in research. Part of the knowledge of organisations is stored in their routines (Nelson and Winter (1982)). It is often not codified, but only remembered by performing and is to a large extent specific to the organisation. This knowledge is not publicly available to other organisations. With respect to the co-ordination and integration of knowledge across the research sector then, communication or even interaction is needed. This can be accomplished by co-operation, strategic alliances, clusters, and networks, all of which install channels along which knowledge can be communicated.

Finally, a country's absorption capability is determined by the organisation of its human capital. To achieve improvement of production technology, i.e. technological progress, on a large scale, relatively more scientists and engineers must be engaged in research directly integrated in production of goods and services as opposed to the university and public research. Notwithstanding that universities and public research institutes play an important role in developing new products and processes, the majority of research is done by firms (Nelson and Rosenberg (1993)). For new products or processes developed by universities or research and development (R and D) institutes, both domestic and foreign, to be implemented in firms' production processes, the innovation must be adapted to firms' specific organisational structure and production processes. This implies that firms understand the innovation and are able to revise it. Firms will have to do research themselves (Cohen and Levinthal (1989)) and might even have to repeat parts of the original research process, since they have only partial knowledge about the innovation. This has important implications for the organisation of R and D personnel: they should be integrated in production as well. More R and D personnel in production of goods and services will increase the possibilities for absorption and diffusion in this sector.[17]

In summary, if the base of human capital is too low, or if there is insufficient mobilisation, co-ordination and integration of different knowledge bases, or too few researchers are directly employed in enterprises, a lagging country is not likely to close the technology gap and will fall behind.

Catching-up potential in the Baltics

It is often argued that the comparative advantage of former socialist countries and the Baltic countries in particular is established by their well educated populations (Sorsa (1994)). Given these well developed stocks of human capital, an indication of which is given by data on enrollment rates in secondary and tertiary education,[18] these countries should export more technologically intensive products in the longer run. However, viewed in the light of the previous analysis, having a well developed stock of human capital may not be sufficient to catch up with the technological frontier and increase competitiveness in technology intensive sectors. We will proceed with an analysis of the science and technology (S and T) systems in the Baltic countries to see whether they fulfill the other prerequisites for catching up.

With the incorporation into the USSR, the research systems in Estonia, Latvia, and Lithuania were transformed along Soviet lines. Former independent research organisations were turned into subdivisions of Soviet research organisations or became research institutes of industrial ministries (World Bank (1992)). The Soviet S and T system was characterised by extreme separation and specialisation. Research was mainly performed in four types of organisations: the Academies of Sciences, state research institutes, universities, and specia-lised industrial R and D institutes supervised by corresponding branche mini- stries. The Academies focused almost entirely on fundamental research, the research institutes of the branch ministries mainly on applied research. Universities engaged in research, too, but only to a limited extent. Professors spent most of their time teaching. The Academies of Sciences were the most important organisations in the research complexes in Estonia, Latvia, and Lithuania. Given the high degree of specialisation, this implies that the emphasis in Baltic research was on fundamental research. There was little interaction between the research organisations. This implies that the channels for the communication of knowledge across the research sector were missing and that there was little co-ordination or integration of different types of knowledge as a result.

Most importantly was the separation between research and experimental development on the one hand, and production on the other.[19] R and D was considered to be of strategic importance for industrialisation and technological progress and was therefore organised centrally. The R and D institutes belonging to the industrial ministries were to develop the innovations for their respective enterprises, which were to absorb them in production subsequently. Enterprises played only a minor role in industrial R and D, they were perceived as production organisations rather than research organisations (Amann and Cooper (1982)). As a result, relatively few R and D personnel were engaged in research integrated in production. Scientists and engineers were primarily employed in the higher education sector, the public research sector, in which the Academies of Sciences were the most important organisations, or the industrial ministries, but not in enterprises (UNESCO (various editions)). In our view, this was a very ineffective organisation of R and D personnel. The separation of R and D and production severely limited the conversion of results of research for productive purposes. In our view, the centralised organisation of R and D has been an important cause for the low adoption rate of new technology by enterprises and the low rate of product renewal in the USSR (Amann and Cooper (1982)).[20]

The socialist legacy weighs down on current S and T systems in the Baltics. There is a striking difference in the organisation of R and D personnel between technological leaders such as the United States, Japan, and Germany, and the Baltic countries. In the former, R and D personnel is mainly employed in the productive sector. These countries are also the ones with the highest level of technology in production, or rapid technological progress in production. In the Baltics very little R and D personnel is integrated in production. It is mainly concentrated in higher education and the general service (public research) sector. In 1994, 60 per cent of the total number of research scientists and engineers in Estonia was employed in higher education and 40 per cent in the general service sector. In Latvia the corresponding numbers were 43 and 45 per cent. This organisation of R and D is more suitable for scientific purposes, in which it has reportedly been succesful in the past (World Bank (1992)). The small percentage of R and D personnel in the productive sector restricts the absorption of scientific inventions in production and is an important source for the low level of production technology in these countries. We conclude that the organisation of human capital in the Baltics does not particularly suit industrial innovation and technological progress.

Moreover, the incorporation into the Soviet S and T system also implied that the purposes of research were dictated by Moscow. The scientific and technological capabilities that the Baltics accumulated during independence were transformed. The emphasis shifted to natural, exact and technical research and a large part of the research in physics, chemistry, mathematics, and engineering was subordinated to serve the Soviet military. In other words, Baltic research was specialised (albeit enforced specialisation). At present, many of these specialisations have become redundant, while disciplines needed for the independent economic development of the Baltic states are not covered in research (World Bank (1992)).

We conclude that the current S and T system in the Baltics is not very conducive for catching up and future technology-induced competitiveness. Knowledge created by Academies, universities, and industrial research institutes has to be integrated, but foremost the separation of research and experimental development, and production should be eliminated. Bringing about a closer integration of R and D and production will need a reorganisation of R and D personnel: it must be decentralised, i.e. more R and D personnel must be employed directly in production. Finally, research in general should move away from socialist commanded specialisations and focus on areas that are important for the economic development of the Baltics.

What implications do these conclusions have for policymakers and enterprises? First and foremost, policymakers should aim at preserving and reinforcing research quality in the Baltic S and T systems, while at the same time ensuring their sustainability. The latter implies that S and T systems have to be rationalised. This can be achieved by reducing the collective research carried out in public institutes like universities, Academies and ministerial research institutes on the one hand, and relocating a large part of industrial R and D into production (i.e. goods and services) on the other. Economic benefits of research yield from its integration in production. The restructuring of the Academies of Sciences into honorary societies only (World Bank (1992)) complies with the reduction of public research. Rationalisation also entails that the remaining public research has to be refocussed. The transition to a market economy will lead to structural adjustment in the sense that industries or activities for which there is no economic rationale will contract or even disappear, while the viable ones increase or emerge. Research efforts should be directed largely toward areas of economic importance, and possibly be intensified. Other research areas should be reduced to affordable sizes. The choices that are involved in creating and preserving sustainable public research require a sound science policy.

Of major importance for the decentralisation of R and D is the restructuring of the former ministerial institutes for industrial research. R and D personnel employed in ministerial research institutes should largely shift into the enterprise sector where they can engage in in-house R and D activities of existing (be it state-owned, privatised or newly established) enterprises, or start up new R and D-intensive production companies or service firms.[21] However, the tasks are considerable. In the first place, there must be incentives for enterprises to engage in R and D and absorb the R and D potential from the ministerial institutes, or to start up R and D intensive activities. The inclination to carry out industrial R and D will increase if enterprises, so as to survive, have to compete with others in terms of prices, product quality and variety. In other words, increasing R and D in the business sector basically requires a transition to a market economy. Thus the government must persistently tend to reform in general like the restructuring of state-owned enterprises and their privatisation, encouraging start-up activity and foreign direct investment (FDI), and financial sector reform. In the short run, new start-up activity has to provide for most of the dynamics in industrial R and D. However, evidence for Estonia (Paasi (1996)) indicates that in 1995 the number of service firms established by employees of former ministerial R and D institutes was very small. Moreover, FDI appeared to occur in activities of little R and D intensity. At the same time, in-house R and D was negligible. As a result, R and D in the enterprise sector remains very limited.

In addition, R and D in enterprises can be stimulated through external funding. The government will be an important source of funding, either directly or indirectly. In this context, the government must design a clear technology policy, and devise or strengthen instruments such as R and D subsidies, tax measures or government sponsored R and D grants and contracts, and agencies to execute the policy. The technology policy should be closely integrated with industrial policies.

Second, and more specific, are the problems of integrating research and production. There is more to integrating research and production than merely increasing the number of research scientists and engineers in enterprises. R and D-intensive production is an organised process: firms have to organise, mobilise, co-ordinate, and integrate different skills and complementary assets so as to generate new knowledge and effectively apply it in production. The managerial capabilities accumulated under socialism are generally of little value in this respect and knowledge about how to bring about horizontal organisational structures and productively organise (complex) interaction between different skills and complementary assets, are generally lacking. Organisational skills can be tought through formal education, or transferred by Western managers, to a limited extent only. Organisational skills are to a large extent tacit so they are best learnt through practical experience Swaan (1994).

Consequently, it will take time before these skills are fully developed. Privatisation and the growth of new enterprises, especially foreign ones, can increase the rate of change and increase the technological capabilities of enterprises.

In order to co-ordinate and integrate various knowledge bases so as to establish a link between science and technology, institutional reform is needed. Let us follow Johnson and Gregersen (1995) in distinguishing between formal and informal institutions. Informal institutions can take many forms like e.g. norms of co-operation, organisational conventions and practices. They are highly qualitative but nonetheless crucial elements in S and T systems, because without them communication between organisations would not be possible. Codes of communication are embedded in a larger framework of habits, norms, routines, established practices and rules, that have been shaped by a country's history, culture, and education. Formal institutions reflect culture as well as government policies, and ideologies. Institutions are formal in the sense that they have been written down. They set standards for the development and quality of new technology, its diffusion, as well as the co-operation in networks. Examples include patent laws, laws and regulation about technical service, joint venture regulations, diffusion oriented public policies.

It is largely up to the governments in the Baltic states to create formal institutions. Informal ones have to be transformed to comply with the newly emerging situation. There is a strong case of path dependence in institutional change. The rate and direction of institutional change are highly dependent upon the historical structure of the institutional set-up. They have been shaped by decades of socialism. It might be here that we find the most fundamental restriction to absorption of international knowledge spill-overs. With the decentralisation and restructuring of the research sector, organisations, relations and alliances change or vanish and new ones have to be set up. Networking and communication are indispensible for knowledge exchange in organised markets (Lundvall and Johnson (1994)). Especially in the beginning of transition when socialist institutions have become obsolete and market institutions have yet to develop, receiver and sender competence in communicating knowledge are weak (Swaan (1994)). Organisations have to develop new and stable codes and channels of communication. The possibilities for formal learning and knowledge transfer from abroad are limited; developing codes and channels of communication is basically a matter of learning by doing. As a result, change will be relatively slow.

Based on this assessment of what needs to be done to create sufficient absorption capability, we conclude that catching up by the Baltics as seen in this light might take longer than assumed in studies that only look at the amount of human capital in these countries.

Can we discern feasible areas for technological development?[22] Industries producing high-tech products are declining or have disappeared more or less. This implies that the basis for integrating research and production has largely vanished. Thus, technological development in high-tech products at present is not feasible. Important industries like wood and base metals appear to be of little technological intensity yet, as indicated by the unit value analysis. However, scientific achievements might well be used as a starting point for the development of clusters around forestry. Estonia, for instance, has a long and succesful record of research in soil technology and ecology; important research fields in Latvia were biology and agriculture (World Bank (1992a, b)). The clusters may go as far as to include the development and production of new machinery used in forestry and the wood industry. The evidence presented in this paper would indicate that the chemical industry is a relatively important sector, at least in Latvia and Lithuania. At the same time, substantial research capacity in the Baltics exists in chemistry, medicine and biology. Sub-areas within the chemical industry must be identified that are important and viable, and that can use the existing research capacity. Yet whether technological development will effectively occur in these industries, or activities, depends mostly on whether the Baltic countries can organise communication of knowledge across various research organisations and eliminate the extreme separation of research and experimental developement on the one hand, and production on the other.

Conclusion

The export structure in Estonia, Latvia and Lithuania has changed drastically since the beginning of the transition process. Under socialism, machinery, light industry and to a lesser extent chemicals were the main export categories. The Baltic republics had relatively high-tech industries like electronics. However, the industries were not technologically advanced enough to withstand competition on world markets after the collapse of the CMEA. This paper argues that the socialist science and technology system was ineffective at generating technological progress largely due to the lack of communication of knowledge across various research organisations and the extreme separation of research and experimental developement on the one hand, and production on the other. So when the CMEA collapsed, exports in these industries went down, too. Main export categories today are of little technological intensity. There is little indication of competitiveness due to technological progress in any of the newly emerging export categories. For technology-induced competitiveness, the current S and T system will have to be restructured drastically. The separation between R and D and production has to be reduced by integrating more researchers directly in production. Channels have to be established for the communication of knowledge across various research organisations. Research has to focus on new areas that are important for the countries' economic development. Restructuring the S and T system in the Baltics requires an incentive climate that induces enterprises to carry out R and D, new managerial skills and a new or at least reformed institutional set-up. This paper argues that this is going to be a time consuming process, as institutional change is largely path dependent. Here, we might find the major barrier to swift catching up and future technology-induced competitiveness in the Baltics.

Notes

1   Financial support by the Netherlands Organisation for Scientific Research (NWO), grant 96/30462 SB107 HSo BD, is gratefully acknowledged. The grant has enabled me to work with the World Bank (Washington, D.C.) for three months.
2   Maureen Lankhuizen, MERIT (Maastricht Economic Research Institute on Innovation and Technology), P.O. Box 616, 6200 MD Maastricht, the Netherlands.
3   It should be noted that the description of the CMEA below applied in full extent to the USSR only. The countries in Central Europe (notably Poland and Hungary) undertook reforms in the 1980s in order to decentralise foreign trade (Kaminski, Wang and Winters (1996)). So the distortions in the latter countries' trade are likely to be somewhat smaller (but still substantial) than in the successor states of the former USSR.
4   The CMEA members were the USSR, Poland, the German Democratic Republic, Czechoslovakia, Hungary, Romania, Bulgaria, Mongolia, Cuba, and Vietnam. Yugoslavia was an associate member.
5   The USSR supplied mostly fuels and minerals to Eastern European countries, and the Eastern European exports to the CMEA members consisted to a large extent of machinery.
6   Prices reflected the importance attributed to products by governments rather than relative scarcity.
7   Within the CMEA, all bilateral accounts were cleared by the International Bank for Economic Co-operation (Schrenk (1992)) and *ex post* 'payments' were made to each country intransferable rubles. These transferable rubles lacked most properties of money (means of payment, store of value and, most importantly, measure of value), it was merely a unit of account. As a result, a surplus could not be used to purchase additional imports from a defecting trade partner. Nor was there a future obligation to supply on the part of a deficit country (Hillman and Schnytzer (1992)). There may have been a downward bias on the volume of trade, as countries tried to prevent running surpluses, since this meant they were implicitly subsidising a deficit country (Schrenk (1992)).
8   See Schrenk (1992) for details on what is called the principle of price of equalisation.
9   Heavy industry was assigned the highest priority since this sector would produce the machinery necessary to achieve industrialisation.The overriding policy objective of the Bolsjevik revolution in 1917 in Russia was to drag the economy out of backwardness and

accomplish modernisation by constructing a socialist state. Ever since then, Soviet type of socialist development has emphasised industrialisation.

10 Exceptions are products which are fairly standard such as fuels and minerals.

11 Within the CMEA framework, over 90 per cent of total exports and approximately 80 per cent of total imports (own calculations based on Watson's (1994) data) in the Baltics were within the USSR. The data do not allow for a distinction in extrarepublic trade between trade with other CMEA members and trade with non-CMEA members.

12 'Under a currency board arrangement, base money must be fully backed by foreign exchange reserves. A central bank is bound by a money creation rule that limits growth in base money to growth in foreign exchange reserves. The extension of central bank credit to commercial banks is limited to the amount of foreign reserves in excess of those needed to provide full backing to the base money issue.' (IMF (1994a), p. 20)

13 From these figures it is difficult to draw conclusions about total trade volumes. The IMF (1994a) estimated output recovery and increased trade volumes from mid-1993.

14 The only exception might be the sector arms and ammunition and products of the Soviet military. Yet, most of this sector has disappeared after the fall of the collapse of the USSR.

15 The chemical industry is a science-based industry. The relatively strong position of the Baltics in this industry might be explained by their emphasis on science research under socialism and their long history in research disciplines like biology, chemistry and medicine (World Bank (1992)). This will be dealt with in greater detail in section 4.2.

16 The statement applies to technological progress in the sense of developing new knowledge by a technological leader as well as in the sense of absorbing knowledge spill-overs by a lagging country.

17 The emphasis is on scientific organisations as the catalysts of technological progress and firms in an assimilating role. Of course, more human capital in production will also raise the autonomous innovative capability of this sector.

18 Data (UNESCO (1996)) indicate that enrollment rates in secondary education in the Baltics are comparable with Western countries, and that enrollment in tertiary education is slightly below Western countries.

19 In the 1970s an organisational attempt to integrate research, development and production is made by creating various kinds of science-production associations. Associations are formed between industrial research institutes and one or several enterprises, and between universities and Academies of Sciences, and one or several enterprises. so as to merge research. For instance, 'the Latvian Academy has reported the creation of five associations on the basis of institutes, design offices and factories' (Amann and Cooper (1982), p. 473). However, the associations fail to establish real unity between R and D and production.

20 Other important factors that account for the low rate of technological progress in Soviet industry are: the lack of incentives, due to the lack of competition, demand, and the need to be cost effective; enterprise size; and the bureaucratic involvement (see Lankhuizen (forthcoming)).

21 Some R and D personnel will be shed all together.

22 An in-depth study would be needed to answer this question concretely. Yet this is beyond the scope of this paper. We only mean to make some preliminary conjectures.

Table 8.1 Interrepublic Trade, 1990 (million transferable rubles)

	Estonia		Latvia		Lithuania	
	export	import	export	import	export	import
Industry:	1745.8	2946.2	3549.6	4643.6	3972.1	7687.4
power	168.3	18.9	131.3	166.7	299.7	148.2
oil & gas	0	516	12.5	1006.1	518	2359.4
coal	0	2.7	0	9.4	0	31.2
other fuels	9	0.1	0	0.1	0	0
ferrous metallurgy	7.2	163.2	114.8	414.7	19.4	357.3
chemicals	244.6	387.7	533.7	477.9	297.7	610.6
machinery	559	1257.5	1565.7	1794.8	1833.4	2417.2
wood & paper	77.8	50.5	77.9	100.4	119.9	135.1
construction materials	27	41.6	49.7	68	63.1	104.8
light industry	302.7	172.1	314.2	184.2	431.9	188.8
food products	294.6	107.4	588.6	80.4	341.3	103.2
other industrial	43.1	65.7	139.3	109.3	36.3	86.4

Source: Watson, R.A.(1994), Interrepublic Trade in the Former Soviet Union: Structure and Implications, in: Post-Soviet Geography, 45 no.7, tables 15 to 17.

Table 8.2 Extrarepublic Trade, 1990 (million transferable rubles)

	Estonia		Latvia		Lithuania	
	export	import	export	import	export	import
Industry:	114.8	315.4	165	873.2	395.3	851
power	0	30.4	0	0	0	0
oil & gas	0	0	0	1.6	161.3	1
coal	0	5	0	32.9	0	0
other fuels	0.3	0	0	0	2.2	0
ferrous metallurgy	15.2	10.5	5.2	10.6	1.7	17.7
chemicals	5.9	38.1	6.2	106.6	12.4	110.1
machinery	26.4	107.5	94.2	311.4	147	400.6
wood & paper	9.5	3.9	13.1	12.3	19.8	7.9
construction materials	1	1.6	3.5	2.3	4.7	8.3
light industry	16.6	69.1	11.4	107.6	13.7	121.9
food products	36.1	42.4	28.5	277	29.5	171.6
other industrial	3.8	4.8	2.9	9.9	2.5	10.8

Source: Watson, R.A.(1994), Interrepublic Trade in the Former Soviet Union:
Structure and Implications, in: Post-Soviet Geography, 45 no.7, tables 15 to 17.

Table 8.3 Trade ($ million) with EU, Estonia

	Exports				Imports			
	1992	1993	1994	1995	1992	1993	1994	1995
products of chemical & allied industries	6.56	8.95	15.08	26.67	4.47	15.02	32.79	102.7
plastics & articles thereof; rubber	0.80	1.71	1.69	17.15	1.62	6.74	14.62	75.15
raw hides, leather, furskin & articles	3.17	2.83	4.20	11.58	0.33	1.02	2.40	11.93
wood & articles of wood	1.75	13.08	40.35	151.9	0.06	0.64	0.99	15.67
pulp of wood; paper & paperboard	0.59	0.35	0.81	7.10	0.86	3.27	5.02	56.69
textiles & textile art.	5.68	22.55	31.85	149.4	5.91	17.67	31.55	151.6
footwear, headgear, umbrellas, ...	0.64	2.35	5.52	17.04	0.51	2.14	7.53	23.09
articles of stone, plaster, cement, ...	1.87	2.17	1.92	8.18	0.64	1.78	5.10	32.28
precious & semi-precious stones, ...	0.48	4.0	0.92	3.65	0.14	0.17	0.27	4.07
base, metals & articles of base metal	4.62	21.92	26.5	78.47	1.50	5.64	12.41	97.08
mechanical & electrical machinery	1.74	4.64	5.36	147.5	18.11	38.74	75.82	376.0
transport vehicles	3.31	2.42	2.08	26.19	12.40	34.72	38.69	92.75
optical instruments & apparatus, ...	0.11	1.06	0.73	7.84	1.28	7.63	13.65	36.08
arms & ammunition	0.0	0.01	0.0	0.01	0.05	0.51	0.49	0.49
miscellaneous manufact. articles	5.86	7.81	15.98	62.13	1.44	4.02	7.78	54.35

Source: Statistical Office of Estonia (1996), Statistical Yearbook of Estonia, pp. 236-242.

Table 8.4 Trade ($ million) with EU, Lithuania

	Exports		Imports	
	1994	1995	1994	1995
products of chemical & allied industries	96.25	94.23	52.28	62.16
plastics & articles thereof; rubber	10.85	24.09	31.02	49.27
raw hides, leather, furskin & articles	14.85	15.68	3.88	5.36
wood & articles of wood	41.53	79.68	3.95	8.18
pulp of wood; paper & paperboard	3.98	2.88	16.61	28.14
textiles & textile art.	98.92	152.8	82.88	113.8
footwear, headgear, umbrellas, ...	5.07	5.42	5.88	3.80
articles of stone, plaster, cement, ...	2.18	4.44	7.19	12.62
precious & semi-precious stones, ...	7.57	0.94	0.55	1.33
base, metals & articles of base metal	51.12	89.06	25.85	43.03
mechanical & electrical machinery	23.60	48.02	191.5	183.5
transport vehicles	15.40	9.89	60.40	82.09
optical instruments & apparatus, ...	1.95	2.0	19.58	27.63
arms & ammunition	0.02	0.04	0.60	0.46
miscellaneous manufact. articles	14.27	14.55	15.58	18.38

Source: Lithuanian Department of Statistics (1996), Lithuania's Statistical Year-book, pp. 66-68.

Table 8.5 Total trade ($ million), Latvia

	Exports				Imports			
	1993	1994	1995	1996.I	1993	1994	1995	1996.I
products of chemical & allied industries	69.93	72.71	83.41	21.74	69.14	126.3	198.2	56.72
plastics & articles thereof; rubber	6.07	8.85	13.49	2.51	17.24	36.03	65.96	16.71
raw hides, leather, furskin & articles	15.49	17.88	21.57	5.75	3.63	4.59	6.16	1.77
wood & articles of wood	88.94	201.8	344.6	71.28	2.79	6	14.14	2.68
pulp of wood; paper & paperboard	8.03	8.41	15.19	6.18	13.29	36.94	77.28	22.55
textiles & textile art.	127.5	130.9	182.6	54.9	44.55	73.37	139.5	36.95
footwear, headgear, umbrellas, ...	22.43	17.3	8.97	2.72	10.55	10.71	12.72	2.81
articles of stone, plaster, cement, ...	13.78	12.97	26	6.76	10.42	17.41	30.08	7.02
precious & semi-precious stones, ...	7.65	2.11	2.41	0.33	0.94	0.95	2.03	0.37
base, metals & articles of base metal	85.85	100.2	103.3	17.46	42.7	62.05	112.6	25.76
mechanical & electrical machinery	72.44	91.66	113.7	29.5	95.98	200.8	305.5	77.7
transport vehicles	125.3	98.4	83.19	17.18	88.06	83.42	142.8	32.17
optical instruments & apparatus, ...	6.19	6.05	5.79	1.06	10.11	30.14	35.47	10.84
arms & ammunition	0.23	0.18	0.12	0.02	0.95	1.63	2.04	0.19
miscellaneous manufact. articles	34.77	44.6	57.81	13.15	12.51	22.16	41.21	10.05

Source: Central Statistical Bureau of Latvia (1996), Macroeconomic Indicators of Latvia, Quarterly bulletin no. 1, pp. 86-95.

Table 8.6 Unit Value Ratios, Latvia

Harmonised commodity	unit value ratio (export/import)			
description	1993	1994	1995	1996.I
products of chemical &				
allied industry	21.4	2.48	1.92	1.66
plastics & articles thereof;				
rubber	1.44	1	0.88	1.07
raw hides, leather, furskin &				
articles	1.44	1.82	1.57	1.64
wood & articles of wood	0.41	0.23	0.27	0.28
pulp of wood; paper &				
paperboard	0.97	0.64	0.44	0.64
textiles & textile articles	1.1	0.84	0.85	1.05
footwear, headgear,				
umbrellas ...	0.5	0.5	0.4	0.35
articles of stone, plaster,				
cement, ..	0.88	1.17	1.67	1.45
precious & semiprecious				
stones, ...	0.32	0.99	0.33	0.88
base metals & articles of				
base metal	1.62	0.75	0.41	0.42
mechanical & electrical				
machinery	0.48	0.46	0.49	0.38
transport vehicles	0.87	0.6	0.79	0.68
optical instruments &				
apparatus, ...	0.56	0.6	0.27	0.6
arms & ammunition	0.18	0.3	1.48	0.89
miscellaneous manuf.				
articles	0.37	0.42	0.33	0.63

Source: Calculations based on Central Statistical Bureau of Latvia (1996), Macroeconomic Indicators of Latvia, Quarterly bulletin no. 1, pp. 86-103.

References

Amann, R. and Cooper, J. (eds) (1982), *Industrial Innovation in the Soviet Union*, New Haven and London: Yale University Press.

Cohen, W.M. and Levinthal, D.A. (1989), 'Innovation and Learning: The Two Faces of R&D', *The Economic Journal*, 99, pp. S.569-596.

Hillman, A.L. and Schnytzer, A. (1992), 'Creating the Reform Resistant Dependent Economy: Socialist Comparative Advantage, Enterprise Incentives and the CMEA', in Hillman, A.L. and Milanovic, B. (eds), *The Transition from Socialism in Eastern Europe: Domestic Restructuring and Foreign Trade*, Washington: The World Bank, pp. 243-262.

IMF (1994a), *Economic Reviews: Lithuania*, no. 6.

IMF (1994b), *Economic Reviews: Estonia*, no. 7.

Kaminski, B., Wang, Z.K. and Winters, L.A. (1996), *Foreign Trade in the Transition: The International Environment and Domestic Policy*, Washington, D.C.: The World Bank.

Lavigne, M. (1995), *The Economics of Transition: From Socialist Economy to Market Economy*, Houndmills: MacMillan Press Ltd.

Lundvall, B. and Johnson, B. (1994), 'The Learning Economy', *Journal of Industry Studies*, Vol. 1, No. 2, pp. 23-42.

Nelson, R.R. and Rosenberg, N. (1993), 'Technical Innovation and National Systems', in Nelson, R.R. (ed.), *National Innovation Systems: A Comparative Study*, Oxford: Oxford University Press, pp. 3-21.

Nelson, R.R. and Winter, S.G. (1982), *An Evolutionary Theory for Economic Change*, Cambridge MA: Harvard University Press.

Paasi, M. (1996), *The Absorptive Capacities of Estonian Firms: Can a Technology-based Industrial Strategy Succeed?* The Research Institute of the Finnish Economy, Discussion Papers, Keskusteluaiheita, no. 554.

Schrenk, M. (1992), 'The CMEA System of Trade and Payments: Initial Conditions for Institutional Change', in Hillman, A.L. and Milanovic, B. (eds), *The Transition from Socialism in Eastern Europe: Domestic Restructuring and Foreign Trade*, Washington, D.C.: The World Bank, pp. 217-242.

Sorsa, P. (1994), *Regional Integration and the Baltics: which way*, Policy Research Working Paper 1390, Washington, D.C.: The World Bank.

Swaan, W. (1994), *Behavioural Constraints and the Creation of Markets in Post-Socialist Economies*, paper prepared for the Fourth Trento Workshop 'Centralisation and Decentralisation of Economic Institutions: Their Role in the Transition of Economic Systems', European Association for Comparative

Economic Studies, Department of Economics, University of Trento, Italy, February 28th - March 1st, 1994.

UNECE (1990), *Economic Bulletin for Europe*, vol. 42.

Watson, R.A. (1994), 'Interrepublic trade in the former Soviet Union: structure and implications', *Post-Soviet Geography*, Vol. 35, No. 7, pp. 371-408.

World Bank (1992a), *Estonia: The Transition to a Market Economy*, A World Bank Country Study, Washington, D.C.

World Bank (1992b), *Latvia: The Transition to a Market Economy*, A World Bank Country Study, Washington, D.C.

World Bank (1992c), *Lithuania: The Transition to a Market Economy*, A World Bank Country Study, Washington, D.C.

9 A Long Way to Go
The Hungarian science and technology policy in transition
ATTILA HAVAS

Introduction[1]

Neo-classical and mainstream economics focus on rational decision-making, assuming a given set of resources. It is a rather static approach as it tends to neglect changes in general, and technological changes – introduction of new products and processes – in particular, as subjects of other disciplines (engineering sciences, history or sociology). Further, this school of economic thoughts postulates a single, 'time-less' – that is, ahistoric – institutional framework, namely a sophisticated and inter-related system of perfectly and smoothly working factor and product markets. Therefore it is neither interested in the rich variety of economic institutions across countries nor institutional changes in a given economic entity – be it a region, a nation or a greater system – over time.[2]

Managers and policy-makers, however, do realise the importance of technological changes as a key factor to underpin the competitiveness of products, services, firms and even broader economic entities (regions, national economies, supranational 'alliances', e.g. the EU, NAFTA). They devise and implement strategies and policies, respectively, aimed at fostering the development and the diffusion of new products, services and production techniques. Managers are also aware of the decisive impacts of various institutional settings, especially those exposed to different environments via working for multinational companies and/or highly export-oriented ones.[3]

More recently technological and institutional changes are making inroads into the textbooks of different economics schools, to a significantly different extent, though. Some subscribers of mainstream economics mention innovation just as an exception to the rule, that is, an example of market failures. Other scholars, still following this tradition, have developed the so-called *new growth theory* in an attempt to incorporate research and development expenditures into the set of major variables of their models. What seems to be more promising is another school of thoughts, called evolutionary economics or economics of technological and institutional changes. Yet, *nomen est omen*: these new attempts are still evolving, and thus seem significantly less axiomatic. Even so, the basic theorems provide a more solid base to understand the process of innovation, and hence to devise adequate policies.[4]

These recent theoretical developments can be tested – corroborated or rejected – by analysing the on-going transition process in the former planned economies which also draws one's attention to institutional changes. The Central European cases, including the Hungarian one, highlight the importance of institutions even more sharply as they are of somewhat different nature in this large and diverse group of countries, given their different history. Briefly, before World War II there was a market economy in place in Central Europe – as opposed to most Eastern European countries and former Soviet republics – based on private property. These economies were linked to the wider European economic space via foreign trade, subsidiaries of, and joint ventures with, foreign firms operating there and subsidiaries of Central European firms active abroad. Then they went through two similar historical periods, namely the planned economy and right now the transition process, but again with some non-negligible differences. Hence three rather distinct socio-economic systems and their impacts on the national system(s) of innovation (or institutions, loosely defined) can be observed in these cases. In other words, it is a large, 'living', laboratory where evolving institutions, including re-emerging old ones, can be observed. Thus it seems worthwhile studying these cases in-depth as they might provide a number of important, perhaps eye-opening, lessons for more general theorising.

This chapter aims at analysing the recent institutional changes in Hungary from the point of view of science and technology (S and T) policy via pulling together some recent theoretical developments in the economics of innovation and a fairly descriptive approach. The underlying question is whether it is possible to devise a coherent, feasible S and T policy and implement it in an efficient, or at least satisfactory, way in a transition economy, or whether S and T policy, together with other major institutions, is also evolving. In other words, is S and T policy an outcome of conscious, well-designed and co-ordinated efforts (can it be?) in this period, or should it be seen as a resultant of deliberate and unintended consequences of actions and interactions of a host of actors?

Privatisation of the formerly state-owned enterprises and the establishment of new, privately owned firms are the core of transition towards market economy, thus one might expect privatisation being the core of this paper, too. Further, firms are the engine of the innovation process, and hence might also be the 'driving force' of this chapter. Given the above aim and the selected method, however, neither the techniques (and results) of privatisation applied in Hungary, nor the role of firms in the innovation process will be analysed here.

The topics to be taken up are as follows: Theories and models of innovation as theoretical foundations for S and T policy are briefly outlined in part 2. Then the focus moves to Hungary in part 3 which describes the legacy of central planning. Recent changes in the science and technology institutional system are analysed in part 4, and policy conclusions are presented in the final part.

Theoretical foundations

The process of innovation and economic theories

Competition is a crucial idea both in neo-classical economics and economic reality. If we consider further basic notions, however, this harmonious relationship between reality and that kind of theory disappears. Competition, innovation, information (as well as knowledge and skills) asymmetries, disequilibrium and profit opportunities are almost identical phenomena in the real world, in that they are various sides of a multi-faceted, complex, entity, called market economy.[5] They might seem to be different and separable when the very phenomenon of market dynamics is seen from different angles. This separation might be necessary and useful in order to better understand certain aspects of this complex process. Neo-classical economics, however, not only separates these features but constructs another world. It speaks of competition among identical firms ('representative agents') leading to general equilibrium (treating – or dismissing – disequilibrium as an exemption to the general rule of equilibrium).[6] This school of economic thoughts is centred around the notion of rational decision-making – optimal allocation of given set of resources –, while innovation – indeed change in general – are excluded from 'scientific' investigation as story-telling.

In evolutionary theorising, however, innovation – defined as 'the search for, and the discovery, experimentation, development, imitation, and adoption of new products, new production processes and new organisational set-ups' (Dosi [1988a], p. 222) – is the hallmark of analysis. Innovation results in variety (diversity), and competition – both conducive to innovation and induced by innovation – selects among firms (or organisations, more generally).

In spite of the apparent similarity with biological processes, one should not mistakenly equate evolutionary economics with evolutionary biology. Freeman

[1994b] highlights two fundamental differences. First, selection is at least partly conscious in the innovation process as decision-makers can choose between various 'mutations' (that is, new products, processes and organisational forms). Moreover, their expectations, hopes, plans and values also shape the 'evolution' of these 'mutations'. Therefore ethical and social considerations play an increasingly important role in the innovation process, notably in the development and utilisation of nuclear energy and biotechnology, as opposed to the process of biological evolution. Second, selection is taking place at a number of levels in the course of competition: among products, firms (organisations), sectors, regions, countries and socio-economic systems. There are some autonomous rules and laws of the selection process at these different levels, however, strong interrelations and interdependencies can also be observed: technological innovations are shaping not only their natural, but also socio-economic environment, while the success of innovations strongly depends on their environment, including the quantity, quality and distribution of accumulated capital in the form of production equipment, roads, railways, communications networks, bridges, etc., as well as institutions, policies, attitudes and norms. Therefore it would be as serious a misconception to copy biological analogies in economics as it is misleading simply 'importing' equilibrium models of mechanics – where they are appropriate and functional, no doubt – and centre economic analysis around them.

While rational agents in the models of neo-classical economics can optimise via calculating *risks* and taking appropriate actions, 'innovation involves a fundamental element of *uncertainty*, which is not simply the lack of all the relevant information about the occurrence of known events, but more fundamentally, entails also (a) the existence of techno-economic problems whose solution procedures are unknown, and (b) the impossibility of precisely tracing consequences to actions' (Dosi [1988a], p. 222 – emphasis added). Thus the notions of *optimisation* or *maximisation become meaningless.*

As opposed to the 'time-less' world of neo-classical economics, '*history counts*: past technological achievements influence future achievements via the specificity of knowledge that they entail, the development of specific infrastructures, the emergence of various sorts of increasing returns and non-convexities in the national set of technological options' (Dosi [1992], p. 183). In other words, technological change is a *cumulative, path-dependent* process, and hence increasing returns are at least as important as diminishing returns.[7] Closely related notions, also in the heart of evolutionary thinking, are *learning by doing, using and interacting* (Freeman [1994a]).

Mainstream economics is mainly concerned with the availability of *information* (or information asymmetries in its jargon). Both the theoretical and empirical literature reflect, however, the growing recognition that the success of firms – regions and nations – depends on their accumulated *knowledge,* both codified and tacit,[8] and *skills* as well as *learning capabilities.* Information can be simply bought, and hence mainstream economics is comfortable with it. Knowledge – and *a fortiori* the types of knowledge required for innovation – on the contrary, cannot be mistaken with goods which can be purchased and used instantaneously; one has to go through a learning process to acquire knowledge and skills.[9] It obviously takes time and involves the process and costs of *trial and error.* Thus the uncertain, cumulative and path-dependent nature of innovation is reinforced.

Cumulativeness, path-dependency and learning lead to *heterogeneity* among firms, and hence another methodological cornerstone of mainstream economics, namely the axiom of 'representative agents', can be seen crumbling. Moreover, sectoral characteristics of the innovation process should also be taken into account while devising strategy or policy.[10]

A vast body of empirical literature has also clearly shown that innovators are not lonely (sometimes even depicted as lunatic) scientists. While some path-breaking scientific or technological ideas might come indeed from individuals, successful innovations can only be generated by a close collaboration of different organisations such as: university departments, government and/ or contract research labs, firms and specialised service-providers. Forms of their co-operation can also be varied widely from informal communications at the one extreme through highly formalised R and D contracts to alliances and joint ventures at the other extreme.[11]

The above antagonistic differences in notions and assumptions applied in various schools of thought reflect, and result in, fundamental theoretical and policy divergence. Given the scope and nature of this study only the latter ones are discussed briefly below.

Implications for S and T and innovation policy

Policy proposals arising from the neo-classical paradigm are based on the so-called market-failure argument. Government intervention is justified on three interconnected grounds:

- private firms would not engage in R and D to an 'optimal' extent because they could not appropriate all the benefits of their efforts (investments)

- outputs are not predictable from inputs
- there are indivisibilities in the process of innovation.

All in all, positive externalities, or spillover effects, do exist. In other words, the social return to R and D exceeds the private return, and thus supporting private R and D efforts improves aggregate welfare. Therefore public money can and should be used to subsidise private R and D to lower costs, to introduce an effective intellectual property right system in order to increase payoffs (improve appropriability) and/or generate technological knowledge at publicly funded universities and laboratories. An implicit assumption of this reasoning is that scientific research leads to technological development which, in turn, would automatically result in new products and processes, to be introduced by firms. This is the so-called linear model of innovation, where the wide variety of interactions among the players in a real-world innovation network is ignored.[12]

The market-failure justification for government intervention is heavily criticised by the evolutionary school on two grounds. First, it is inconsistent: following the axiom of trade theory that technology is a free commodity at world level, and can be moved without costs across national borders, governments must not use tax-payers' money to support the creation of new technology.[13] Second, it provides no guidance for policy makers:

> 'While market failure provides a general rationale for policy intervention, it is inherently imprecise in its detailed prescription: a firm may spend too much or too little on innovation, it may innovate too quickly or too slowly, it may undertake excessively risky projects or be too conservative.' (Metcalfe and Georghiou [1998], p. 81)

Evolutionary account of the innovation process leads to some sobering lessons: in a world of uncertainty policy cannot bring about the optimum either. The policy maker is not 'a perfectly informed social planner correcting imperfect market signals to guide private decisions toward more desirable outcomes'. (Metcalfe and Georghiou [1998], p. 94) Of course this is not easy to accept, especially for those trained in the paradigm of rationality, maximisation and optimisation:

> 'For obvious reasons, many economists prefer models that provide precise policy recommendations, even in situations in which the models are inapplicable to the world of our existence. Our own view is that, rather than using neo-classical models that give precise answers that do not apply to situations in which technology is evolving endogenously, it is better to face the reality that there is no optimal policy with respect to technological change.' (Lipsey and Carlaw [1998], p. 48)

Further, different forms of 'waste' seem to be unavoidable, e.g. duplication or even 'multiplication' of efforts, given the need to promote variety, as well as 'failures' stemming by definition from trial and error. These types of 'waste', however, are not only inherent in the innovation process, and hence to be accepted, but should be seen from a different angle, too. 'Errors' are in fact important pieces of information on where not to search (Metcalfe and Georghiou [1998], p. 78), while duplication of efforts in reality means learning, accumulating skills and experience in a wider circle. In other words, the more firms are engaged in the search process, the more input is generated for further innovation, and in the meantime diversity is also maintained.

Variety, selection and uncertainty also have repercussions on the very nature of policy. The relevant and potentially successful policy is an *adaptive* one, relying on and learning from feedback from the selection process to the development of further variation (Metcalfe and Georghiou [1998]). In other words, policy making is increasingly becoming policy learning; the process of policy formulation deserves as much attention as the process of innovation (Lundvall and Borrás [1998], Teubal [1998]).

Some more instructive policy implications can also be derived from evolutionary theorising: given the characteristics of the innovation process, public policies should be aimed at promoting learning in its widest possible sense, in other words competence building at individual, organisational and inter-organisational levels. Co-operation and networking among a hosts of actors, including not only researchers and producers but users, too, is a vital element in generating and disseminating knowledge. Commercialisation of R and D results and diffusion of innovations is not a smooth, automatic process. Therefore adequate policy tools should be devised and implemented to foster this process. To sum up, a system-approach is required whereby 'policies recognise the division of labour in the generation of innovation-relevant knowledge, that no individual firm is self-sufficient in its knowledge and skills and that there are corresponding gains from linking firms with the wider matrix of knowledge-generating institutions' (Metcalfe and Georghiou [1998], p. 84). Indeed, a recent trend in science and technology policies of advanced countries is a shift from direct R and D support to infrastructure building, i.e. the promotion of linkages and the so-called bridging institutions among the players in the innovation process.[14]

Other policies, such as investment, privatisation, industrial, regional development, competition, trade, monetary, fiscal, education, labour market and foreign policies, also have certain bearings on innovation and diffusion, and thus should be co-ordinated.[15]

The following parts shift the focus towards the Hungarian case, and hence a more descriptive approach is applied.

The heritage of central planning: fragmented S and T organisations

The Soviet model of both social and economic institutions, including state ownership, central planning, mono-party system, trade unions controlled by the Communist Party, etc., had to be introduced in Hungary, as in all other Central and Eastern European countries dominated by the Soviet Union, in the late 1940s. This abrupt change had far-reaching impacts on the every day life of people, the domestic and foreign politics of these countries, their economies, and hence their science and technology (S and T) systems as well. Several changes have occurred since the 1960s in Hungary. Most importantly the centrally set, mandatory plan targets were abolished as early as 1968,[16] and hence certain norms and attitudes prevailing in market economies disseminated widely among enterprise managers. The standard of living was one of the highest among CMEA[17] countries. The political and economic transition process, of course, brought about much more important changes in the early 1990s. Yet, the legacy of central planning cannot be ignored even now. Hence it is worth highlighting some major characteristics of that period.

Central planning and the rationale of the so-called party-state did not allow to sustain a complex set of various independent economic, social and political institutions, co-operating and co-evolving in a number of ways through horizontal links. Excessive centralisation of all social, cultural, political and economic activities required vertically organised, insulated sub-systems. Relationships among these sub-systems were only established at the very top level, e.g. R and D, production and trade functions were separated not only at firm level, but also at the level of the ministries, and hence co-ordination was only possible at the highest political level. Firms became mere production units, with no responsibility, and no means to conduct R and D, buy raw materials, trade their products or control their finance. As for international relations, the former intense trade and ownership links as well as R and D co-operation with Western firms were cut off, and Hungarian companies became dependent on other CMEA countries both in terms of raw materials and markets. Exports and imports, as well as domestic trade, were also separated from manufacturing firms, and were exclusively conducted by separate state-owned companies.

A rigid system of division of labour was also imposed on S and T organisations: basic research was assigned exclusively to research institutes of the

Hungarian Academy of Sciences (HAS),[18] while applied research and development had to be performed by the so-called branch R and D institutes, supervised by branch ministries. Teaching, on the other hand, became the only task of universities, i.e. departments were not supposed to conduct research projects, and thus were not given resources for such activities. Horizontal links among academia and industry were also cut off.[19] R and D co-operation of Hungarian researchers with Western universities and research institutes was also controlled along political lines, and hence became much more difficult to maintain, thus weaker and weaker (as in the case of firms' co-operation with their Western partners).

The whole system, and thus the S and T subsystem has become far less rigid and more decentralised since the 1960s, e.g. HAS institutes were engaged in applied research and teaching, too, while university departments also started research projects. Yet, hardly any co-operation has evolved among these 'insulated' sub-sectors of R and D.

The highest authority for R and D policy-making was the Science Policy Committee, while science was administered by the HAS and technology by the National Committee of Technological Development (OMFB), set up in 1961.[20]

Financial and institutional changes in S and T system

Although transition has brought about a number of crucial political and economic changes effecting the S and T system, no systematic science and technology, innovation or industrial policies have been implemented since the early 1990s.[21] For methodological reasons it is practically impossible to establish who has blocked various initiatives or why: policy-makers would not disclose any details of these day-to-day negotiations as some important details are confidential, while revealing other details would adversely effect their future 'battles' for funds and influence.[22]

One important reason must have been the lack of adequate funds. Most long-term policies, such as education, infrastructure, innovation, industrial, SMEs, regional, health care, and environment ones, would require either substantial investment projects or generous subsidies, or even both. The transition process, however, has hit most of Central European countries: instead of facing the 'problem' how to spend abundant financial resources they have to cope with significant budget deficits plus find means to tackle more urgent needs, such as rocketing unemployment. One might add, however, that lack of fund would require redoubled efforts to devise policies how to spend scarce resources, rather than not thinking at all on setting priorities.

Sometimes a lack of knowledge about up-to-date policy principles and methods also poses a significant problem, and hence prevents their introduction.[23]

As for S and T policy, OMFB [1995] even summarised and published the most common arguments put against a more pro-active S and T policy, together with counter-arguments, in an attempt to convince politicians and government officials that OECD and EU member countries are not following an extreme 'laissez-faire' ideology.[24]

Even this type of rather unusual reasoning has not been powerful enough. Some financial, institutional and organisational changes, though, have happened since the early 1990s. These are summarised in the following sub-parts.

Finance of R and D

Shrinking R and D funds

R and D expenditures have significantly dropped since the late 1980s. Whereas 2.3 per cent of GDP had been devoted to R and D in 1988, this ratio fell to 0.7 per cent by 1996. Given the shrinking GDP[25] and the rather high rate of inflation in this period,[26] it is a dramatic drop in real terms, indeed. According to a recent CSO estimation, using the so-called purchasing power parities method, R and D expenditures in real terms in 1996 were a mere 36 per cent of those in 1990 (OMFB [1997], p. 27).

To compare, EU countries on average spend around 1.8-2 per cent of their GDP on R and D.[27] This is already a huge difference, moreover, their GDP per capita is three times higher than the Hungarian one.

Table 9.1 Gross domestic expenditure on R and D (GERD) in Hungary, 1988-1996, current prices

GERD	1988	1989	1990	1991	1992	1993	1994	1995	1996
billion forints	32.8	33.8	33.7	27.1	31.6	35.3	40.3	42.3	46.0
GERD/GDP (%)	2.3	2.0	1.6	1.1	1.1	1.0	0.9	0.8	0.7

Source: Central Statistical Office, *Tudományos kutatás és kísérleti fejlesztés*, various years.

Inevitably, R and D personnel has also been cut quite drastically, by some 60 per cent compared to 1988. Aggregate figures, as always, hide important differences. In some cases this cut means the necessary streamlining. In some other cases, however, it represents a severe loss of useful knowledge and skills developed and accumulated over time. In other words, it would not be possible to reproduce these intangible assets immediately once funds were made available. There are no reliable estimates readily available on the share of necessary streamlining and severe loss.

The composition of the total R and D personnel has also changed so that the number of scientists and engineers exceeds that of the supporting staff. Again, the overall picture is mixed. In some cases it is a step towards increased efficiency, but in other cases it causes inefficiency at a social level. When highly qualified scientists have to perform simple tasks, instead of spending their time on resolving scientific problems as they are trained for because of the lack of supporting staff, that is obviously a waste of scarce and expensive resources.

Table 9.2 R and D personnel in Hungary, 1988-1996, full-time equivalent

	1988	1990	1992	1994	1996
Total R and D personnel	45,069	36,384	24,192	22,008	19,776
of which Scientists and engineers	21,427	17,550	12,311	11,752	10,408
Other staff*	23,642	18,834	11,881	10,256	9,268

Source: Central Statistical Office, *Tudományos kutatás és kísérleti fejlesztés*, various years.
* Includes technicians, assistants, administration, etc.

Unexpected shift in the sources of R and D expenditures

Given the experience of market economies, some observers and politicians have expected enterprises to play a decisive role in financing and executing R and D, and, in turn, the government to withdraw. Quite the opposite shift has occurred for obvious reasons, and hence not really surprising. Two major elements of the relevant arguments are discussed here.

Most Hungarian companies are suffering from the loss of markets for two principal reasons, namely the collapse of CMEA, their former major market, and swift import liberalisation. Hence their sales had dramatically declined (by 15-75 per cent in various industries) by the early 1990s compared to the last pre-transition years, 1988-89. Shrinking revenues, in turn, prevent them from generating adequate funds for R and D (see Table 9.3) and investment.

Another element of the explanation is that privatisation only started in 1990, and it has taken time to find investors. In most cases radical re-structuring was necessary both in the organisational set-up and in the product-market mix of these companies in order to prepare for privatisation. Therefore managers were not really in the position to make decisions on long-term issues, including the design and implementation of innovation strategies, for two reasons. First, it would have been somewhat hostile to the would-be owners to tie their hands, which, in turn, would have made the relationship between the (prospective) owners and managers somewhat uneasy. Not surprisingly, managers did not want to cause these types of conflicts. Second, managers were overwhelmed by the prepa-ration for privatisation (re-structuring, cost-cutting, etc.), i.e. by short-term issues. In brief, uncertainties related to the would-be privatisation of companies also hindered innovation until the mid-1990s.[28]

Table 9.3 Breakdown of GERD in Hungary by sources, 1988-1996, per cent

Funding sources	1988	1989	1990	1991	1992	1993	1994	1995	1996
Business	52.1	45.5	38.8	40.3	31.3	28.6	28.7	36.1	37.4
Government	45.7	52.4	58.6	55.8	62.9	65.1	63.0	55.1	51.2
Other*	2.2	2.1	2.6	4.2	5.8	6.3	8.3	8.8	11.4

Source: Central Statistical Office, *Tudományos kutatás és kísérleti fejlesztés*, various years
* Includes foreign sources plus some non-profit, non-government organisations, e.g. foundations

One might find an apparent paradox here: firms do not spend a lot on R and D, yet, fierce competition – loss of former markets, import liberalisation – compel them to introduce new products and/or processes. Indeed, they do so – other-wise would not survive – but in most cases these innovations are not based on their own R and D projects. Quite often they rely on technologies provided by parent companies or other foreign partners, e.g. in a subcontracting agreement. Foreign firms not only encourage their Hungarian suppliers to introduce new products, processes and managerial techniques, but sometimes they even provide licences and know-how free of charge.[29] In other words, R and D expenditures cannot be used as a proxy variable for innovation.

Finally, the significant differences behind these aggregate figures should also be noted. Foreign-owned firms do spend more on R and D than indigenous ones,[30] moreover, they can also rely on the R and D results achieved, or bought, by their parent company.

Short-term issues, that is, radical cost-cutting to avoid insolvency and preparation for privatisation, prevent companies from elaborating and implementing mid- and long-term actions, such as innovation and investment. The number of R and D units operated by firms, therefore, sharply decreased in the early 1990s, yet, considerably increased by 1996, almost reaching again the 1988 level.[31] In 1997-98 a number of large, foreign-owned firms have either substantially increased R and D spending at their existing R and D units (e.g. GE-Tungsram, Knorr-Bremse, Ericsson) or decided to set up new R and D facilities (Audi, Nokia). The expanding number of R and D units in higher education is also worth noting.

Table 9.4 Number of R and D units, 1988-1996

Type of organisations	1988	1990	1992	1994	1996
Research institutes	69	69	68	63	73
Higher education	944	940	1071	1106	1120
Firms	235	174	98	183	220
Other*	75	73	50	49	48
Total	1323	1256	1287	1401	1461

Source: Central Statistical Office, *Tudományos kutatás és kísérleti fejlesztés*, various years.
* Includes R and D units operated at/by national and regional archives, libraries, museums, hospitals and ministries.

Foreign aid projects have also eased the severe financial situation to a certain extent. Although foreign funding has increased significantly in relative terms (a significant part of 'Other' sources in Table 9.3 comes from abroad), these grants have not been able to counterbalance the aforementioned dramatic drop in R and D expenditures, given their low weight. Nonetheless, they have made a significant impact via diffusing new methods to allocate grants (e.g. emphasis on individual projects rather than financing institutes, the importance of project assessment and monitoring). It is also of importance that some vital projects have been continued and significant new ones could be started due to these funds.[32]

Renewed financial support schemes

The most promising development in the transition period has been the renewal of some former R and D schemes and introduction of new programmes (but as already stressed, allocating shrinking funds in real terms). In most cases applicants can initiate projects in any discipline, technology or sector, i.e. the so-called 'bottom-up' approach is applied. In other words, the formerly prevailing 'top-down' approach, whereby government bodies selected certain disciplines, technologies or sectors eligible for R and D subsidies, has been abandoned. Another major institutional change has been the setting up of councils to allocate grants or favourable loans, relying on a peer review system. The three most important funds are as follows:

Higher Education Development Fund (FEFA) to finance the development of the infrastructure of higher education. It is administered by the Ministry of Culture and Education.

National Scientific Research Fund (OTKA) to finance basic research. It is administered by the OTKA Office.

Central Technological Development Fund (KMÜFA), administered by OMFB, to promote technological development.

The role of OMFB

OMFB operates a number of support schemes using KMÜFA money to improve R and D infrastructure, finance applied R and D and the so-called national projects. Grants or favourable loans awarded through these schemes are available for practically all Hungarian researchers or organisations (firms, university departments, other R and D units). Before providing some details of these schemes it should also be stressed that KMÜFA used to be financed directly via a special levy, and hence was not part of the budgeting process, but now is financed from the central budget. This way spending of the tax revenues can be controlled by the Parliament, and hence it can be regarded as a step forward.

This change also raises questions, however, whether sufficient funds are allocated for R and D in the complex bargaining process in which the central budget is set. Table 9.5 clearly shows that KMÜFA funds varied quite substantially in 1991-1997. Until 1994 roughly the same amount was available in nominal terms, that is, a marked drop in real terms. 1995 saw a dramatic decline even nominally, which was not compensated by the modest growth in 1996. Then a further increase in 1997 meant to reach again the 1992-1993 level, nominally. Long-term issues, such as innovation, would require a bit more stable environment and less hectic financial decisions, to say the least.

Table 9.5 KMÜFA funds, 1990-1997 (million Ft)

	1991	1992	1993	1994	1995	1996	1997
Residue from the previous year	1,314.8	5,122.4	3,057.3	1,769.2	2,472.8	3,417.1	4,225.1
'Fresh' funds from the central budget	8,253.5	4,814.6	6,786.5	7,139.5	3,485.6	4,158.4	5,947.0
Total	9,568.3	9,937.0	9,843.8	8,908.7	5,958.4	7,575.5	0,172.1

Source: OMFB [1998]

R and D infrastructure projects

This 'bottom-up' scheme was introduced in 1991. Major goals include (a) to upgrade the R and D and educational infrastructure, e.g. to provide grants to purchase PCs and various instruments, and (b) to facilitate the dissemination of R and D results, e.g. grants to attend conferences abroad if the applicant's paper is accepted, and contribution to organise conferences in Hungary. A growing amount had been spent until 1994, and then a marked decrease occurred (Table 9.6) because procurement of instruments has been supported from other sources since 1995.

Table 9.6 Spending on R and D infrastructure projects, 1991-1997 (m Ft)

1991	1992	1993	1994	1995	1996	1997
397	2,162	2,977	2,151	852	307	331

Source: OMFB [1998].

Applied R and D projects

This is another new 'bottom-up' scheme, also introduced in 1991. Project proposals are evaluated by independent technical and financial experts in three rounds. In most cases an interest-free loan is provided. The amount spent under this scheme has varied from 600 million to almost 4 billion forints since 1991 (Table 9.7).

Table 9.7 Financial support for applied R and D projects, 1991-1997 (m Ft)

1991	1992	1993	1994	1995	1996	1997
586	2,653	2,087	1,881	1,908	1,189	3,861

Source: OMFB [1998]

Target-oriented national projects

This is a 'top-down' scheme, as opposed to the aforementioned ones. It was introduced in 1992. Four major goals were selected to be supported from public funds: deposition of nuclear waste (165 million forints were spent up to 1996 and none in 1997), development of geographic information systems (589 million forints), food processing and packaging technologies and machinery (342 million forints), and automotive technologies (140 million forints).

Besides these aforementioned schemes, 2,046 million forints were spent to promote the competitiveness of Hungarian exporters through technological development in 1990-97, and 207 million forints to finance patent application fees abroad in 1992-96.[33] Innovative SMEs have also been eligible for financial support since 1989 (297 million forints were spent in 1990-1996). 780 million forints were granted to finance the National Informatics Programme in 1990-97. A new scheme was introduced in 1996 to support those Hungarian researchers who participate in a project financed by the 4th RTD Framework Programme of the EU, with 122 million forints being spent in 1996-1997. Regional innovation initiatives are supported from 1997, together with the regional chambers (327 million Ft). The development and diffusion of information and communication technologies is also promoted by a new scheme launched in 1997 (459 million Ft spent).

Finally, the Ministry of Industry and Trade also administers applied R and D funds available from the repayment by firms of former R and D loans provided by the ministry.[34]

Legislation for a new S and T policy framework

New legislation on higher education and on the Hungarian Academy of Sciences became effective in 1994.[35] These steps certainly contribute to the formulation of a new framework for science policy. Yet, some other bills have also to be passed in order to provide a sound legal and institutional basis for technology and innovation policies. In other words, the current challenge is to build a new environment conducive to technological changes, broadly defined, in a comprehensive, systematic way. Current changes in legislation are summarised in the following subparts.

Act on Higher Education

The Bill on Higher Education was passed in early 1994. The new Act has strengthened universities' autonomy. Among other changes, PhD degrees now are awarded by them, as opposed to the former system, when HAS used to exercise this right. Curricula are evaluated by a new body, called National Accreditation Committee, in a systematic way, and thus it is hoped that the level of higher education will be improved.

Another significant change is that all universities, previously operated under the control of a number of different ministries, are supervised by the Ministry of Education. The 'Hungarian Rectors' Conference' has also been set up as an independent association of universities. Its major role is to act as an advisory body to the Ministry of Education in professional, scientific, legislative and organisational issues concerning higher education. Universities are also encouraged to co-operate with each other and with HAS research institutes through new financial schemes.

New legislation on HAS

A Bill on HAS had already been prepared before 1990, i.e. prior to the political changes, marked by the 1990 general elections. Nonetheless, internal conflicts, namely those between HAS headquarters and research institutes, on the one hand, and between members of HAS and researchers employed by HAS institutes, on the other, as well as ideological battles in the Parliament blocked the legislation procedure for almost five years. Eventually the new legislation was enacted in May 1994.

The new Act changed the structure of the highest authority of HAS. Previously the General Assembly only consisted of members of HAS, now delegates of scientific degree holders also join this body, and have 50 per cent of votes. The Act also stipulates a guaranteed annual support from the central budget. The network of HAS research institutes is subordinated to the HAS and governed by the 'Council of Academic Research Institutes'. Research institutes, however, enjoy a certain degree of autonomy. Financial support is allocated by three research councils on the basis of research evaluation. A new scientific degree, namely 'Doctor of Sciences' is awarded by HAS. It is a prerequisite for becoming a member of HAS. Co-operation with universities is also promoted by this Act.

Intellectual Property Rights

A number of measures have also been taken to strengthen intellectual property rights. Under the previous law so-called process patents also used to be registered in Hungary. Hence pharmaceuticals companies, for instance, were able to 're-invent' drugs by finding new methods to produce molecules known from others' medicines. Obviously it was cheaper than to develop original drugs or pay a licence fee. Since July 1994, however, this 'smart' method cannot be applied any more. Sales of software packages, audio tapes and CDs are also checked regularly, and illegal copies are destroyed in a demonstrative way.

Reorganised government bodies

Major government bodies have also been reorganised. Hence the role of the government in R and D and innovation is still evolving.

The former Science Policy Committee was dissolved in 1994, its secretariat moved from the Prime Minister's Office into the Ministry of Culture and Education, and a new committee, chaired by the Prime Minister, was set up. It was reorganised again in February 1999.

OMFB has also been reorganised. In 1990-94 its President was a member of the cabinet in the capacity of a minister without portfolio, responsible for technological development. In the new organisational set-up it was supervised by a designated member of the cabinet from 1994 to1998,[36] and by the minister of economic affairs from January 1999. Besides the usual tasks, such as elaboration of technology policy, provision of financial support for technological development, and the organisation of international S and T relationships, a new responsibility has been added, namely to conduct technology assessment and technology audits. Strategic issues are decided upon by the Council, consisting of representatives of certain ministries and independent experts who are appointed by the Prime Minister for three years.

The foregoing subparts suggest that important organisational and legislative changes have occurred in recent years. Yet, more co-operation and co-ordination among the major players would be desirable. That would promote commercialisation and diffusion, what is perhaps the most important task for any S and T policy, but it is definitely 'the' crucial task in Hungary.

New initiatives to promote commercialisation and diffusion

Central planning has had far-reaching bearings on the Hungarian R and D and innovation system since the late 1940s. The most important one has been the lack of economic exploitation of the internationally respected R and D results achieved by Hungarian scientists and engineers.[37] Thus it is of crucial importance to introduce innovation policy tools capable of promoting the commercialisation and diffusion of new technologies.

Following the above realisation the Hungarian government has decided to establish new types of applied R and D institutes. The aim is to facilitate a closer, mutually beneficial co-operation among universities, R and D institutes and industry, following the German Fraunhofer Institutes' model. These new institutes are partially financed by the *Zoltán Bay Foundation*.[38] Three Bay institutes have been inaugurated since 1993, devoted to biotechnology (in Szeged), logistics and production technologies (in Miskolc), and materials sciences (in Budapest).

The *Hungarian Innovation Association* has established its own *database* of development capacities (skills of R and D and engineering consultancy groups) in an effort to act as a catalyst between technology suppliers and users. Another major step taken by them has been to found a *Business and Innovation Centre* in Budapest together with the *Chamber of Small and Medium-Sized Enterprises*, the *Hungarian Chamber of Commerce* and *Innotech kft.*, relying upon a *PHARE* grant.

Liaison offices and science parks have also been set up at technical universities to facilitate academia-industry relations. Preliminary experience, however, suggests that it takes time to find an appropriate mission, strategy and internal organisation, let alone adequate funds and skilled managers, for these new institutions amidst the complexity of the transition process.

The Hungarian Foundation for Entrepreneurship has set up a number of regional offices to help establish new businesses and the diffusion of information on new products and technologies.

Several foreign funds have helped to set up information and knowledge transfer organisations. As a systematic, thorough evaluation of their activities has not been conducted, it is not known whether these organisations are effective. Sporadic evidence, e.g. interviews with their directors, indicates that firms frequently use their free services, especially information services. In other words, firms are happy to have a free lunch but nobody knows whether fledgling SMEs or the government will be able to finance these organisations (through fees and/ or grants, respectively) once foreign aid projects conclude.

Policy conclusions

Although innovation is a fairly complex, non-routine, non-foreseeable socio-economic process, and hence no panacea can be prescribed for how to foster it, some policy conclusions can be drawn from recent research projects.[39]

Evolutionary economics, based on thorough empirical analyses of the innovation process, has provided a new policy rationale, a different one from that based on neo-classical economics. This new approach is gaining ground in more and more advanced countries. Some important organisational and legislative changes have occurred in Hungary, too, on the whole in line with the recent international trends. Yet, a deliberate, systematic innovation policy is still lacking for a number of reasons. The heritage of the former socio-economic system, current economic and social difficulties caused and/or revealed by the transition process, and partly ideological, partly socio-psychological stands against the apparently increased role of government all constitute obstacles on the road. Moreover, there are vested interests against concerted efforts. In short, there is a long way to go. There is a lot to learn from recent theoretical results and poli-cy approaches, and an even more demanding task is to devise and implement a coherent socio-economic strategy with innovation in its centre.

Methodology of policy making

History clearly shows the interdependence of technical, economic and social change. Policy decisions should, therefore, be based on an *integrated approach*, taking into account the systemic aspects of the relationships of technology, competitiveness and growth together with the importance of social, institutional and cultural factors in a country's ability to profit from technological change.

Techniques and methods to support this approach include:
- regular conduct of *foresight studies* to identify critical issues, major technological. market and social trends so as to improve quality of life and competitiveness;
Foresight exercises are aimed at achieving a cultural change; better communication, mutual understanding and co-operation between the scientific community, industry and government departments. The first Hungarian Technology
Foresight Programme was launched in 1997, to be completed by 1999.

- strong(er) representation of *local and regional interests* so as to harmonise
those with the national ones.

Policy decisions should be integrated in a technical (pragmatic) sense as well:

- innovation, industrial, investment, privatisation, competition, trade, monetary,
fiscal, education and labour market policies must not be devised, implemented
and evaluated separately since all have considerable impact on enterprise
behaviour, and hence innovation;

- former and current actions should also be seen in an integrated way: (a) the
legacy of previous measures simply cannot be ignored, moreover, (b) an
extensive use of information on their impacts is inevitable when designing the
new ones, i.e. regular *monitoring* and *evaluation* of all the major policy
measures should be devised.

Policy measures

Experience of successful countries suggests two major lessons: it is the *firms'*
task to undertake the bulk of innovative activities, however, *governments* can,
and indeed should, also play a vital role by shaping the institutional characteristics of the *national system of innovation* and providing favourable *international relationships* within which it operates. The overall, twin, objectives are
to improve international competitiveness of firms and the economy as a whole
and to enhance the quality of life. The above '*networking*' *activities* can
considerably contribute to achieving these ultimate goals via creating
environments conducive to innovation. This includes the task to establish an
appropriate physical and institutional infrastructure to advance the *generation
of new technologies, skills and knowledge* as well as to facilitate the *diffusion,*

that is, both adoption and adaptation, of technologies in order to improve the system's ability to take advantage of technological change.

Transition poses specific challenges, too. A major one is that financial difficulties together with exaggerated market ideologies might lead to policy suggestions aimed at further 'marketisation' of R and D. It seems needless to stress that this would be a fatal misconception.

It is also of importance to learn from the mistakes made by industrialised countries' governments. Hence the Hungarian government should avoid: policies that seek to pick winners, and creating 'islands' of innovation through selective support of certain high technology industries.

Notes

[1] This chapter is a revised and updated version of a paper prepared for *Central and Eastern Europe: Institutional Change and Industrial Development,* a workshop organised by Aalborg University at Tannishus, Northern Jutland, Denmark, on November 20-23, 1997. Comments on the previous version by Anne Lorentzen, Mihály Laki and Brigitta Widmaier are gratefully acknowledged. The usual disclaimer applies.

[2] For a more detailed analysis see Freeman [1994a], Nelson [1995], Nelson and Winter [1982] and von Tunzelmann [1995].

[3] Politicians and political scientists, of course, are also keen on institutional changes, broadly defined, for their own professional reasons.

[4] See, e.g. Ergas [1987], Freeman [1982] and (1995), Freeman and Soete (1997), Foray and Freeman (1992), Dosi 1988], Dosi (1992), Dosi *et al.* 1988], Dosi *et al.* 1994], Dosi and Nelson 1993], Lundvall (ed.) (1992), Mowery and Rosenberg (1989), Nelson (1993), Nelson and Winter (1982), OECD (1992), Rosenberg (1983).

[5] Metcalfe and Georghiou (1998), referring to Richardson's book on Information and Investment published already in 1960, explain it in two plain sentences: 'Without asymmetry there can be neither novelty nor variety. Indeed innovations and information asymmetries are proper synonyms and it should not be forgotten that a profit opportunity known to everybody is a profit opportunity for nobody.' (p. 81).

[6] Evolutionary economists strongly disagree with this vision of economic reality, e.g. Metcalfe and Georghiou (1998) opens by a simple, but powerful, blunt thesis: 'Capitalism and equilibrium are fundamentally incompatible concepts' (p. 76).

[7] In neo-classical economics, of course, the dominance of the latter is a crucial postulate.

[8] For a brief but highly informative discussion of codified and tacit knowledge - and the policy relevance of this distinction - see Lundvall and Borrás (1998) (especially pp. 31-33) and the literature they refer to.

[9] Borrowing a sparkling parable of Dosi (1988b), although there are market conditions of access to information e.g. there is a market for textbooks and economic conditions of access to higher education (the level of registration fees, the availability or scarcity of grants for students), 'in any proper sense of the word, getting a PhD is not simply acquiring information, and it is even less true to say that there is a market for PhDs' (p. 1130).

[10] A seminal taxonomy developed in Pavitt (1984) identifies supplier-dominated sectors, specialised suppliers, scale-intensive and science-based sectors.

[11] Freeman (1995) provides a thorough literature survey, see also Lundvall and Borrás (1998), the papers on the role of networks in the 1991 October issue of *Research Policy* and the 'national innovation system' approach, e.g. Lundvall (ed) (1992), Nelson (1993) as well as the on-going OECD project on this topic.

[12] Rothwell (1993) describes 5 generations of innovation models, and explains the importance of interactions, feedbacks, system integration and networking.

[13] 'The 'free-riding', non-interventionalist government would just leave it to their domestic firms to tap into the free pool of global knowledge' (Lundvall and Borrás (1998), p. 44). For further critical remarks see op. cit. pp. 49-50, 52, as well as Lipsey and Carlaw (1998).

[14] Metcalfe and Georghiou (1998) provides an overview of S and T policies in EU member countries (pp. 85-93), see also further contributions in the special issue of *STI Review* on *New Rationale and Approaches in Technology and Innovation Policy* (1998, No. 22), as well as Lundvall and Borrás (1998). This new approach can also be observed in a recently proposed distinction between science, technology and innovation policy. Dodgson and Bessant (1996) define science policy 'concerned with the development of science and the training of scientists', while technology policy 'has as its aims the support, enhancement and development of technology, often with a military and environmental protection focus'. Innovation policy, however, 'takes into account the complexities of the innovation process and focuses more on interactions within the system' (cited in Lundvall and Borrás (1998), p. 42).

[15] See also Havas (1995), Lundvall and Borrás (1998) and Radosevic (1994) for a more detailed discussion.

[16] A more decentralised planning system, together with the so-called indirect economic control tools, on the whole giving more room of manoeuvring to companies, replaced the former system.

[17] Council for Mutual Economic Assistance, the trade organisation of the former Soviet Bloc

[18] HAS was established in 1825 by a rich, enlightened aristocrat, István Széchenyi.

[19] Until the 1940s large companies had intense co-operation with universities. In addition to the usual way, that is, commissioning university departments to conduct certain research projects, some of these firms were actually spin-off firms from universities (e.g. MOM, an optical company), while others even set up new university departments (e.g. Tungsram established the nuclear physics department at the Technical University in Budapest).

[20] For an excellent, detailed analysis of the Hungarian R and D system and related issues see OECD (1993). A shorter overview can be found in Balázs et al. (1990).

[21] Policy proposals, however, have been drafted, see, e.g. IKM (1993), IKM, OMFB, PM (1993), OMFB (1995).

[22] It would go beyond the scope of this paper to speculate about political reasons. At a rather general level, however, some, mostly ideology-driven, arguments can be summarised. Given the political and economic legacy of central planning most politicians have been either against any sort of strategic thinking conducted, and actions taken, by the government, or not wanted to 'fight' hopelessly for these ideas, like industrial policy, even if they believe in them. Policy-makers, for obvious reasons, have followed these lines. Ironically, though, quite a few politicians, as ministers, pursued rather etatist policies in their day-to-day decisions, sometimes with rather long-term repercussions, both in 1990-1994 and

1994-1998 when the two governments in power had rather different political backgrounds. A more detailed analysis of their economic policies, declared and actual ones, would, obviously, require a separate paper.

[23] For example a recent study, Glatz (1998) still treats 'science' as a separate entity, i.e. not in the broader context of innovation.

[24] The prevailing arguments against a more pro-active S and T policy were as follows: 1) Government actions in, or subsidies for, technical development is part of the 'socialist past' (i.e. should be discontinued). 2) Scientific results automatically generate technological development. 3) Know-how and other R and D results should be purchased from abroad (in other words, economic results cannot be expected from indigenous research). We should wait for economic successes that generate resources for technology-intensive development.

[25] In real terms GDP dropped by some 20 per cent by 1992 compared to the 1988 level due to the so-called transformation recession. Although the late 1990s saw significant growth (e.g. above 4 per cent in 1997), the GDP is likely to reach the 1988 level in real terms only in 1999 (author's calculation based on CSO data for 1987-97 published in the *Statistical Yearbook of Hungary 1997* and the government's estimation for 1998-99).

[26] The rate of inflation (consumer price index) has been fluctuated between 20-28 per cent a year until the mid-1990s, and was still around 18 per cent in 1997 (Central Statistical Office Yearbooks).

[27] The European Commission urges them to increase this ratio in order to catch up with the US and Japan. (EU 1996) The latter two countries spent 2.5-2.8 per cent of their GDP in 1985-1996 (OECD (1998]).

[28] For a detailed analysis of these issues see György and Vincze (1992), Havas (1997b), Havas and Inzelt (1994), Inzelt (1994], Inzelt *et al.* (1991), Tóth, G. L. (1994) and Vincze (1991).

[29] For such cases in the automotive industry see Havas (1997a).

[30] According to a recent CSO census, cited in Inzelt (1998), manufacturing firms located in Hungary spent on average 0.86 per cent of their revenues on R and D in 1995. This ratio was 0.97 per cent for (partially or wholly) foreign-owned firms on average, but 1.59 per cent for firms in which foreign ownership was above 75 per cent. Fully Hungarian-owned manufacturing firms, however, only spent 0.64 per cent of their revenues on R and D.

[31] Besides economic reasons behind these changes, there might be some methodological ones, too. Given the organisational and ownership changes occurring on a massive scale, quite a few companies might have not been reached by the Central Statistical Office. Moreover, a number of those reached by the CSO survey might not have answered. The situation has become more settled by the late 1990s, and CSO has also learnt important methodological lessons. Thus more recent statistics provide a more sound base for analysis.

[32] As the Cold War ended, radical changes have also occurred in international scientific and technological relations. Hungarian researchers and R and D institutes can now join mutually advantageous international projects. Hence basically all major international programmes and organisations, such as the 4th and 5th EU RTD Framework Programmes, COST, PHARE ACCORD, EUREKA, CERN, OECD, NATO Scientific Projects and ESA are now open for Hungarian participation.

[33] The former scheme was introduced in 1986, while the latter one in 1992.

[34] En web-udgave af programmet kan findes på adressen:
Prior to the introduction of the aforementioned new schemes, i.e. until the early 1990s, KMÜFA had been allocated among various ministries to fund R and D projects initiated by organisations supervised by them.·

[35] For a more detailed description on the new legislation on HAS and higher education see Balázs (1994).

[36] It was not stipulated in the government decree on the responsibilities and organisation of the OMFB who was to be its minister. In practice it was the minister of industry, trade and tourism.

[37] Havas (1994) discussed this general problem using the example of laser technology.

[38] Zoltán Bay (1900-1992), working for a major Hungarian company, Tungsram, as a physicist, made the first ever radar contact with the moon in 1946. A few years later he emigrated from Hungary to the USA.

[39] This part draws on Havas (1995), as well as on empirical and policy studies mentioned in references.

References

Balázs, K. (1994), Transition crisis in Hungary's R and D sector, *Economic Systems*, 18, pp. 281-306.

Balázs, K., Hare, P. and Oakey, R. (1990), The management of research and development in Hungary at the end of the 1980s, *Soviet Studies*, 42, pp. 723-741.

Dodgson, M. and Bessant, J. (1996), *Effective Innovation Policy: A new approach*, London: International Thomson.

Dosi, G. (1988a), The nature of the innovative process, in Dosi *et al.* (eds.) (1988).

Dosi, G. (1988b), Sources, procedures and microeconomic effects of innovation, *Journal of Economic Literature*, 26, pp. 126-171.

Dosi, G. (1992), The research on innovation diffusion: An assessment, in: Nakicenovic, N. and Grübler, A. (eds.): *Diffusion of Technologies and Social Behaviour*, Berlin: Springer-Verlag.

Dosi, G., Freeman, C., Nelson, R.R., Silverberg, G. and Soete, L. (eds) (1988), *Technical Change and Economic Theory*, London: Pinter.

Dosi, G., Freeman, C. and Fabiani, S. (1994), The process of economic development: Introducing some stylized facts and theories on technologies, firms and institutions, *Industrial and Corporate Change*, 3, pp. 1-45.

Dosi, G. and Nelson, R.R. (1993), Evolutionary Theories in Economics: Assessment and prospects, IIASA Working Paper WP-93-064.

Ergas, H. (1987), The importance of technology policy, in: P. Dasgupta and P. Stoneman (eds): *Economic Policy and Technological Performance*, Cambridge: Cambridge University Press, pp. 51-96.

EU (1996), *Green Paper on innovation*, Brussels - Luxembourg: ECSC-EC-EAEC.

Freeman, C. (1982), *The Economics of Industrial Innovation* (2nd edn], London: Pinter.

Freeman, C. (1994a), The economics of technical change: A critical survey, *Cambridge Journal of Economics*, 18, No. 5, pp. 463-514.

Freeman, C. (1994b), Marching to the Sound of a Different Drum, paper presented at the EUNETIC Conference on 'Evolutionary Economics of Technological Change: Assessment of results and new frontiers', Strasbourg, 6-8 October.

Freeman, C. (1995), The 'National System of Innovation' in historical perspective, *Cambridge Journal of Economics*, 19, No. 1, pp. 5-24.

Freeman, C. and Soete, L. (1997), *The Economics of Industrial Innovation* (3rd edn), London: Pinter.

Foray, D. and Freeman, C. (eds) (1992), *Technology and the Wealth of Nations*, London: Pinter.

Glatz, F. (1998), *Tudománypolitika az ezredforduló Magyarországán* (Science Policy at the Turn of the Millennium in Hungary), Budapest: MTA.

György, K. and Vincze, J. (1992), Privatization and innovation in the pharmaceutical industry in a post-socialist economy, *Rivista internationale di Scienze sociali*, 100, pp. 403-417.

Havas, A. (1994), Incentives to innovate in transition: The case of laser technology in Hungary, *Economic Systems*, 18, pp. 197-214.

Havas, A. (1995), Science and technology policy in Hungary, in: Parissakis, G. and N. Katsaros (eds): *Science Policy and Research Management in the Balkan Countries*, Dordrecht: Kluwer Academic Publishers, pp. 193-208.

Havas, A. (1997a), Foreign direct investment and intra-industry trade: The case of automotive industry in Central Europe, in: Dyker, D. (ed.): *The Technology of Transition*, Budapest: Central European University Press, pp. 211-240.

Havas, A. (1997b), Restructuring precision engineering industry in Hungary, in: Lorentzen, A. and M. Rostgård (eds): The *Aftermath of 'Real Existing Socialism' in Eastern Europe*, Volume 2: *People and Technology in the Process of Transition*, Basingstoke: MacMillan, pp. 210-236.

Havas, A. and Inzelt, A. (1994), A Bumpy Road for the Diffusion of New Technologies in Hungary, mimeo, Budapest: IKU.

IKM (1993), *Iparpolitika a 90-es évekre* (Industrial policy for the 1990s), Budapest: Ministry of Industry and Trade.

IKM, OMFB, PM (1993), *Innovation Policy*, Budapest: Ministry of Industry and Trade, National Committee for Technological Development and Ministry of Finance.

Inzelt, A. (1994), Privatization and innovation in Hungary: First experiences, *Economic Systems*, 18, pp. 141-158.

Inzelt, A. (1998), A külföldi befektetõk kutatás-fejlesztési ráfordításainak szerepe az átalalkuló gazdaságban (The Role of R and D Expenditures of Foreign Investors in an Economy in Transition), Külgazdaság, 42, pp. 59-75.

Inzelt, A., György, K., Havas, A. and Vincze, J. (1991), Privatisation and Innovation, background paper for OECD (1993), Budapest: IKU.

Lipsey, R. G. and Carlaw, K. (1998), Technology policies in neo-classical and structuralist-evolutionary models, *STI Review*, No. 22, pp. 31-73.

Lundvall, B-Å. (ed.) (1992), *National Systems of Innovation: Towards a theory of innovation and interactive learning*, London: Pinter.

Lundvall, B-Å. and Borrás, S. (1998), *The Globalising Learning Economy: Implications for Innovation Policy*, Luxembourg: Office for Official Publications of the European Communities.

Metcalfe, J.S., and Georghiou, L. (1998), Equilibrium and evolutionary foundations of technology policy, *STI Review*, No. 22, pp. 75-100.

Mowery, D. and Rosenberg, N. (1989), *Technology and the Pursuit of Economic Growth,* Cambridge: Cambridge University Press.

Nelson, R.R. (ed.) (1993), *National Innovation Systems: A comparative study*, New York: Oxford University Press.

Nelson, R.R. (1995), Recent evolutionary theorizing about economic change, *Journal of Economic Literature*, 33, pp. 48-90.

Nelson, R. and Winter, S. (1982), *An Evolutionary Theory of Economic Change*, Cambridge, Mass.: The Belknap Press of Harvard University.

OECD (1992), *TEP: The Key Relationships*, Paris: OECD.

OECD (1993), *Science, Technology and Innovation Policies: Hungary*, Paris: OECD.

OECD (1997), *Creativity, Innovation and Job Creation,* Paris: OECD.

OECD (1998), *Science, Technology and Industry Outlook*, Paris: OECD.

OMFB (1995), A kormány muszaki fejlesztési koncepciója, Eloterjesztés a kormány részére (The government's concept on technological development: A proposal for the government), *OMFB Híradó*, November.

OMFB (1997), *Tudományos kutatás és kísérleti fejlesztés alakulása 1990-1996* (Research and Technological Development Indicators, 1990-1996), Budapest.

OMFB (1998), *A Központi Mûzaki Fejlezstési Alapapprogram 1997. évi felhasznásáról* (Report on the Use of the Central Technological Development Fund), Budapest.

Pavitt, K. (1984): Patterns of technical change: Towards a taxonomy and theory, *Research Policy*, 13, pp. 343-373.

Radosevic, S. (1994), Strategic technology policy for Eastern Europe, *Economic Systems*, 18, pp. 87-116.

Rosenberg, N. (1983), *Inside the Black Box: Technology and economics*, Cambridge: Cambridge University Press.

Rothwell, R. (1993), 'The Fifth Generation of Innovation Process', in: Oppenländer, K. H. and Popp, W. (eds): Privates und Staatliches Innovations- management, München: ifo, Institut für Wirtschaftforschung.

Teubal, M. (1998), Enterprise restructuring and embeddedness: An innovation systems and policy perspective, paper presented at INTECH Conference on *The Economics of Industrial Structure and Innovation Dynamics*, Lisbon, 16-17 October.

Tóth, G. L. (1994), Technological change, multinational entry and re- structuring: The Hungarian telecommunications equipment industry, *Economic Systems*, 18, pp. 179-196.

Vincze, J. (1991), Kutatás-fejlesztés és K+F finanszírozás a gyógyszer- és vegyiparban (R and D Activity and Financing of R and D in the Hungarian Chemical and Pharmaceuticals Industry), mimeo, Budapest: IKU.

von Tunzelman, G.N. (1995), Technology *and Industrial Progress: The foundations of economic growth*, Aldershot: Edward Elgar.

Section 4:
Transition and the Path Dependency of Innovation Strategies

Introduction

ANNE LORENTZEN, BRIGITTA WIDMAIER, MIHÁLY LAKI

One of the decisive factors influencing the outcome of post socialist transition is the adaptive capacity of economic agents such as firms, households and other economic institutions. Individual attitudes and social networks have developed during the long period of soviet socialist economy and they are often incompatible with the principles of a market-led economy in a democratic political order. In other words, the question which is the central issue for this chapter could be formulated: is *homo sovieticus* (accommodated to and involved in socio-economic relationships of the Soviet socialist economy) *able* or motivated to embark on the rules of the Western type market economy? Is the knowledge and experience, also known as human capital, which has been accumulated and the enterprise culture developed under different conditions useful or rather a hindrance in the process of adaptation? As a frame of reference it is asked what the differences between the rules and institutions of the planned economy and the market economy are that call for adaptation?

The chapters in this section approach the above questions from different levels: While Baca's contribution is based on research about intra-enterprise aspects, Laki's empirical focus is the small and medium sized enterprise area, whereas van Zon has directed his interest towards the comparison of two national economies. All three of them mainly focus on the post socialist economy but, instead of dealing with exclusively *economic* transactions within companies, governments or households, van Zon, Baca and Laki include socio-cultural and historical factors influencing the behaviour of economic agents. They describe and analyse how the accumulated knowledge and experience from the socialist past influences the decisions and transactions of economic agents even though their environment has changed into something quite different, namely a market-oriented economy.

Baca has done field work in several foreign-owned Hungarian firms. She has interviewed both non Hungarian and Hungarian managers of these companies about difficulties encountered when introducing Western management practices, how problems may have been overcome, and how behaviour by local employees is to be explained or understood. Consulting with Hungarian experts and scientists who have done research in Hungarian companies, the author found that they gave different explanations for what often to non Hungarian managers appeared as irrational and counterproductive behaviour. The difference between interpretations given by foreign managers and Hungarian experts shows that wide-spread attitudes and beliefs based upon common historical and social experience (i.e. national culture) influence the frames of reference used by different groups involved in this study. The relevance of informal networks, for example, was not visible for foreign managers while it was repeatedly mentioned by expert informants as a major element in explaining some issues.

Laki begins by showing that the economic share of private activities was quite substantial in Hungary before the transition. His thesis is that people active in the private sector were very aware of the political risks involved but, on the other hand, the risk involved in market transactions was outweighed by the existence of shortage-induced demand. Based on this experience, many Hungarians developed a business strategy which gave them a chance to adapt successfully to the circumstances of the changing socialist business environment. After the collapse of socialism the number of small private businesses rapidly increased but the vast majority of them have been unable to expand. As could have been expected, general politically driven institutional changes have made small businesses vulnerable, and the saturation and contraction of markets has confronted them with new difficulties. The new institutions established through small business protection policies seem thus far unable to counterbalance the negative effects of these current trends.

Van Zon presents a comparative analysis of Ukrainian and Polish post socialist development. He challenges the idea that all CEE countries follow similar development paths, although at different speed, from socialism to capitalism. He argues that a time-lag between developmental stages in Poland and Ukraine is not a sufficient explanation. A long list of historical, cultural and structural differences between the two countries is used to describe why the economic performance of these two countries of the post socialist transition differ so much from one another. The case of the big Ukrainian factory Avtozaz in Zaporozhye strengthens the argument that path-dependent structural differences exist, and it is shown that such differences are observable even in the events of everyday practice.

A general conclusion of the chapters in this section is that a remarkable amount of knowledge has been accumulated during the period of socialism, and has proven useful in surviving the collapse of the socialist system and the first years of post socialist transition. Countries in which the rigid (non-reformed) planning system existed faced many more disadvantages than did those that had undertaken reforms earlier than 1998 (van Zon). Flexible adaptation of legal forms or diversification of activities (Laki) and sophisticated informal networks within large firms (Baca) are based on the controversial heritage of the socialist past. Creative entrepreneurs and managers have modified and developed these elements of business strategy so that they are also able to use them in the new context of privately owned companies.

The authors emphasise the importance of the heritage of socialism, but it would be misleading to overestimate the efficacy of this heritage. Without learning business strategies used in market economies, (including marketing, business planning, and advertisement) private firms cannot develop the adaptive capacities which are necessary to master the transition processes successfully.

10 Industrial Development and Institutional Diversity in Central and Eastern Europe

The cases of Ukraine and Poland

HANS VAN ZON

Does history matter?

The aim of this contribution is to bring order in the numerous actors and factors determining the variety of industrial development paths in Central and Eastern Europe after the collapse of communism. To this end industrial development of independent Ukraine will be compared with that of Poland. It will be argued that socio-economic dynamics in post-socialist Poland and Ukraine are qualitatively different, mainly due to the different institutional and historical legacies of both countries.

It is conspicuous that the economic gap between Western Europe on the one hand and the former communist bloc countries on the other hand has become much greater than it was in pre-socialist times (see Table 10.1).

Table 10.1 Per capita GNP in Central and Eastern Europe, 1910, 1990 and 1997

	1910	1990*	1997*
	Western Europe=100	EU =100	EU =100
Eastern Europe**	45		
Russia	45	39	23
Hungary	58	37	37
Bulgaria	42	29	19
Romania	48	26	23
Poland		27	32
Czech Republic		62	57
Slovak Republic		47	42
Ukraine		29	11

* GDP per capita at current Purchasing Power Parities (USD)
** the part of Europe that underwent the socialist experiment
Source: for 1910 Berend and Ranki,1982, p. 158; for 1990 and 1997 Podkaminer 1998, p. 19.

It raises the question of the impact of socialist industrialisation. Within post-socialist Europe differences in development levels are now much greater than they were during the 1980s. For example, whereas GDP of Poland in 1997 was above the level of the late 1980s, Ukrainian GDP is now approximately on one third of its 1990 level. Whereas in 1990 Ukraine's GDP per capita (at current purchasing power parities) was 106 per cent of Poland's, it was in 1997 only 35 per cent (Table 10.2).

Table 10.2 GNP per capita at current Purchasing Power Parities (USD), from 1998 constant PPPs 1996

	1990	1997
Poland	4221	6298
Ukraine	*4490*	*2195*
Bulgaria	4487	3768
Croatia	4811	4852
Czech republic	9526	11319
Hungary	5750	7249
Romania	1120	1327
Russia	5995	4480
Slovakia	7313	8399
Slovenia	9225	11290
EU average	**15440**	**19816**

Source: Podkaminer, 1998, p. 19 and Economic Commission for Europe,1997

In terms of differences in development level, the pre-socialist economic geography seems to have re-emerged again in Central and Eastern Europe. The countries that were not, or almost not industrialised in pre-socialist times, face now the threat of complete de-industrialisation, while the countries that had known industrialisation under capitalist conditions are recovering easier and faster and are able to find ways to regenerate their industrial capacities.[1] A rough yardstick for economic regeneration and attractiveness for foreign investors is the per capita inflow of foreign direct investment that varies highly across Central and Eastern Europe (Table 10.3). Apparently, history matters very much for the capacity of the post-socialist countries to regenerate their economies. Also, the question emerges to what extent socialism has created a base for modern economic development.

Table 10.3 Cumulative per capita inflow of FDI
(1991-1996, US$)

Poland	126
Ukraine	*23*
Bulgaria	65
Croatia	123
Czech republic	617
Hungary	1256
Romania	61
Russia	42
Slovakia	128
Slovenia	325

Source: Podkaminer, 1998, p. 19 and Economic Commission for Europe, 1997

Ukraine in the light of the Polish experience

The question of the role of history, as well as the general theme of diversity of development paths in Central Europe will be addressed by analysing the cases of Poland and Ukraine. These countries are on the extremes of the spectrum of development paths in Central and Eastern Europe. A short account of transition in Ukraine will be given referring to Polish transition, highlighting differences between the two countries in order to come to grips with the dynamics underlying their development paths. In short, the question is why Poland emerged as the fastest growing economy in Europe, while the Ukrainian economy has faced the steepest economic decline among the European transition economies and has, by early 1998, still not bottomed out.[2] (See table 10.4).

The description can, of course, not be exhaustive. It will be a provisional enumeration and grouping of factors and actors that are, most probably, important in explaining differences in development paths.

For ages the larger part of Ukraine has been part of the Russian Empire. Ukraine hardly had known genuine capitalism, while Poland, more particular the South Western part, has had some, albeit shallow, history of capitalist development.[3] The larger part of Ukraine had known more than 70 years of communism, unlike Poland, that had less than 45 years of communist rule.

In 1991 independence came in Ukraine more or less as a gift. The nationalist movement is rather young and was mainly active in Western Ukraine, especially those provinces that were under Polish rule during the interbellum. Independence did not primarily come as a result of the activities of the nationalist movement but above all as a result of external forces that brought about the dissolution of the Soviet Union. Ukraine has never been an independent state and nation. It means that a new state apparatus had to be build up as well as the competence to govern a country. This task was complicated as the nation was not ethnically homogenous, like Poland, because approximately 20 per cent of Ukrainian's population is Russian.[4]

Table 10.4 Ukraine and Poland, some economic indicators

	Poland	Ukraine
Population (1996)	38.6 mn	50.9 mn
GDP (1997)	137 bn USD	49.7 bn USD
Industry as share of GDP	39%(1993)	34 % (1995)
Agriculture as share of GDP	7% (1993)	12 % (1995)
Exports of goods (1997)	27.106 bn USD	14.431 bn USD
Imports of goods(1997)	37.721 bn USD	17.128 bn USD

Source: Podkaminer et al, 1998, Economist Intelligence Unit.

The Ukrainian economy was much more integrated into the Soviet economy than was the Polish. Approximately 90 per cent of exports were in 1991 with other republics of the former Soviet Union. Poland had in 1991 only 18 per cent of exports with the former Communist bloc.[5]

Especially the dependence on imported energy was striking. In 1996, 52 per cent of Ukrainian imports consisted of energy, mainly from Russia and Kazakhstan. While Ukraine paid only 3 per cent of the world market price for oil in 1990, now it is on the world market level.[6] Apart from the oil price shock, there was the problem of interruption of energy supplies that interrupted the working of industry. In 1996, for Poland net imports of energy constitute only 4 per cent of total imports.[7] Already from the mid-1970s and onwards, Poland began to pay prices for energy that were following world market prices.

Ukraine was, unlike Poland, very isolated up to 1991, and the crisis of socialism was much less visible compared to Poland. Poland was the weakest link in the communist bloc. Ukraine was, on the other hand, one of the bastions of communism. In 1991, there was in Ukraine not much popular support for the change over to market economy and parliamentary democracy. This in sharp contrast to Poland where a popular movement was a major factor in the demise of communism. Nevertheless, communist rule was in Ukraine much sharper than in Poland. Millions of Ukrainians died as a result of Stalinist repression. During the 1930s, millions of Ukrainians starved as the result of the politically induced famine.

Whereas communist rule in Ukraine was almost totalitarian, trying to regulate every domain of life, it was authoritarian in Poland. In Poland a countervailing force to the communist rule was the Catholic Church. In the shadow of this church an embryonic civil society could develop. Civil society hardly developed in Soviet Ukraine.

This partly explains the lack of support for reform policies in Ukraine. Another factor is the lack of a revolutionary elite in Ukraine. It is the former nomenclature, the co-opted Communist elite that took over power in Ukraine, in the absence of a countervailing force. There were and are hardly interest groups advocating market-oriented reforms.

In Poland there was, apart from the recognition by a large part of the ruling elite that communism was a complete failure, a strong second economy that developed under communism.[8] Also, a private agricultural sector always existed in communist Poland. Moreover, Poland has had the experience of market-oriented reforms under socialism, that taught Polish leaders about the limits of reform of centrally planned economy. In Poland, a powerful coalition across the political spectrum developed which supported market-oriented reforms. The reformed communist party, transformed into a social democratic party and in government during 1996-1997, also pursued a policy of strengthening market economy with, of course, a social face. This does not mean that there are no powerful forces hampering marketization. For example, the Polish coal industry up to now successfully resisted marketization. However, in Poland market economy attained a critical mass.

In Ukraine, on the other hand, there are no powerful pro-reform forces identifiable. Political parties are rallied around persons and not so much around ideas. In parliament, that has a big impact upon policy making, the overwhelming majority has taken an anti-reform stand, especially after the elections of March 1998 in which the communist party appeared as by far the largest political party.

In Poland there seems to be a broad consensus about the market as the major co-ordinating mechanism in the economy.

In Ukraine privatisation is in its early phase and the economy is still state dominated. The government is issuing a flood of decrees regulating economic

Scheme 1.10 Development paths of Ukraine and Poland compared

	Ukraine	**Poland**
Pre-socialist history	almost no experience with cap. development	industrialisation in South-West
	very week civil society	civil society more developed
	no experience of independent state	experience, although short, with nation state
	new nationalism	old nationalism
	strong collectivism/weak individualism	week collectivism/strong individualism
		experienced epochal changes of Reanissance and Enlightenment
Socialist history	70 years communist experience for lager part of Ukraine	40 years communist experience
	Stalinist socio-psychological syndrome	
	isolation from world society/-economy	more open compared to Ukraine
		more links with developed West
	totalitarianism	authoritarianism
		significant private sector (agriculture, second economy)
		countervailing force of Catholic Church
		history of economic reforms
	integration in Soviet economy	
	enterprise centre of social and pol. life	
Economic system	state dominated, bureaucratically	critical mass of market economy
	controlled economy	
	shadow economy 60 per cent of econ.act. corruption	
	involution	evolution
Economic structure	12 per cent of GDP agriculture	7 per cent of GDP agriculture
	52 per cent of imports energy (1996)	
	ind. enterpr. hardly adjusted	industrial, restructuring, corporate restructuring

	25 per cent of industry used to produce for military large share of intermediate products heavy emphasis on heavy industry	
Economic polidy	protectionism control mania of bureaucracy	liberal import policy
	a-liberal policy 'social market economy' Ukrainian style no commitment to reform	liberal economic policy market economy shock therapy
Economic environment	very weak state very low level of economic competence GDP decline 97/98 66 per cent impoverished population de-industrialisation very low level of social capital	GDP growth 97/98 8 per cent economic dynamism industrial regeneration
International env.	partnership agreement EU	association agreement EU prospective EU member
	far away from prosperous markets Ukraine very weakly inserted in European institutional set-up	bordering European Union gradually integrated into EU
	Ukr. products not competitive on OECD markets	prospective markets EU
	no protection for import competition	import competition furthers domestic competition
	very low level of FDI manageable debt, but very dependant upon IMF support conflict potential with Russia	moderate level of FDI moderate debt burden
	low level of trade with OECD	much trade with OECD

activity in such a way that the economy looks more like a planned economy than a market economy.[9] Even price setting is still controlled in many ways. Whereas in Poland 45 per cent of the work force is in small business, it is in Ukraine only 10 per cent (1997).[10]

Each transition economy is faced with the problem of conflicting time scales; transition in one field is proceeding faster than in other fields and this friction causes adaptation problems. In Ukraine these conflicting time scales seem to be of another nature than in Poland. There is the example of adjustment of indu-strial structures to international competition. In Poland industry emerged from socialism more competitive than Ukrainian industry. This is related to the fact that, due to the Polish history of market-oriented reforms, Polish industry was better prepared for competition. This being better prepared is also related to the fact that Polish industry was less integrated into the communist bloc than Ukraine and the weight of military production was less overwhelming in Poland. All these factors made Polish industry, on average, less vulnerable for international competition than Ukrainian industry. Import competition, introduced during the 1990s, has contributed greatly, coupled with the slow pace of reform, to the demise of the larger part of Ukrainian industry. [11] Although Polish industry was faced with a steep decline in industrial production immediately after the opening up of the economy, import competition combined with restructuring and marketization has laid the base for impressive growth figures since the mid-1990s.

Given the above mentioned factors influencing development paths in Poland and Ukraine it is not surprising to see that Poland in the mid-1990s has become the fastest growing economy in Europe while Ukraine has been one of the fastest declining European economies. In Poland there seems to be a critical mass of market economy, that can function as a motor for growth.

The conclusion is that different development paths of Ukraine and Poland are related to transition policies, institutional set-up, historical legacies and different international environments. It is certainly not one factor, for example transition policies that can be blamed for the worse performance of Ukraine.[12]

Institutional diversity and path dependence

Many observers of the transition process assume that the difference between Poland and Ukraine, and other Central and Eastern European countries, is mainly a phase difference. This approach is especially prominent in the publications of international institutions like IMF, World Bank, OECD and European Bank.[13]

The assumption is that all transition countries have to go through a specific sequence of phases and that the end result will be, if all policy recommendations will be followed up, a smoothly functioning market economy, with, of course, its own national traits.

The idea of similarity of development paths will be challenged here. Taking the economies and societies of Ukraine and Poland, important structural differences emerge, although both socio-economic systems are still fluid. Two of these structural differences will be shortly described.

Different modes of interaction between the state and the economy

There is the different role of the state and the state bureaucracy. Given the overriding role of the state in economic life it is obvious that the state bureaucracy in Ukraine plays a much more important role than in Poland.[14] There are, however, also distinct bureaucratic cultures. It seems that in Ukraine, control mania of the bureaucracy has always been much more pronounced than in Central European countries, like Poland.[15] This is not only related to the long communist past but also to the Tsarist legacy.[16] Moreover, corruption in the state bureaucracy has become much more a way of life in Ukraine compared to Poland. A recent survey of the European Bank found that the countries of the former Soviet Union scored higher in the world corruption league than any other region in the world. Ukraine received the highest possible ranking for corruption among officials.[17] The bureaucracy in Ukraine can be characterised as parasitary, whereas the bureaucracy in Poland seems to move in the direction of a facilitative bureaucracy.[18] What does 'parasitary' mean for small business in terms of money? It means that in Ukraine on average a total amount of about 2000 dollars in bribes is needed to be allowed to start a business.[19] Thus, barriers to entry are in Ukraine almost prohibitive, while relatively low in Poland. A jungle of often contradictory laws and the absence of the rule of law facilitate corruption in Ukraine.

With respect to the decision-making process, one can not speak about a clear division of power in Ukraine, whereas this seems to be the case in Poland. According to the constitution, the president and parliament fulfil tasks that in other countries are fulfilled by government. In Ukraine the new state, an arena for clan-infighting, seems to become disintegrated without a clear demarcation of competencies between president, parliament and government. More important in this respect is the fact that political power in Ukraine gradually has become criminalized. Mafia, police and bureaucracy are not only co-operating but also intertwined. According to a report for Ukrainian president Leonid

Kuchma, organised crime poses an immediate threat for the stability of the state.[20] Although Poland also has problems with bureaucracy, corruption and crime the role of the state seems fundamentally different compared to Ukraine. In Ukraine, the state is increasingly unable to influence the behaviour of public and private actors. The Ukrainian state has become a classical weak state, unable to resist all kind of pressure groups, especially those around leading clans. Whereas in Ukraine the main organizing principle governing state-economy interactions has become of a pre-modern traditional nature, that is patronage relationships, in Poland informal arrangements, albeit still important, increasingly have been replaced by modern organizing principles, with due respect to the rule of law.[21] In Ukraine the distinction between private and public is increasingly blurred while this distinction has become more important in Poland. Related to this, one can say that in Poland there is an increasing institutional encapsulation of agency, i.e. the guidance of agents through formal and informal institutions, while this process has hardly started in Ukraine.[22]

In Ukraine institutional consolidation hardly occurred. Elster et al (1998) define the degree of 'horizontal differentiation' as the conceptual criterion for consolidation. A measure of such differentiation is the degree of insulation of institutional spheres from each other and the limited convertibility of status attributes from one sphere to the other.[23] State socialism is an order that systematically obstructs horizontal differentiation and maximizes inter-domain convertibility of resources. In this respect Ukraine is still very close to state socia-lism, while the extraction process from socialism is in an advanced stage in Poland.

Related to the specific role of the state in Ukrainian economy is the role of the shadow economy, that is the non-registered part of the economy that has attained enormous proportions. The Ukrainian government assesses the share of the shadow economy at approximately 60 per cent of estimated Gross National Product. This is higher than in most other countries in the former Soviet Union and much higher than in Poland, where the share is around 30 per cent of GNP.[24] It means for Ukraine that it is almost impossible to implement an effective economic policy. The high level of taxation and corruption within the state bureaucracy furthers the shadow economy. It means that there are powerful lobbies, also within the state, that are interested in a large shadow sector. Experts of the Ukrainian Centre for Social and Economic Research think that in Ukraine the shadow economy is constituting not only a shadow sector in the economy but a parallel illegal power that grows and begins to duplicate the most important functions of the state.[25]

A lot of illegal money is earned with foreign trade.[26] Estimates of illegal capital exports since 1991 vary from 20 to 100 billion dollars.[27] Dimensions of illegal trade and capital flight are higher than Poland ever has known.

It seems that in Ukraine the state has lost control over economic development, although the registered part of the economy is still state dominated, whereas in Poland the economy is still governable. In Poland the state seems to provide the backbone of an institutional framework that allows market economy to develop, while in Ukraine the state constitute the backbone of an institutional environment that prevents a market economy to develop. Institutional environment should be interpreted here in the broad sense. Institutions do not only include formal organisations, but also more informal conventions, habits and routines, which are sustained over time (and through space).[28] North (1993) defined institutions as 'the humanly devised constraints that structure human interaction'. They are made up of formal constraints (e.g., rules, laws, and institutions), informal constraints (e.g., norms of behaviour, conventions, self-imposed codes of conduct) and their enforcement characteristics. Together they define the incentive structure of society and specifically economies.[29]

Comparing Ukraine and Poland in terms of incentive structures, one can say that in Ukraine formal and informal constraints prevent people and enterprises to produce efficiently. In Ukraine one can rather speak of a disincentive structure, paralysing society and economy. In Poland, although numerous obstacles exist for enterprises to produce efficiently, the marketization of the economy is progressing continuously.

In Ukraine the registered part of the economy is still state dominated, highly regulated and redistributive in character. Early 1998, it was still more rewarding for many economic sectors and regions to lobby for state subsidies than to enhance development potential in their own sector or region, related to the fact that profits are immediately siphoned off to the centre.[30] A network of powerful lobbies supports the reproduction of this redistributive mechanism. At the national level, the ruling elite, how diverse it may be, seems to be interested in the maintenance of this mechanism in order to keep the weak Ukrainian state together. The redistributive mechanism has been, hitherto, a major instrument of control.

In Poland, where the state is much stronger and centrifugal forces weaker, there was and is comparatively less support for the maintenance of the redistributive mechanism.

Attitudes and economic behaviour

It is especially in the sphere of attitudes, habits and routines that barriers for market-oriented development exist. Many observers of change in transition economies share the idea that attitudes constitute a formidable barrier in the transformation process. For obvious reasons, this attitudinal complex hardly has been studied.[31] This attitudinal syndrome is especially pronounced in Ukraine and other states of the former Soviet Union. The communist and Tsarist past has produced a system of values, norms and behavioural patterns that is quite persistent. The properties of the syndrome can be summarised in the following way: the Tsarist and communist past have created a cult of power that made the attribute of power, and therewith also the lack of it, of overriding importance in social life. Absolutist power was the rule. Self-organisation of society was almost absent, also in Tsarist times. Later, the wish of the party-state to control all aspects of social life produced a control mania. A correlate is the aversion to delegate power and with employees, an aversion to assume responsibility.[32] Initiative was not rewarded but punished. The state took, in principle, care for almost everything in the individual's life, there was care from birth to grave. This stimulated a general passiveness.

Independent thinking was discouraged, also in the universities. The party-state promoted a simplistic world outlook, based on exclusion, i.e. all opinions other than that of the party are not true. The disregard of truth in public life, absolutist power and lawlessness created distrust in public life. In recruitment mechanisms for influential posts, the nomenclature system, loyalty was of utmost importance, less so competence. This furthered incompetence on all levels. Competent people were often marginalised. The utmost importance of obedience created people who comply with anything that is imposed upon them.

The properties attributed to the socio-psychological syndrome became most pronounced in Stalin's time, although many of these properties already developed in Tsarist times and are described in 19th century Russian literature.[33] The constituent elements of the syndrome form an interrelated whole, reinforcing each other. Therefore it is so tenacious. Seven years after independence of Ukraine and the collapse of the party-state it appears that this syndrome is very persistent, although with transition to market economy the circumstances in which Ukrainian citizens lived changed fundamentally. For example, whereas in Soviet times own initiative was often punished, nowadays it is crucial for survival.

The set of values, attitudes and behavioural patterns is hindering economic development in many ways. For example, trust is a basic value in developed market economies, underpinning economic growth. Ukraine is an ideal-typical example of a low-trust society.[34]

Regular visitors of Ukraine and Poland will notice, that the syndrome as described above for Ukraine, is in Poland much more shallow and less pronounced, related to the fact that communist institutions were less deeply rooted in Polish society.

Elster et al (1998) argue that Soviet-type communism could absorb the basic concepts and perceptions of an agrarian society and use it to its own ends. They bring forward the hypothesis that agrarian societies are more receptive to a Soviet-type forced industrialisation than advanced industrial societies. Under Communism as well as in pre-revolutionary Russia, obligations of personal obedience tend to be essentially unlimited. There was a personal view of authority. 'Power is seen as a means of control of society rather than a social relation whose skilful design releases it creative and learning capacities'.[35] Elster et al (1998) conclude that 'while communism promoted industrialisation, urbanization, mass education, and the secularization of society, it did not aim at and in fact accomplish the creation of primarily individualistic values such as toleration of inequality, open-mindedness for the diversity and plurality of values, attitudes, and life styles'.[36] Soviet-type communism means industrialisation without modernisation.

Different modes of extraction from centrally planned economy

Poland and Ukraine constitute two quite different modes of extraction from centrally planned economy. The institutional transformation towards capitalism in Poland already began before the demise of centrally planned economy and the party state. In Ukraine the abolition of centrally planned economy came, more or less, as a result of the implosion of the Soviet Union. Thus, extraction from centrally planned economy occurred in Poland much earlier than in Ukraine and in a completely other context. This gave Poland the scope of manoeuvre for shock therapy.

In Ukraine transformation costs are much higher than in Poland, as communist institutions are much deeper rooted in Ukrainian society compared to Polish society and the distortion of economic structures at the end of communist rule was in Poland less pronounced compared to Ukraine.

Although the basis of the redistributive state is eroding quickly and the state has less means available to redistribute, the redistributive system is reproduced as the state and criminal groupings are burdening profit making industrial enterprises in a prohibitive way. The economic system that has emerged in Ukraine leads to involution, a system that eats its own economic base, whereas Poland's economic system allows evolution.[37] In Ukraine, capital is systematically channelled from the sphere of production to the sphere of exchange.

The economic system of Ukraine can be described as an archipelago of economic subsystems with quite different operating mechanisms. There is the large sector of state owned enterprises where the state interferes continuously, the bazaar economy with its petty traders, the emerging commercial-financial sector, etc. The redistributive mechanism keeps this archipelago together. This mechanism prevents a productive capitalism to develop. Conversely, in Poland, the market economy emerged as the dominant subsystem and can expand at the expense of other subsystems. Although in Poland some sectors, like the coal and steel industry, are hardly restructured and still dependent on state support, they are gradually encapsulated in a more competitive environment and budget constraints are hardening.

Many observers of transitional economies implicitly assume that the emer-ging 'market sector' is so dynamic that it will push aside other, less dynamic economic subsectors and that the market will become the dominating operating mechanism because it will prove policy makers to be superior. However, many countries and regions in the less developed world show that politically constituted involution may be a structural phenomenon. There is also the example of Sicily, where social and economic development is structurally retarded by the criminalisation of society and economy, although Sicily is embedded in the Italian nation state, which is part of the developed West.[38]

According to Hayek, the public order in the context of a developed market economy, as based on general rules rather than specific commands, is able to co-ordinate behaviour while allowing wide latitude for individual choice and variation.[39] It seems that in Ukraine such a public order is largely absent.

Economic and social systems are generally both enabling and constraining. Comparing the Polish and Ukrainian economic systems, it seems that in Ukraine the evolving economic system is mainly producing prohibitive constraints. The Polish economic system is producing more enabling constraints.

Given the structural character of above mentioned constraints, it seems that Ukraine is moving in another direction than Poland and that the difference in the social and economic situation in both countries does not merely reflect a phase difference.

What is the industrial legacy of socialism?

Again, the question emerges to what extent socialism has created assets for modern economic development. Although the question can not be answered satisfactory, some of the author's experiences in the Ukrainian town of Zaporozhye may be instructive.[40]

Zaporozhye had developed in Soviet times into an industrial town, with almost one million inhabitants, with a lot of high value added production, like transformers, aircraft engines and cars. There is the example of Avtozaz, the local car manufacturer with a capacity of 300.000 cars, that used to produce in 1993 150.000 cars. Ukrainian newspapers write that it is one of the most modern factories in Europe, with a new assembly line installed in 1992.

Having visited the factory several times and after numerous informal talks with employees the following can be said: Avtozaz was a monopolist of cheap cars for the former Soviet Union. It was also known for its poor quality cars which quality deteriorated even further after disruption of supplies since independence of Ukraine in 1991. Import competition since 1991 meant the death of Avtozaz and in 1996 only 7000 cars were produced. The factory is outmoded and even the new production line, one out of three, is not very modern as it is not fully automised.

Production organisation hardly has changed since independence. There is the example of quality control. Although on paper quality control exists, it does not work in practice. If a component of the car is missing, the assembly is not halted as is usual in car factories in developed Western countries. Employees are expected to write down what is missing so that it can be later inserted. Very often, employees forget to do so.

Employees are often very negligent. Drinking on the work place is common. Alcoholism very much affects the production process. Girls work on the assembly line with tasks that they are not strong enough to perform.

To be short, behind the facade of so-called modern production developed in Soviet times, a Soviet style production organisation and outmoded production outlays are hidden. Management runs the enterprise with an engineer's mentality with little attention to the social aspects of production. The management revolution as occurred in the developed market economies, went unnoticed. In Zaporozhye, skills are very much devalued, due to long standstill in production, brain drain, and the deficient work organisation.

Daewoo recently decided to go into a joint venture with Avtozaz and to invest, over a period of six years, 1.3 billion dollars. However, Daewoo cars will be produced at the Avtozaz-plant in Illichevsk, near Odessa, and not in

Zaporozhye. In the first phase, production will be confined to assembly, which requires few skills. The question is also if the promised investment will indeed materialise, given the enormous difficulties that generally exist for industrial producers in Ukraine.

The example of Avtozaz shows that the existence of high value added production created under socialist conditions does not say much about the potential for high value added production under conditions of competition. Modern production assumes innovative capacities and here was the weak point of production organisation developed under socialist conditions. Whereas human capital in Ukraine, in terms of technical knowledge of individuals, may be, on average, on a rather high level, although shrinking rapidly, social capital, that refers to features of social organisation, such as networks, norms and trust, that facilitate co-ordination and co-operation for mutual benefit, is on a very low level in Ukraine. This social capital is crucial for modern economic development.[41]

It can be said that socialist industrialisation has meant channelling huge resources in establishing the facade of a modern industrial society, ignoring the complex social fabric that is underpinning it. In the developed market economies, this social fabric is the result of a long evolution, involving learning and unlearning, the creation of new institutions, the establishment of competition as well as co-operation.

The concept of path dependence

The industrial development path followed under socialist conditions does not tell us much about the industrial trajectories to be followed in post-socialism, under conditions of competition. The socialist experience has had an adverse impact on social capital, that is a crucial ingredient in any industrial innovation trajectory. On the other hand, the cases of Poland and Ukraine show that the pre-socialist past, mainly reflected in informal institutional arrangements, shapes to a considerable extent present industrial development paths.

This is not to say that the industrial future is pre-determined and that there is no scope of manoeuvre for policy makers.

Generally, for most policy-makers in the relative stable Western countries, it is clear that the scope of manoeuvre is limited. Governments have to dance with chains on their ankles. In destabilized countries these limitations are even stricter. The interplay of different logic in the political and economic process delimits very much the manoeuvring space of governments. The art of governing is partly to know the limits of governing, i.e. to know path dependence.

It becomes clear that governments can not impose transformation policies irrespective of the various interests which are at stake. Transformation policies are the outcome of pacts and negotiations between various interest groups and this outcome may differ significantly from government declarations and adhered ideologies.

Numerous authors have emphasized that the transition of Central and Eastern European economies does not mean an abrupt break with the past, although there are qualitative changes, but an institutional reconfiguration in which new elements are merged with elements of the past order. David Stark (1990), for example, described the emerging property relations in Hungary as recombinant property, a quite diffuse mixture of private and public.[42] Various studies dealing with network analysis in post-socialist countries found that new networks evolved organically out of old.

The structure of the historically grown social and economic system, implemented policies and the impact of the changing international environment determine path dependence. The various industrial development paths should be seen in the context of their path dependencies.

Trajectories of development paths can be outlined by excluding specific development paths. A spectrum of probable development paths can be outlined on the basis of identifying major structural constraints that differ from country to country and even differ across industrial sectors in the same country.

The list of structural constraints as outlined for Ukraine, by contrasting it with the Polish case, makes it plausible that in the short or medium term Ukraine will not be able to emulate the Polish trajectory.

The way in which Ukrainian and Polish transformation paths were described, contrasting the Ukrainian path in the light of the Polish experience, may have given too rosy a presentation of Polish transformation as Poland scores in all comparisons better than Ukraine. However, also Poland faces many constraints that have not been analysed here. Here, it should also be noticed that in this analysis countries, that is Poland and Ukraine, have been taken as a unit of analysis, contrasting two countries on the extreme of the transformation spectrum in Europe. However, travelling from Eastern Ukraine to Western Poland, change is less abrupt as above description might suggest. Regional variations exist, reflecting the multi-layered character, also from a geographical perspective, of transformation. Eastern Ukraine and Western Poland conform more to the description above than do Western Ukraine and Eastern Poland.

Although factors influencing economic development and explaining divergence in development paths between Poland and Ukraine have been divided into various subgroups, the overview of factors seems to be a sea of unrelated facts (scheme 4).

The comparison of differences between Ukraine and Poland led to the following conclusions:

a. The weight of various factors determining development paths can not be determined and a comprehensive assessment of differences in economic development paths is almost impossible. The overview clarifies why Ukraine is performing worse than Poland, but it is not so clear what is the weight of the various factors. What is, for example, the weight of the over-integration of Ukraine into the Soviet economy and the subsequent dissolution of the Soviet Union, and what is the weight of the energy shock, the weight of the slow pace of reform and the weight of attitudinal barriers.

b. In any explanation of the transformation process, factors at the three following levels: legacies, institutions and policy making, should be taken into account.

c. With respect to industrial development paths and conditions for innovation, many relevant factors mentioned above, such as typical behavioural patterns, modes of interaction state-economy and the shadow economy, are not subject of study and often not tangible. The study of transformation generally does not take into account the general social and economic environment, including formal and informal institutional framework. It is exactly the institutional diversity that explains to a large extent variety of industrial development paths within Central and Eastern Europe.

d. The mode of interaction state-economy seems to be a crucial variable explaining difference in path dependency between Ukraine and Poland.

e. Communism has had an adverse impact on social capital that is a crucial ingredient for modern economic development and any industrial innovation strategy. The apparent re-emergence of the pre-socialist past in present patterns of industrial development can be linked to the shallow nature of socialist industrialisation.

f. In Poland and Ukraine, socio-economic formations are emerging that are qualitatively different.

Notes

1 Per capita industrial production as a share of average per capita industrial production in Europe was in Russia, in 1990, 34 per cent, in Austria-Hungary 82 per cent, in Bulgaria and Romania 33 per cent (Berend and Ranki, p. 159). For that year no figures are available for the territory of present-day Hungary, Poland, Czech Republic and Slovakia. Historical evidence points out that those territories were more industrialized than the above mentioned East European countries.

2 11 June it was announced that over the first five months of 1998, GDP grew by 0.1 per cent. According to the State Statistics Committee, this is the first time since 1989 that GDP has increased (Radio Free Europe, 12 June 1998). However, at the same time Ukraine is faced by a severe financial crisis. Debt servicing over the first quarter of 1998 was more than total income of Ukrainian government over that period. The International Center for Policy Studies expected that Ukraine would see no real GDP growth in 1998 (Eastern Economist 5 June 1998).

3 Industrial development took off in the regions of Donetsk and Krivoi Rog from the second half of 19th century onward.

4 See Pirie, O.S.,1996.

5 Boss, H. ,1993, p.25, and, Economic Commission for Europe, 1992.

6 Boss, H. 1993, p. 7.

7 Economist Intelligence Unit, 1997.

8 The political and economic situation of Poland during the second half of the 1980s was widely perceived within the communist political elite as a deadlock situation. This is widely documented, among others in interviews with former communist leaders and memoirs. The memoirs of former Prime Minister Rakovsky are telling. This perception of deadlock situation led the communist leaders to the round table negotiations with Solidarnosc that lead to the first free elections.

9 Von Hirschhausen, 1996, brought forward the thesis that Ukraine is currently embarking on a path from non-monetary socialism to a monetary planned economy. 'An incredible amount of planning activity is observed in almost all spheres of economic life. We provide proof of that through empirical case studies, carried out personally in about 50 industrial enterprises all over the country. We conclude that the 'window of opportunity', during which substantial reforms can be pushed through based on a large social consensus, is over' (p. 2).

10 See Economist Intelligence Unit, 1998.

11 According to Ukrainian Economic Trends (April 1997), the index of real industrial production in Ukraine was in 1997 42.1 per cent (1990 = 100).

12 For example, von Hirschausen relates the distinct development path of the CIS countries, compared to Central European countries, exclusively to the result of an economic policy that was insufficiently market-oriented (p. 5).

13 See, for example, the yearly Transition Report (EBRD, London), World Development Report (World Bank, Washington) and Cornelius et al, 1997.

14 State expenditures as percentage of GDP were in Ukraine 49.5 per cent of GDP in 1997 and 43.2 per cent of GDP in 1996 (Ukrainian Economic Trends, December 1997).

15 Within Central Europe, Poland is notorious for its bureaucratic red tape. Within the 1998 World Competitiveness rankings, Poland got a low ranking (place 45, Russia place 46, Hungary 28, Czech Republic 38), mainly due to these problems and corruption (Ukraine did not get a ranking)(International Institute for Management Development).

16 According to Walther, 1998, the major reason why Ukraine is so slow to implement reforms '..may lie with the implementation of these reforms in a classic, bloated, imperial Russian bureaucracy - encrusted in a Soviet policy - and reluctant top officials'.

17 The Guardian, 4 November 1997.
18 Poland is the transition economy with the most far-reaching reforms in public administration and local government (see Wiatr,1995)
19 Business Central Europe, June 1997.
20 Zerkalo Nedeli, 10 February 1996, p.6.
21 See Cirtantas, 1995.
22 See Elster, J., Offe, C., Preuss, U.K., 1998, p. 27.
23 Elster et al, p. 31
24 The Guardian, 3 January 1998, p. 2. The size of the black economy compared to the official economy is estimated by the Economist as 45 per cent for Poland, 24 per cent for Italy, 15 per cent for France and 9 per cent for the USA.
25 Ekonomika Ukraini, November 1996, p.11.
26 Zviglyanich, 1996, p. 132.
27 International Herald Tribune, 10 April 1997.
28 Amin and Thrift, p. 16.
29 D. North, 1993, p. 360, ff.
30 The share of funds allocated in the Ukrainian government budget for assistance of enterprises has declined significantly since the early 1990s. However, there are hidden subsidies as the non-payment of the energy bill, and exemption from taxes that allow value-subtracting enterprises to survive.
31 One of the few analyses made of this attitudinal problem are to be found in D.N. Shalin, 1996, and Etkind, A., Gozmann, L. 1992.
32 This is related to the lack of 'horizontal differentiation', mentioned earlier. As Elster et al (1998) notice: 'tight coupling (of institutional spheres) nurtures irresponsible behaviour as it provides ample opportunity, as well as incentives, to either blame others if things go wrong or to positively exploit others (as in the case of 'soft budget constraints' (p. 31).
33 Gontsharov (*Oblomov*) can be mentioned, later Dostojevsky (*Demons*), Tsjechov (*The Cherry Orchard*) and Gogol (*Dead Souls*). The philosophers Berdjaev and Rosenov wrote extensively about the lack of initiative of the Russian intelligentsia.
34 With respect to attitudes, behavioural patterns and organizational routines, important differences between Eastern and Western Ukraine exist, as they also exist between Eastern and Western Poland. For example, Western Ukraine is more entrepreneurial than Eastern Ukraine, related to the fact that some Western provinces only had known socialist rule for approximately 50 years, and were incorporated in the Austrian Empire.
35 Elster et al, (1998) p. 298.
36 Ibid.,p. 301
37 See for an elaboration of the concept involution Bulawoy, 1996,
38 See Putnam, R.,1993.
39 M. Mueller, Z. Tan, 1996, p. 6.
40 See van Zon et al, 1998.
41 See for a thorough analysis of the concept 'social capital', Woolcock, M. 1998.
42 Stark, D. 1990.

References

Amin, A. (1995), *Globalisation, Institutions and Regional Development.* Oxford: Oxford University Press.

Berend, I.T., Ranki,Gy. (1982), *The European Periphery and Industrialization.* Budapest: Akademiai Kiado.

Burawoy, M. (1996), 'The State and Economic Involution: Russia Through a China Lens', *World Development*, Volume 24, nr 6, pp 1105-1117.

Cirtantas, A.M. (1995), 'The Post-Leninist state in a conceptual and empirical examination', *Communist and Post-Communist Studies,* Vol. 28. nr. 4, December.

Cornelius, P.K., Lenain, P.(eds) (1997), *Ukraine: Accelerating the Transition to Market.* IMF: Washington.

Economic Commission for Europe (1993), *Economic Survey of Europe in 1992-1993.* UN: New York, Geneva.

Economic Commission for Europe (1997), *Economic Survey of Europe in 1996-1997,* UN: New York, Geneva.

Economist Intelligence Unit (1998), *Country Profile Poland 1998-1999.* London.

Economist Intelligence Unit (1998), *Country Profile Ukraine 1998-1999.* London.

Elster, J., Offe, C., Preuss, U.K. (1998), *Insitutional Design in Post-communist Societies.* Cambridge Cambridge, University Press.

Etkind, A., Gozmann, L. (1992), *The Psychology of Post-Totalitarianism,* Centre for Research into Communist Economies, London.

Hirschhausen, C. von (1996), *Industrial Restructuring in Ukraine: from socialism to a planned economy?* Discussion Paper No. 144. Deutsches Institut fur Wirtschaftsforschung. Berlin, November.

Mueller, M., Tan, Z. 1996, China in the Information Age, *The Washington Papers,* The Center for Strategic and International Studies, Washington.

North, D. C. (1993), *Institutions, institutional change and economic performance.* Cambridge: Cambridge University Press.

Pirie, O.S. (1996), 'National Identity and Politics in Southern and Eastern Ukraine', *Europe-Asia Studies.* November.

Podkaminer, L. et al. (1998), 'Transition Countries: 1997 External Deficits Lower Than Feared, Stability Again a Priority', *WIIW Research Reports.* No. 243, February.

Putnam, R.D. (1993), *Making democracy work. Civic traditions in modern Italy.* Princeton: Chichester Princeton University Press.

Shalin, D.N. (1996), *Russian Culture at the Cross Roads - paradoxes of postcommunist consciousness,* Westview Press.

Stark, D. (1990), 'Privatization in Hungary - from 'plan to market' or from 'clan to plan', *East European Politics and Societies*, Vol. 4, nr.3, pp. 351-392.

Walther, M. (1998), 'The trouble with IFOS', *Eastern Economist,* 25 May 1998, pp 5-8.

Wiatr, J. (1995), 'The Dilemmas of Re-Organizing the Bureaucracy in Poland during the Democratic Transformation. *Communist and Post-Communist Studies*, Vol. 28, No.1.

Woolcock, M. (1998), 'Social capital and economic development: Towards a theoretical synthesis and policy framework', in *Theory and Society,* 27, 1998, pp 151-208.

Zviglyanich, V. (1996), 'The State and Economic Reform in Ukraine: Ideas, Models, Solutions' Ukrainian *Quarterly,* Vol. LH, no 2 - 3, Summer - Fall.

Zon, H. van, Batako, A., Kreslavska, A. (1998), *Social and Economic Change in Eastern Ukraine - the example of Zaporizhzhya,* Aldershot: Ashgate.

11 Industrial Policy and Small Private Businesses in Extreme Situations

The Hungarian case

MIHÁLY LAKI

In this chapter we shall focus on the development of the Hungarian small business sector before and after the collapse of socialism. Our argumentation is based on research which was made in the period of 1993-1995. The main sources of information are in-depth interviews concerning the detailed history of 50 small businesses which operate in two small Hungarian towns, Eger and Nagykanizsa. We interviewed members of the two local governments responsible for small businesses as well. Moreover we had the opportunity to consult with leading figures of local and of nation-wide business organisations. In co-operation with experts and specialists of ministries and of other governmental bodies we also analysed several documents of industrial policy.

Small businesses in socialist economies

Marx, Lenin, Stalin and other famous designers of communist-socialist society were true believers in mass production and big factories. The disciplined work-forces and high efficiency of big industrial companies and nation-wide organisations in market economies (railway and postal systems) strengthened their hopes that the 'one factory one nation model' would not only be adaptable in the future socialist society but *more efficient* than the existing decentralised capitalist economy based on market co-ordination (Róna-Tas 1997). When and where communists came to power whole economies were nationalised in a short period of time. Small businesses in towns and peasants' farms in the country-side were collectivised as well. Small nationalised units were concentrated (centralised) into big state-owned companies or huge co-operatives. After the brutal or 'voluntary' liquidation of small businesses there was/is no meaning in speaking about any special industrial policy or to search for special institutions responsible for the small businesses.

There were a few exceptions. The majority of the agricultural sector in Poland, a more than marginal part of the service sector and a few small industrial firms in the GDR (during the period of 1949-1972) and in Hungary remained in private hands.

The *strategic* attitude of ruling groups of communists towards these businesses was like in other socialist countries negative discrimination. Moreover communist rulers, both reformers and fundamentalists declared several times that private small businesses were only *provisional elements* of the structure. These transitory forms of ownership would be transformed into co-operatives or into other collective forms of ownership at a higher level of socialism.

The main reason for the expected *temporary existence* of the private sector was the bad (much lower than planned) performance of state-owned companies. There were several signs that since the beginning the robust and highly centralised Stalinist command economy had worked in a very inefficient and chaotic manner. Controversial plan targets, lack of managerial skills and inefficient investments disturbed inter-firm relations and, as a consequence of these negative tendencies, permanent shortages of goods and services characterised the everyday life of the socialist economy. People tried to counterbalance these negative tendencies with spontaneous legal or illegal transactions. This unexpected development was evaluated by the ruling group of communists in different ways. The fundamentalists *victimised* this part of the population because of these activities. They were convinced that the socialist system was workable and even more efficient than the capitalist one. Therefore the transactions were nothing but sabotage of plan targets and of other directives which could be seen as conscious breaking of the law. The official propaganda suggested that these anti socialist activities were managed and stimulated by former capitalist landlords and their clients, supported by foreigners, mainly imperialists and Fascists.

Another group of the leadership realised that these permanently repeated defects were not mistakes or diversive actions of the enemy but were produced by the system. The task was therefore - they argued - *to reform* the system of planning. Instead of victimisation reformers tried to *canalise* into the socialist economic system the legal and illegal private activities of the population.

Institutions of repression and discriminative regulation

We could interpret the waves of reforms and of anti reform periods in Hungary and in other former socialist countries therefore as stages of victimisation or canalisation of legal and illegal private activities. Based on this interpretation we may reconstruct the institutional order and industrial policy concerning small private businesses.

Institutions serving the *rapid elimination* of the small private business sector were established in 1949 when the dictatorship of the proletars was introduced in Hungary. The voluntary associations of small artisans were dissolved. Instead new nation-wide associations were established.

Old and new associations differed remarkably:
1. Membership was free in the old and *mandatory* in the new ones. Every legal small businessman was obliged to join the newly established associations.
2. Old type small business associations were politically independent. Their representatives were elected by the membership. The new ones were *subordinated* to the Communist Party. The management of these associations was selected and delegated by central or local Communist Party organisations.
3. Associations existing in the pre-socialist period usually articulated and defended the interests of their members. The newly formulated associations were not more than a special subsystem of planning. They transferred rules and plan targets to the community of the formally independent small businesses.

Not only associations but other parts of the planning system (tax office, branch ministries) took part in the regulation of small business activities. There were several forms of negative discrimination:
- Small artisans had to have special permission to buy several inputs.
- Entry and exit of local markets were restricted. Small private businesses for example were excluded from markets of other towns.
- State-owned companies were not allowed to subcontract private businesses. Private firms had no permission to deliver goods or services to the state sector,
- Small businesses usually paid more than state-owned firms for the same good or service (discriminative pricing).

There were cases when brutal physical repression and intimidation of private businessmen (peasants) served the discriminative activity of the communist party.

Small private entrepreneurs were excluded from the general system of pensions and of health care. Children of private entrepreneurs were discriminated negatively against the admission policies of secondary schools and universities.

These seriously discriminative initial conditions of small private businesses regulation were gradually modified by economic reforms. Licensing of procurement, prohibition of private-state contracting was abolished in the late fifties. Entry of non local markets by small private businesses was liberalised a few years later. The negative discrimination of children of small business families was abolished in 1962-63. The system of discriminative prices was mainly liquidated by the radical reform in 1968. The 'residue of reforms' (Seleny 1991) increased remarkably but we have to take into consideration here that the rules were *modified only to a certain extent*. Limitation of business activities (limits of size) never has changed. The party-state's superstructure responsible for small business and its internal hierarchy was never reorganised. Associations of small businesses were controlled and managed by local and central communist party organisations and by delegated members of the nomenclature till the collapse of the socialist system.

Throughout the period there were *no guaranties* that the process of liberalisation of the private sector would not be reversed. There were a lot of cases in anti reform periods when discriminative rules were revitalised or new restrictions were introduced.

Special structure of risks

There were two main components of the uncertainties and risks of legal private activities in socialist economies. The risk of market transactions differed from the risk caused by regulative activities of state authorities (or by *the change* of these regulations).

The risk of market entry or of market transactions was relatively low. The permanent shortage and the rigid market behaviour of state-owned enterprises produced several 'empty' market segments and niches which gave the opportunity to small private companies to make profitable businesses. The other side of the coin was that risks produced by the negative discrimination of the political system was high, especially in anti reform periods. In reform periods the political risk of *starting a business* was lower than before. But as we have mentioned, reformers emphasised the *temporary* character of the recovery of the private sector. Therefore private entrepreneurs had no chance to estimate how long this period would be. That is the main reason why it remained relatively risky to maintain or to extend a small business in reform periods.

Successful business strategy

The low risk of market transactions and the unexpected waves of political risk, which is a very *unique composition* of risk elements produced a special but efficient strategy of small businesses (It is not the purpose here to discuss *why* these people took the risk instead of remaining under the umbrella of state employment).

Based on our research we are convinced that the core of their business strategy was not only making a substantial amount of profit but to avoid or to diminish risks. Private entrepreneurs' strategy consisted of several special elements serving this aim. One of their methods was *the temporary interruption* of business activities. In bad times people involved in private activities stopped their activities and in better times they started their businesses again. Moreover private entrepreneurs were masters of *changing the legal form* of their businesses. Legal forms of private or semi private activities supported by reform minded political leaders improved the chances of survival. Another basic element of risk avoiding or diminishing strategy was when they *divided their economic activities*. They were part time private entrepreneurs and were employed by state-owned companies as well. In the last years of socialism about 34 per cent of private craftsmen were parallelly employed by the state. The owners of the 1.5 million household plots were at the same time members of agricultural co-operatives. In connection with this strategy the majority of private entrepreneurs *minimised the size of the firm.*

Temporary interruption, change of legal forms, division of economic activities and growth avoiding behaviour were efficient but *passive* forms of adaptation. The strategy also consisted of *offensive innovative elements*. *Multi-purpose investment* was the most important part of the offensive strategy. They invested very little in buildings and equipment which served *only* production or trade. But households involved in private businesses accumulated a lot of goods and assets which were *used in reform periods in production but in periods of forced contraction of private activities they became objects of private consumption*. The best example was multi-purpose utilisation of family houses and other buildings. Cars, telephone lines, gardens belonging to the family served similar purposes. Savings in cash or in bank accounts was an important part of this multi-purpose strategy.

Physical assets owned by families played an important role in small business development but the main source of accumulation was the capitalisation of family labour. We have to emphasise here the *long term/evolutive/protractive character* of this strategy. Protraction improved the chances of market entry and market development. Moreover socialist entrepreneurs were able to eliminate several negative effects of the bad performance (of missing services) of banks and of other financial institutions in a long term (sometimes interrupted or delayed) investment process.

The long term evolution of private enterprises gave better chances to build up *sophisticated networks* of friends, colleagues and of members of the family. Instead of legal institutions (voluntary associations, banks, centres of information and marketing) these networks were the main sources of information on business partners, on factors of production and of course on the changes of regulations including taxes, and of the ups and downs of the economic policy. Networks were also an important source of illegal loans.

Table 11.1 Space of maneuvre of small businesses

Employment	Multi-purpose assets of households	
	Consumption	Production
State	A	B
Private	C	D

Table 11.1 helps us to understand the space of manoeuvre of the small businesses in socialist countries. The original aim of the communist designers of the system was to keep people in block A where they were employed by the state and consumed goods made by state-owned enterprises. For a number of different reasons people tried to *move out* from the block A to block D in reform periods or move back from D to A in periods of dogmatic-fundamentalist domain. There were move outs in the direction of B and of C as well. The typical case of B was out-working in which participants employed by state-owned companies produced goods for the company at home. The typical case of C was when state-employed people started a private business but instead of using the assets of the household they used them as productive assets.

Transition instead of perestroika

In the last years of the communist system a few people expected or forecasted the collapse of the Soviet Empire. Intellectuals (dissidents as well as radical reformers) and the general public expected nothing more than radical reforms. In other words: they calculated that a less risky political environment combined with the usual risk of market transactions would be favourable for the development of the private sector. They were convinced that this development would happen *within* the reformed socialist economy dominated by the state sector. In a public opinion poll made in 1988 'only a little minority of the people (10 per cent) hold the opinion that the Hungarian economy has to be built on small businesses. According to the majority this sector has to play only a supplementary role only'. According to the poll 'the majority (59 per cent) opposed the idea that big enterprises should have been owned by private persons' (Public opinion in 1988).

Manifestos and other documents of illegal opposition groups and later political programmes of alternative political organisations shared this opinion. In these documents *a new mainly negative industrial policy was formulated* focusing on the 'not to do anymore' elements. Among others there was argumentation about the elimination of negative discrimination against small private entrepreneurs.

Privatisation of large state-owned companies was missing from these programmes. Regarding the business cycle no recession was expected in 1987-88 in these documents. Plans and forecasts of the last communist government also presented an optimistic scenario. The main task of the government was 'cooling' the economy because of inflation caused by the expected acceleration of economic growth.

Based on these programmes and promises in the last years of socialism a lot of Hungarians expected that the risk of private enterprise would diminish with market risk remaining low and political risk being smaller than before) *in the framework of the reformed socialist economy.* Using the symbols of Table 11.1 a lot of people (families) were going to move from block A to other blocks, mainly to block D.

Conventional business protection policy

Instead of the expected radical reform the socialist system collapsed in 1989. The new Hungarian government and its opposition agreed that new institutional order and an industrial policy were needed which were in harmony with the nature of the market economy dominated by the private sector (Gray C. W. - Hanson R. J. - Heller M. 1993). There was a consensus among experts that the elimination of negative discrimination was necessary but not enough to counterbalance the disadvantages of the small private business. The crucial point of their analysis was that post-socialist small business suffered *not only* from disadvantages caused by the socialist heritage. Experts of industrial policy and of market regulation also emphasise that there are *structural* disadvantages or handicaps which negatively influence the competitiveness of small firms *in market economies*. Unit costs of several activities are higher in small than in big companies (typical cases: costs of R and D personnel or of market entry). The reason is obvious: because of the *indivisibility* of these inputs the unit costs are higher than in big companies which diminishes the competitiveness of small companies.

There are advantages related to small size as well. A remarkable proportion of these firms are more flexible and innovative, and costs of inside information and of decision making are less in small than in big companies. But in a lot of cases these advantages cannot counterbalance the above mentioned disadvantages. This negative balance is the main *microeconomic* reason for the small business protection policies in market economies.

There are also *macroeconomic* and *political* reasons for this business protective behaviour of governments. Empirical and statistical evidence shows that the small business sector is the main job creator in several countries. The flourishing small business sector helps to stabilise local communities and/or regions.

There is a long debate about the *efficiency* of small business protection in market economies. The core of the critique is that in relation to projects and programmes supporting small businesses, real outcomes are less attractive than declared aims. Preferential loans with state guaranties, the aim of which is to eliminate disadvantages of the small business, are very advantageous for big companies because their small subcontractors share the benefits of these loans with them. Moreover these loans are distributed by state authorities or local governments which are not exclusively interested in profit and/or efficiency. The results are less than suboptimal: not only successful or promising small firms but also inefficient ones are protected by projects delivering preferential loans. Similar problems occur when tax preferences or subsidies are adapted.

Because of these negative results of *direct* protection different forms of *indirect* small business protection have become more popular over the last two decades. Instead of cheap loans and tax preferences, creation of a favourable climate for (small) business including business friendly institutions such as networks for information and education have become the most important elements of small business protection and/or industrial policies in advanced market economies.

The system of small business protection after 1989

Based on West European examples a network of new institutions was established in the post-socialist period to counterbalance the disadvantages of small businesses. The Ministry of Industry Trade and Tourism (MITT) is responsible to the government for this policy. A Council for Protection of Business Development was organised, subordinated to the MITT. Delegates of other ministries involved in small business affairs, representatives of business associations and respectable members of the business community (invited by the minister) comprise the members of the Council. The main task of this body is 'to improve the level of communication between business and government and to formulate consensual statements in strategic questions' (The planned governmental tasks...1997).

Local governments in big towns also built up institutions of small business protection. In smaller towns or in villages local governments have their specialists responsible for these activities. Moreover there are several private institutions the aim of which is to help small businesses.

The *Hungarian Business Development Fund* (HBDF) is the central body of small business protection in *non agrarian sectors*. It was established in 1990 as an independent institution. Its capital to start with was 4.2 billion HUF (financed by the central budget). The aim of this fund was to help the development of existing small (less than 150 employees, less than 300 million HUF income/year) businesses and to contribute to start ups of new enterprises. The main forms of protection are: preferential loans, guaranties and non repayable subsidies.

A centralised organisation is unable to fulfil these tasks. Therefore a nation-wide network of local business centres and advisory offices were established. There were 19 local business centres and about 150 local offices managed by the HBDF in 1997. The aim of these offices is to help small businesses and to stimulate start ups of new ones. These centres formulate programmes or projects of local or regional small business protection, and they also manage educational programmes for small artisans.

These centres are non-profit foundations. Local governments, business associations and banks contribute to their expenses but the main source of their budget is the contribution of the Hungarian Business Development Fund and funds from the EU. The *Start Guaranty Fund* (established by the HBDF) brings into motion different *systems of preferential loans*. For example the so-called Reorg-Start loan is available only for small businesses employing not more than 3 persons. Money from the EU is available for small- and medium-sized companies where the share of the Hungarian state or foreign investor is less than 50 per cent. Hungarian agriculture has its own system of small business protection. There are more than 10 different preferential loans available for agricultural small businesses. Different programmes of the Ministry of Labour aiming to protect working places are very favourable for small businesses too.

The Hungarian government built up a system including loan guaranties and interest support. The Ministry of Finance, the Ministry of Industry, Tourism and Trade and the Ministry of Agriculture have their own systems of protection. The size of protected enterprises varies but companies employing more than 500 persons are excluded from these projects. The government has also established *The Company Limited for Loan Guaranties*. The aim of the Company is to help lending activities of firms employing not more than 300 persons. The Guaranty Fund of Agrobusinesses has the same purpose.

Table 11.2 Number of popular forms of economic organisation

	company limited number	prev. year=100%	individual proprietorships number	prev. year =100%
1989	17341		320619	
1990	26807	154.6	393450	122.7
1991	43439	268.0	510459	129.7
1992	60762	164.0	608207	119.1
1993	86867	142.9	715105	117.6
1994	121128	139.4	778026	108.8
1995	106245	87.7	791496	101.7
1996	125940	118.5	745247	94.2
1997	147388	117.0	659690	88.5

Source: Statistical Yearbook of Hungary (1997)

Statistical evidence

This short overview shows that post socialist Hungarian governments eminently accepted the conventional argumentation of small business protection. There is a sophisticated system of small business protection similar to the ones existing in market economies. But how efficient is this system?

The number of small businesses has increased very quickly. Based on the last surveys there are more than 1 million licensed enterprises in Hungary (The population of the country was 10.1 million in 1997).

Important positive *structural changes* have taken place during the post socialist period. The number of new firms in service and trade sectors increased in this period much faster than the number of new firms in industry and agriculture. The sector of financial services and mortgage businesses expanded extremely fast. The rate of growth was much lower in industry and agriculture than in other branches.

The Hungarian economy was dominated by big state-owned companies during the period of socialism. The overcentralization and its negative outcomes (monopolistic markets) are over because the majority of companies are *very small*. As much as 97 per cent of them employs less than 10 persons in 1996. (Statistical Yearbook of Hungary 1997) Ownership structure underwent transformation too. The majority of new companies are owned by private persons or by other private firms.

No doubt these indicators of small business development are very impressive. But we have to take into consideration that about 20 per cent of these enterprises never worked. There is no measurable output and input and therefore no tax is paid by them. A remarkable portion of the active firms work only occasionally. In spite of these corrections we may claim that the active business community grew very quickly during the period of 1989-1996.

Another not so impressive, indicator of small business development is the low level of investment activity. The share of small businesses in loans lent by banks diminished during the period of 1993-1996. One of the unfavourable consequences of this trend is that more than 2/3 of the small businesses have no physical assets.

Behind the statistics: different groups and different strategies

In our statistical analysis we implicitly assumed a homogenous small business community. But based on sociological research we may go into a more detailed analysis. We have to distinguish here the group of 'single issue firms' established for making a few transactions only from the group of those which have a long-term surviving or expansive strategy. The two groups have different risks and therefore different costs and benefits. The 'single issue firms' may not take into consideration the impacts of shrinking markets of discriminative lending of banks, etc.

The group of businesses established for making a few transactions also consists of subgroups. There are firms the aim of which is tax avoiding or making a single business to enjoy some subsidies. There are 'empty' firms which are *parts of networks* usually owned or controlled by a group of entrepreneurs. There are situations in which these owners have 'activised' the firm or its accounts. Other firms from this group are not empty but have no real business strategy. The best example is when workers and companies make contracts with the aim of paying fewer social security fees. The formal status of the worker is licensed small business but he or she is working at the same workplace before.

We cannot say that the behaviour of these occasional enterprises is irrational. On the contrary: in a fast changing environment careful and conscious analysis of costs and benefits may increase the number of occasional firms.

But how may we explain the behaviour of firms with a long-term strategy? We have to take into consideration that (as we have seen earlier) important elements of the strategy designed and used successfully during the socialist era became useless in a post socialist environment.

Using the terminology of microeconomics the strategy of these firms consists of a package of methods. A part of them may help to overcome or *postpone* acute difficulties. The most important technology of surviving is *tax avoiding* while another well-known method is *slower or delayed paying*. Moreover there are chains or rings of debt. This is not only a sophisticated method of lending or borrowing which may help overcome liquidity problems. Sometimes the entrepreneur *consciously develop chains or rings of firms* including empty ones. These technically unified but legally decentralised conglomerates are very efficient in distributing the risks we mentioned earlier.

Other methods are parts of a long-term strategy. We are not able to present a consistent strategy but we may observe some elements of it. A *careful selection of members of the staff* is very important for Hungarian entrepreneurs. In connection with this they make serious efforts *to improve the work environment*. The wage system of these small firms is performance oriented including a functional relationship between wages and the performance of the firm.

Another part of the strategy puzzle is the *selection of markets* or submarkets. There are several methods of selection. Some of the firms have contracts with big industrial or trade companies while others focus their efforts on a local market or on a narrow nation-wide market of a specialised good or service. Sometimes these small firms even agree on how to share their markets.

A third group of small firms use the well known method of *diversification*. There are cases in which companies organise production units but we can observe opposite expansions in which producers build up departments for sale.

And of course there are a lot of small Hungarian companies which use traditional methods of the small business like *quality oriented production* or *price differentiation or sponsoring and advertising*. And a little minority is interested *in investing in technical development and innovation*.

Impacts of small business protection

Can we evaluate the performance of the new small business protection policy based on this statistical and sociological description of post socialist development? The main methodological problem here is how to separate the impacts of this policy from other factors influencing the behaviour of the small business community.

No detailed evaluations of the efficiency of the new small business protection policy are available. Cost benefit analysis of the projects is missing as well. That is the reason why we have no direct answers to these questions. Instead we may use *indirect* indicators: There are sporadic but interesting data about the effects of the actions of institutions involved in small business development.

A survey made by HBDF showed that only 11 per cent of small businesses were in some form of connection with local business centres and offices (Czakó-Vajda 1993). The number of those who *used* the services offered by the offices, centres or banks involved in small business protection projects is much smaller. Based on calculations of Teréz Laky, in the first four years only 7000 small businesses borrowed using preferential loans (Laky 1994). In another programme which helped unemployed persons in starting a business the number of participants was about 20.000 during the same period. A project to save and to defend workplaces managed by the National Employment Fund accepted 389 applicants between 1992-1994 from mainly small and medium size enterprises who promised to save about 35.000 workplaces (Neumann 1996). If we take into consideration that the number of small businesses was about 1 million in these years the protective activity of the state authorities has not been remarkable in the post socialist period.

Conclusions

These sporadic figures show that the activity of newly established institutions for small business protection played only a *secondary* role in the development of this sector of the post socialist Hungarian economy. *Deregulation,* namely the abolishment of the system of negative discrimination gave the main impetus to rapid development. The *accumulated knowledge* of small businessmen based on experiences during reform periods is another decisive part of the success of this sector. The negative side effect of this positive development was that in a lot of cases businessmen postponed technological change and they were not motivated to invest. These types of activities were observable only within a little group of small businesses. On the other hand, it was not so much the mistakes of the institutions responsible for small business protection but first and foremost the unexpected transitional recession that can explain the negative side effects of this development.

The policy makers in Hungary face a serious dilemma: The main positive impacts of deregulation are over and only rather expensive programmes could help the future development of the small business sector. Such programmes are not necessarily successful but a random of spontaneous development of small businesses is not enough to change the innovation and investment avoiding attitudes of small Hungarian entrepreneurs.

References

A kis és középvállalkozás fejlesztés tervezett kormányzati feladatai (1997), Ipari Kereskedelmi és Idegenforgalmi Minisztérium (mimeo). (The planned governmental tasks of the small business development).

A közvélemény 1988-ban (1988), *Magyarország Politikai Évkönyve R-Forma Kiadó,* Budapest (Public opinion in 1988).

Czakó, Ágnes,- Vajda, Ágnes (1993), *Kis és Középvállalkozók Magyar Válalkozásfejlesztési Alapítvány Kutatási Füzetek 2.,* Budapest (Small- and medium-size entrepreneurs).

Gray C.W., Hanson R.J., Heller M. (1993), *Legal Reform for Hungary's Private Sector,* Acta Oeconomica, Vol. 45. (3-4) pp.269-300.

Laki, Mihály (1998), *Kisvállalkozás a szocializmus után Közgazdasági Szemle Alapítvány*, Budapest (Small business after socialism).

Laky, Teréz (1994), *Vállalkozások a Start hitel segítségével Magyar Vállal kozásfejlesztési Alapítvány Kutatási Füzetek 1*. Budapest (Business with the help of the Start loan project).

Neumann, László (1996), *Az OFA munkahelymegtartó támogatási programjának értékelése*. Kutatási Zárótanulmány Munkaügyi Kutatóintézet, Budapest (Evaluation of the workplace defence programme of the OFA).

Róna-Tas, Ákos (1997), *The Great Surprise of the Small Transformation. The Demise of Communism and the Rise of the Private Sector in Hungary*, The University of Michigan Press, Ann Arbor.

Seleny, Anna (1991), *Hidden Enterprise, Property Rights Reform and Political Transformation in Hungary*, (mimeo).

Statistical Yearbook of Hungary (1987), (1990), (1997), *Compiled by the Dissemination Department of the Central Statistical Office of Hungary Central Statistical Office*, Budapest.

12 Cultural Perspectives on Management Issues in Hungary

Foreign-owned production companies in transition

SUSAN BERRY BACA

Introduction: A cultural focus on foreign-owned production

Foreign investment in Hungarian production companies has been playing an important role in the transition process to a market-oriented economy since the early 1990s. Foreign buyers have brought to Hungary both access to export markets and the necessary and scarce resources needed for company transition. Necessary and scarce resources include not only investment capital, though this has certainly been an important input, but also the market-oriented management skills needed to guide transition processes within companies.

Although Hungary had been moving towards a market system since the reforms of 1968, the majority of large production companies remained state-owned and to a large extent centrally governed, carrying on the practice of politically oriented management (Hare and Oakey 1993, p25). Only after the radical reforms of 1989 began opening Hungary to the West did large-scale privatization of production and a real market orientation begin to emerge. As a natural consequence, experienced managers were, for the most part, ill prepared to guide their companies through the transition to market orientation.

Foreign buyers typically came in as joint venture partners, but almost invariably with a controlling interest in a company and plans to buy up remaining shares as they became available and when changing legislation allowed. They filled key management positions with people experienced in their own company, i.e., with non-Hungarians or, to a lesser extent, with Hungarians who had been living in the West for most or all of their working lives. These ex-pats, as members of the former group call themselves, are gradually being replaced with Hungarian managers as the later can be trained to take over positions, or as young candidates can be lured from other foreign-owned companies where they have received extensive training and experience.

Replacement of ex-pat managers with local ones has generally gone more slowly than expected, and a majority of foreign-owned companies are led by expats who stay in the country for a period of two to five years, to be replaced by another home-office appointee. Some international companies have a policy of rotating top managers from one country to another which ensures an international management group in all involved countries. In those foreign-owned companies in Hungary that today employ only local managers, the presence of the foreign owner is still felt through required reporting systems and regular visits from the home office, and of course a battery of systems and procedures that have been installed by the parent company.

The reason for focusing a cultural study on foreign-owned production companies lies not so much in the presence of individual ex-pats, or groups of them, as in the transfer of management techniques, procedures, and rationales that were developed in and adjusted to operations in cultures very different from that in which they are now being applied. Of course many locally-owned and some state-owned companies are also adopting Western management practices,[1] but one must suppose that within these companies the process will be less thorough and, at the same time, more insightful regarding local cultural contexts.

This chapter, then, looks into the proposition that history – in the form of culturally founded patterns of construing reality – matters at the level of company transition to a market orientation. It is not so much that which has popularly come to be called 'organizational culture' that is of interest here, but that of the broader, some would say national, culture, since patterns of perception generally shared throughout the population are much more likely to have a profound influence on the path(s) ultimately taken under transition to a market economy. This is so because those patterns most firmly rooted, or deeply seated, in the culture of the larger society will, according to cultural theory, be the most stable over time. The decision to focus on foreign-owned production companies is based upon both the presumed importance of these companies to national strategies for economic advancement, and the opportunity they present for investigating the consequences of implementing Western management practices[2] within a culture to which they have been largely foreign. Understanding the degree to which ensuing dynamics can be attributed to the culture of the host country can also give an indication of necessary adjustments, changes or innovations in Western market-oriented management techniques as an alternative to the 'one best way' attitude often prevalent among Western managers.

The meaning of the term 'culture' is a much contested one, and thus an in-troductory explanation of the way it is used here may be necessary by way of orientation (a fuller discussion can be found in section 3 of this chapter). Hans Gullestrup's (1992) broad definition of culture, including prevailing views of life, values, norms, as well as their material and immaterial artifacts, and his dynamic model distinguishing between manifest and core culture and their respective levels, is used as a classification guide for identifying elements of culture and their relationships to one another. This conceptualization is somewhat deterministic in its approach, however, assuming that persons are 'programmed' by their cumulative cultural experience. That individuals within one macro culture are also members of other cultural groups at different levels of aggregation, and function according to the appropriate cultural context at any given time is later elaborated in Kuada and Gullestrup (1997), though the assumption is still that experience within different cultural contexts is determinant for the functioning of the group and individuals within the context of the group. While the above described body of theory is well suited for evaluating the influence of history in patterns that can be currently found, it does not account for the occurrence of innovation, but tends to disregard the possibility. The symbolic approach to cultural theory, on the other hand, focuses strictly on 'webs of significance', or constructions of meaning, used among groups of people at any given time, recognizing that signifiers (be they words, actions, silence, artifacts, or some other bearer of significance), can have different meanings for the same people at different times, depending on the context. The creation of meaning between or among people is assumed to be an ongoing process, and thus innovative patterns of meaning, and the manifesta-tions they give rise to, are an ever-present possibility.

The concept of culture used in this chapter recognizes both the cumulative influence of history and the ongoing process of the creation of meaning. It assumes that individuals, groups, and collectivities are informed by historical experience in the on-going process of meaning creation, that access to this experience is necessarily finite and variable, and that possibilities for innovative meaning creation are infinite.

The above named assumptions concerning the conceptualization of culture are reflected in the research method developed for this study. As a means for discovering where rationales prevalent in the Hungarian cultural context might impact on the attempt to introduce Western market-oriented management practices, interviews were carried out to identify what are here called 'manage-ment issues'. Management issues have to do with instances in which responses from local employees did not match the expectations of the (Western) ex-pat managers and consultants who attempted to introduce new systems and/ or practices in the sample companies. Qualitative interview guides were used for identifying management issues in keeping with the assumption that both historically influenced and innovative creations of meaning could affect the actions and reactions of the local employees, thus ruling out a priori categorization of possible issues. During the same round of interviews, explanations were sought from both ex-pat and Hungarian managers as to why named issues arose. The empirical information thus obtained was used to identify types of issues, which in turn were used in a following round of interviews with Hungarian researchers and practitioners familiar with the field of inquiry. The aim of these interviews was to explain, from a broad Hungarian perspective, the attitudes and circumstances, both historical and current, which support the types of actions and reactions involved on the part of Hungarian employees. Put in other words, these interviews were used in an attempt to learn something about the Hungarian way of construing meaning when confronted with Western management practices.

While space does not allow for a full presentation of each of the issues identified and their explanations from a Hungarian perspective, three of them are dealt with at length in the following sections. The analysis that then follows is based upon the entire corpus of data.

Identifying management issues

The empirical research upon which this paper is based was carried out during three visits to Hungary during 1994 to 1996, the first two of which involved identifying management issues. The topic of management issues was chosen for empirical research based on the theoretical assumption that incongruities between imported Western market-oriented management practices and rationales and the Hungarian cultural context would be most likely reflected in such issues.

During the first visit managers in fifteen production companies, eight foreign-owned and seven Hungarian-owned,[3] were interviewed to gain insight into the differences between Hungarian-owned and foreign-owned operations and to get an idea of the types of issues arising in foreign-owned companies. Companies visited were within the food and machine production industries and were located in three different regions of Hungary.

Method of issue identification

During the second visit in 1995, case studies were carried out in three companies in the food production industry, again in three different regions. Controlling ownership resided in the hands of one British, one American, and one Danish company. The selection process depended in large part on the willingness of companies contacted to agree to interviews, but was also conditioned by the necessity of English or Danish speaking management being present. That case studies represent two Anglo Saxon and one Danish company may influence the results found, since it has been suggested that Austrian, German, and Italian mother companies, in particular, have a greater understanding of the Hungarian context and subsequently have fewer adjustment problems.

In the three sample companies, qualitative interviews were conducted with at least nine upper, middle, and lower managers in each company, as well as four production workers in each of two of the companies. The bulk of the manager interviews were carried out in English, though Danish was used in one interview and translators were used in five. All production workers were interviewed with the help of a translator.

From the case study interviews, nine issues were derived from statements made by both Western and Hungarian managers, but are stated below from a Western perspective. Eight of them were mentioned in all three of the case study companies, while the last one was mentioned as an issue in only two of them. It is included in the following presentation of issues because it is presently an issue for Hungarian workers and may increasingly become problematic for managers as well. Other issues mentioned in less than all three companies are not included.

It should be stressed that the issues derived from interviews are put in focus as a result of the research method used and should not be interpreted as a generally felt negative attitude towards Hungarian managers or the Hungarian workforce. This would be a gross misrepresentation since *all foreign managers interviewed in fact expressed very positive reactions to the situation found in Hungary in general, both social and work-related.*

Issues delineated

Following is the list of management issues arrived at from case study interviews. For three of the issues, examples of the way the issue was stated are given, followed by the reason(s) why it is problematic for companies, explanations offered as to why the issue occurs, and methods used to deal with it.

Issue no. 1: *Managers, and others, do not feel and act like 'company owners', i.e., it is difficult to get them to take the initiative or responsibility to influence and change what they can see needs changing in the company,* was expressed in the following ways:

'(There is) a certain attitude of the people, or the manager, that they do not seem to be a real manager or a real owner of the specific field. They behave, even the managers, as employees, not managers of the specific field. ... and do not feel that they have really the opportunity to influence certain things. They are just expecting decisions from the bosses, and they would like to carry through as good as possible. So this kind of attitude is missing from our managers, even at a very high level.'

'You know, the only bad decision is no decision. But make a damned decision.'

'Now we have our freedom, we can think, but.. Generally, what we do, there is always, somebody has to decide at the top.'

Examples illustrated that the tendency to avoid taking responsibility can be found at all levels of company structure. Foreign managers felt that their time was wasted when they were asked to make decisions that lower managers were actually more qualified to make themselves. What is perhaps more crucial is the situation in which a new system that required immediate decision making at lower levels had been put into place, a situation not atypical of transition changes. When people failed to take responsibility for making decisions and acting upon them, the new system didn't function, or it functioned only poorly. This was a source of frustration not only for foreign managers, but also for Hungarian managers who had been given the responsibility for making a new system work.

Explanations offered as to why the issue occurred included fear of doing something wrong, fear of being blamed for a problem, compartmentalization of functions or areas of responsibility that are hard to change, a feeling of being lost because of all the changes, lack of understanding, lack of information, expectations that the director should make all decisions, the 'old way of thinking', and a preference for stability in job functions rather than flexibility.

Measures for dealing with the issue always involved training of various types, both in-house and in foreign countries. Changes in company structure were often accompanied by detailed explanations of managers' areas of responsibilities. One foreign manager said that he tried to make himself less accessible, so that lower managers were forced to make their own decisions. The same manager also noted that improved methods for creating operations information and for making it available to all managers improved the situation. Another manager, Hungarian, related that he tried to fill management positions with people who had experience working for other foreign-owned companies because they showed more initiative and were more flexible. Yet another manager, Hungarian, reported that taking the time to explain new systems fully to each lower manager, daily communication, and monetary reward for a job well done was effective in changing the attitudes of even people who had worked many years in the old system. All agreed, however, that the shift from waiting for orders from above to taking responsibility oneself was a major attitude change that took time and consistent reinforcement to achieve.

Issue no. 2: *Some managers resist change, making changes in the company difficult.*

Issue no. 3: *It is difficult to establish direct communication and cooperation between functional departments within the company.* Examples of the way in which this issue was expressed are:

'Because of the traditional organization, and traditional way of thinking of the people, the whole company is too much segmented. I mean, the different departments, manufacturing and the technical department, finance, personnel. I see some problems how to establish better cooperation, better understanding of each other's problems and goals.'

'We're too functional, very functional at all levels. We go up and down, up across and down. You know, the board is the focus of that. We don't push enough down, so there isn't enough interaction at lower levels.'

'What we're fighting with at the moment is coordination between the departments, because they haven't learned that yet. When I say copy, now we have a plan here and everyone must have copies, they don't get sent unless I say they have to be sent over there so they know what is happening. They keep them to themselves. This is my area, this is up to me, others have no business mixing. They haven't gotten over that yet. We're fighting with that at the moment, no question about it.'

'When I first got here I says, well, what's your plan? He says, I don't have that. That's top secret. Quote unquote.'

According to those interviewed, resistance to direct communication and cooperation resulted, in practice, in slower reaction to market changes, inhibition of improvements or innovation within departments, conflicts between departments, longer down-time or reduced output on production lines, lower efficiency than desired, and more waste.

Explanations offered as to why the issue occurs included the persistence of old, established ways of doing things, distrust, narrow areas of knowledge, resentment of new employees who were considered different from existing employees, departmental self-interest, status struggles, communication problems with non-Hungarian speakers, a 'traditional' type of organization, too much decision making at top management levels, and secrecy.

Measures used to deal with the issue included mixing people from different departments in training groups, combining divisions, new product development teams comprised of people from all departments involved, explanations to all managers about the functions and importance of a new department, direct orders from a non-Hungarian manager backed up with the threat of dismissal, dissemination of detailed information about who can be called upon to deal with specific problems or needs, replacement of non-compliant managers, daily production meetings involving cross-departmental problem solving, and centralized information gathering and dissemination. Only the last three measures were reported to have been successful.

Issue no. 4: *The company structure is too steep. There are too many managers in proportion to production workers.*

Issue no. 5: *Local managers respond to outside criticism and direction by stepping back from the situation and saying, you do it then. As soon as a person who has put in a new system goes away again, the people just stop doing the system, or do it only partially,* was expressed in the following ways.

'I think that they (home office) assumed that the people here weren't good at their jobs, and whoever they brought from the West was better. (...) I think how it affected (...) was that the managers here just said, well, okay then. You do it. And took a step backwards from the situation. (...) If you know best, you do it.'

'So there are systems in place, but people don't adhere to them. People don't look after them. It's easy to put a system in; it's easy to develop a new way of working. It's a lot harder to actually keep working like that and not fall back into old habits. And I think that's what's happened here, that people have put a new system in, and then as soon as the person who has put the system in has gone away again, then they just stop doing it.'

'We broke away from that (control by the mother company on a new installation). The more control they tried to get, the less control they had. Meaning that the only person that really ended up with control was (the supplier).'

While this issue could be seen as a subset of resistance to change generally, it is also a more particular set of behaviour that was given attention by interviewees, and is therefore handled as a separate issue here.

Examples of how this particular type of resistance to change, or noncompliance, occurred in practice included instances in which work simply stopped when the outside (Western) expert left; local managers and line workers alike delivered required documentation without carrying out the functions which were ostensibly documented; or that local managers boycotted a new system, refusing to produce required documentation.

Explanations offered as to why the issue occurs were varied. In the case of equipment installation, it was assumed that local managers expected, or required, the presence of the outside expert if he indeed intended to control the process. In the case of delivering documentation without carrying out functions, it was assumed that the people involved didn't really understand the purpose of the new system, even if they said all of the right things, or that they thought it was meaningless. Boycotting a new system was interpreted by the foreign manager as a result of fear that previously existing positions would be made obsolete by the new system and as reluctance to bypass the old hierarchy. In another case, criticism by a home-office evaluation team was seen as insulting to local managers and therefore as a hindrance to promoting trust and local initiative.

Dealing with the issue ranged from repeating a train, control, train cycle, hoping that employees would eventually understand or be convinced that the system was worthwhile, to discharging outside experts and giving responsibility to local, on-site managers. In some instances, more detailed instructions in the form of orders were given to middle managers to ensure that not only the documentation but also the processes being documented were completed. In one instance it was reported that local trainers played a support role in imported (Western) training programs and would eventually take over the training process. Only the method of giving responsibility to local managers was reported to have been successful in a case study company, while a manager in another company reported to have had success with the method of train, control, train in another Hungarian acquisition by the same mother company.

Issue no. 6: *People are not highly motivated.*

Issue no. 7: *The Hungarian way of thinking is wasteful, not well enough defined, not effective, in comparison to the Western way of thinking.*

Issue no. 8: *Communication problems exist between Hungarian and Western managers who don't speak the other's language, as well as between non-English speaking Hungarians and international contacts.*

Issue no. 9: *Western owners generally don't want to provide social benefits beyond what the law requires, but workers see benefits as part of their rightful remuneration, and resist their elimination.*

Discussion of issue designation

The above identification and naming of issues is admittedly and necessarily an artificial one in that the inductive method used requires creating one's own categories from the empirical information gathered. Creating categories is useful in this case for generalizing about perceived management issues within foreign-owned companies and for further analysis of issues from a cultural perspective.

Several of the issues described above are obviously interrelated, but without further background information (here I am referring to emic, or insider information, as well as results from other related research) and analytical frameworks, distinctions as to how and why issues are related, or not related, remain hazy. Treating management issues as cultural phenomena can, as illustrated in subsequent sections of this paper, provide different ways of interpreting the same phenomena and show how they are elements of other issues or frames of reference within the Hungarian context.

External validity

The question remains as to whether or not the nine categories of management issues presented above can be seen as representative of recurring issues within Hungarian transition industries in general, only within foreign-owned Hungarian companies, only within the food-production industry in Hungary, or as representative at all. Regional influences were controlled for as far as possible by conducting case studies in three different regions of the country (Budapest, the economically depressèd north-east region, and the relatively wealthy north-west region).

Researching the above question through a written questionnaire survey was originally planned but this method was discarded after consultation with other researchers, both Danish and Hungarian, who had obtained unusably low return rates from similar Hungarian populations. Two possibilities remain: finding other empirical research results that either confirm or contradict my findings, and deducing the likelihood of generalizability through further analysis.

In pursuance of the first possibility, a thorough and lengthy search of English-language literature has revealed that empirically based research dealing with the fit of Western management techniques within the Hungarian context is notable mostly for its absence. Numerous authors advocate that Western managers and mother companies take a greater interest in learning about the Hungarian cultural context, but to date empirical research on the subject is at best sparse. While the consideration of related literature is a part of the larger research project, it is not included here for reasons of limited space.

The second possibility, of deducing the likelihood of generalizability, follows as a result of the cultural analysis dealt with in following section of this paper. In this regard, however, I will stress the word *likelihood*, for as Clifford Geertz (1973), from a symbolic perspective, reminds us, '..culture is not a power, something to which social events, behaviours, institutions, or processes can be causally attributed; it is a context, something within which they can be intelligibly (..) described,' (p14). The deduction of a likelihood, then, depends upon identifying and describing those Hungarian contexts within which the issues in question become intelligible, and endeavouring to discover the degree to which such contexts are likely to serve as frames of reference for those people involved in company transitions.

Cultural perspectives

It should perhaps be noted that it is not the intention of this research to undertake a description of Hungarian culture in its entirety. What is relevant here is to gain insight into those cultural contexts that can explain, from an Hungarian perspective, the actions and reactions described above as management issues. Put in more auspicious terms, 'Our double task is to uncover the conceptual structures that inform our subject's acts, the 'said' of social discourse, and to construct a system of analysis in whose terms what is generic to those structures, what belongs to them because they are what they are, will stand out against the other determinants of human behavior,' (Geertz 1973, p27).

For a symbolic perspective (more specifically termed semiotic ethnographic) that is open to innovative impulses, I will agree with Geertz that 'man is an animal suspended in webs of significance he himself has spun' and 'take culture to be those webs,' (1973, p5). It should perhaps be restated here that the spinning of webs is taken to be an on-going process.

For an historical perspective, I will understand, with Gullestrup (1992) culture to encompass:

...the view of life and the values, norms and actual behaviour - as well as the material and immaterial productions resulting from these - which man takes over from a previous generation, and which he passes on to the next generation, possibly in a modified form; and which in one way or another distinguishes him from people belonging to other cultures, (as translated in Kuada and Gullestrup, forthcoming).

In refinement of this very broad understanding of culture, Gullestrup (1992) distinguishes between three dimensions, the horizontal, the vertical and the temporal, which respectively account for the common tasks incumbent upon a given culture, a gradation of layers from manifest symptoms to a fundamental philosophy of life within a given culture, and the ways cultures respond to different pressures for change over time. The first two dimensions are summarized in the following diagram:

Figure 12.1 The Static Cultural Model

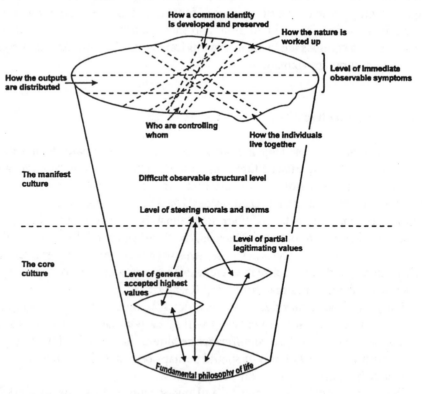

Source: from Kuada and Gullestrup, forthcoming.

Inherent in this conception of culture is the idea that the deeper the level in the vertical dimension, the more resistant it is to change. This would indicate that the deeper the cultural links, the more likely issues are to be persistent and, therefore, the more indicative they are of adaptations to be made on the part of the foreign owner.

Cultural contexts: levels of aggregation

There is a great deal of confusion and disagreement in the literature as to the degree to which anthropological conceptions of culture can be applied to supra, sub and transnational aggregations of people that form lasting and to some degree predictable affiliations. This holds true particularly with regard to organizational culture as some authors, for example Kleppestø (1998) argue that the functionalistic concept of culture is inadequate for explaining the dynamics of mergers and acquisitions, while others, mostly following Schein (1985) apply a functionalistic concept of culture derived from anthropology to explain and guide organizational dynamics.

Of the few authors who address the difference between organizational and national cultures, the empirical studies carried out by Hofstede (1991) and Sackmann (1991) are particularly noteworthy. Hofstede (1991) concluded that the basis for what is popularly known as organizational culture is shared perceptions of daily practices rather than shared values. The latter is, according to his theory, the basis for national culture. Sackmann (1991) found in her case study of a single multi-divisional company that guiding philosophies and values were known only to the leaders of the company, while other levels of employees shared knowledge of and attitudes towards daily practices.

In my opinion, national and organizational cultures are not of the same magnitude with regard to their impact on members. Referring again to Gullestrup's model of culture (see page 12), one can say that the two deepest levels of culture, 'level of generally accepted highest values' and 'fundamental philosophy of life' belong to national culture, while the higher levels, including all of the 'manifest culture' and possibly the 'level of partially legitimating values' can also be formed at an organizational *level of aggregation*. This distinction makes it possible to explain the phenomenon of 'leaving one's hat at the factory gate'. In other words, people construe meaning according to the context within which they are functioning. They are not automatons who think and act according to a ruling culture, but thinking and feeling beings who act and react according to what they consider to be appropriate frames of reference.

In contrast to most functionalists, then, I hold that the unconscious level of culture that is commonly attributed to national cultures, and believed to be in place by the time of adolescence, cannot be attributed to organizational cultures. People take deeply seated values ('generally accepted highest values', in Gullestrup's terms) and world views ('fundamental philosophy of life', in Gullestrup's terms) with them into the workplace. However, these orientations are normally not challenged, but mutually taken for granted or unconsciously assumed, at least in the context of companies indigenous to the same national culture as its employees.

Whether or not the deeper levels of core culture are challenged within foreign-owned companies during the process of transition must remain an unanswerable question. According to Gullestrup (1992), understanding another culture at this level is not a possibility for non-members who necessarily bring their own cultural orientations with them to the research site. Furthermore, members of the culture in question cannot answer your questions or tell you what you need to know about its deepest levels, for much is, on this level, subconscious, taken to be 'natural', unquestioned and unquestionable. One may deduce the fundamental orientations of a culture not one's own, but this is unavoidably a very risky undertaking.

Given the constraints imposed by my non-Hungarian background and inability to speak Hungarian, as well as ever-present time and funding constraints, the methods chosen for researching the cultural side of management issues relied on interviews with Hungarian experts and published literature. Even though the methods of inquiry used in this research are not those of semiotic ethnography, the words of Clifford Geertz (1973) once more seem applicable:

> Cultural analysis is intrinsically incomplete. And, worse than that, the more deeply it goes the less complete it is. It is a strange science whose most telling assertions are its most tremulously based, in which to get somewhere with the matter at hand is to intensify the suspicion, both your own and that of others, that you are not quite getting it right (p29).

It is thus the aim, in the following section, to identify as best possible the frames of reference and their wider cultural contexts at various levels of aggregation, that can be used to intelligibly describe those actions and reactions within foreign-owned Hungarian companies that give rise to management issues. In other words, I will address the question: How do Hungarians make sense of what is happening? – without expecting to be able to report complete and indisputable answers.

Perspectives on management issues

The following is a summation of information gathered through interviews in the fall of 1996 with fourteen Hungarian informants and two from 1995. Persons interviewed were mostly academics with research backgrounds in Hungarian production concerns, and working in the fields of entrepreneurial studies, economics, management development, technical development, labour relations, innovation research, sociology, social policy, politics, and history. One of the interviewees was a senior consultant in a management consulting firm, and another involved in a joint venture association. All interviews were conducted in English.

The following concentrates on identifying the Hungarian cultural contexts that likely serve as frames of reference for management issues. As interviews used the individual management issues as topics of inquiry, this section is ordered according to the issues presented earlier, and is limited to the issues that were presented in full.

Issue no. 1: Managers, and others, do not feel and act like 'company owners', i.e., it is difficult to get them to take the initiative or responsibility to influence and change what they can see needs changing in the company.

The factors most operative in producing this issue appear to be experience from the time of the Socialist regime, a question of trust, and time. During the Socialist period, decision making in corporate settings was highly politicized. The better a person was at avoiding responsibility, the more safe he or she was, and the easiest way to avoid responsibility was to let someone higher up in the hierarchy make the decisions. People became very skilful at this tactic, for taking the initiative or responsibility to change something brought no reward while, on the other hand, it could easily cause problems for the person taking the initiative or responsibility.

That this pattern of behaviour tends to persist after changes in both the macro (governmental) and micro (organizational) systems is due not only to force of habit. People had learned, under the Socialist system, not to trust the official rhetoric, for it could change suddenly with shifting political constellations on both the macro and micro level. A lack of trust persists today on the macro level due to the frequent changing of rules, regulations and systems, often without warning. Change is also prevalent on the micro level, not the least in the case of foreign take-overs of existing enterprises. Especially during the first few years, radical changes in company structure and operating practices are more the norm than the exception. The situation is sometimes unwittingly exacerbated by foreign owners who try to implement motivational systems that closely resemble tactics used under the former regime, and which Hungarian people have learned to mistrust. Symbolically speaking, the message received is that the power holders have changed faces but the game remains the same. Why should the new systems or power holders be trusted more than the old? It follows, from this perspective, that taking initiative and responsibility would be an irrational act.

Trust exists within the company, but it is founded upon actual experience and exists among individuals and groups of people who have known each other and learned to trust one another over an extended period of years. Foreign managers rarely qualify for membership in such groups since their length of stay in the Hungarian company is typically limited to a few years. Given the experienced instability of both macro and micro systems, neither can trust in new systems or attendant practices be assumed, as is so often the expectation from Western managers. Time is a necessary component in establishing the credibility of new practices within a company, especially practices that are perceived as potentially dangerous such as taking initiative and responsibility.

Issue no. 3: It is difficult to establish direct communication and .cooperation between functional departments withing the company.

Communication between some departments, such as production and sales, are typically difficult to establish no matter where a company is located. This sort of problem can thus be seen as an organizational problem rather than one specific to foreign-owned production companies in Hungary. Nevertheless, looking at the more general problem from within the Hungarian context suggests ways in which the context has generated localized perceptions which have bearing on the issue.

The privatization situation is in many ways similar to a crisis situation in which there is a great deal of uncertainty and individuals and groups of individuals keep as much information as possible to themselves in order to achieve advantage. Just after an enterprise has been bought by a foreign company, the aim of the foreign investor is not clear and uncertainty persists. Most managers fear that they will not survive the transition, so they keep information to themselves in an attempt to make themselves less dispensable.

As a result of organizational de-layering and implementation of new measurement and reporting systems, both more typical of foreign-owned than Hungarian state-owned companies, a certain amount of the communication and cooperation problems between departments will be eased, but there are still factors that tend to hamper the free flow of information. These are to be found within and outside the company, and involve behaviours and structures with historic roots as well as current realities.

In the Socialist system, the good manager was one who could successfully compete for resources for his department. His focus was thus directed on the department rather than the enterprise as a whole. There was also a very steep hierarchy that made it necessary to please the person directly above oneself in order to obtain a promotion or to secure resources. Horizontal communication was seen as a source of trouble, and spheres of competence were guarded from outside interference. Hierarchical organization was the rule not only within enterprises, but throughout society, and individuals' connections and ambitions were organized through hierarchies inside the enterprise, the sector, and geographically, with Budapest as the centre of power.

An exception came into play when a manager had a problem. Since it was politically unwise to admit problems to one's superior, problem solving took place with the use of personal informal networks. These networks typically involved people from within and from outside the enterprise, the former case possibly giving rise to informal inter-departmental communication and cooperation.

The development and use of informal networks was not solely a work-related phenomenon during the Socialist regime, but came into being as a response to attempts at atomizing society and as a means of creating some security in an insecure environment. In some cases the extended family was the core of informal networks, in others friends made at school or during professional life. As a member of the Communist Party, very sophisticated networks could be established.

Informal networks still exist today, and are still seen in typical Hungarian companies as a necessary qualification for being a good manager. Larger foreign-owned companies have also recognized the efficacy of such networks in the Hungarian context, and make conscious efforts to hire or retain Hungarians with good connections, especially political connections. Among the general populace, it is said to be the norm that people belong to and use informal networks rather than official channels, because networks are more efficient. For some things, the formal legal, institutional systems can be used, but in a crisis situation they are not sufficient.

While the continued existence of informal networks would not per se hamper the free flow of information between departments of a company, their use as the most efficient way of solving problems would tend to negate the use of systems designed to promote inter-departmental communication and cooperation. To the extent that such systems directly challenged one's allegiance to an informal network personally deemed highly valuable, the most rational choice would be to resist the prescribed systems.

> *Issue no. 5: Local managers respond to outside criticism and direction by stepping back from the situation and saying, you do it then. As soon as a person who has put in a new system goes away again, the people just stop doing the system, or do it only partially.*

This is a complex issue with a number of contingencies that will vary from case to case, but there are also structural realities and historically conditioned attitudes that can contribute to the problem when it arises.

It has been the case in Hungary during the Socialist period that educations were highly specialized. Due to the shortage of labour, it was deemed necessary to specialize people rather early in their educations so that they could begin working as soon as possible. Even on the university level, educations could be characterized as producing specialists rather than generalist. People who were educated under this system comprise the bulk of the Hungarian workforce today, and the specialized nature of their educations makes it extremely difficult for them to suddenly take up new tasks that they were not prepared for through their educations. Given that a high value is placed upon expertise within one's area, stepping out of this area can easily be perceived as personally risky. Returning to or continuing established practices would thus be considered the safest alternative in times of uncertainty.

Added to the above is the historically conditioned expectation that innovations at the workplace are not to be taken seriously. The Socialist system required a quota of innovations within enterprises, and people complied with what were considered to be 'fake innovations'. Experience said that nothing would come of them, but one must go through the motions. It is understandably questionable as to whether or not innovations would suddenly be taken seriously just because there are some foreigners now occupying leading management positions in the company.

Western managers regard the Socialist system as it existed in Hungary as irrational, but it would be a mistake to transfer the label to the people in enterprises who were capable of creating rationality within this system. Systematic irrationalities spawned the belief that, 'Of course we should be smarter than them, and we can go around them'. And so they did. People developed expertises in their areas for making things work in spite of the system, accumulating a kind of human capital that made them indispensable for meeting the demands that were placed upon enterprises. Today the demands have changed, and new methods and systems introduced by a foreign owner will almost invariably have the effect of devaluing or negating much of the human capital that exists within a company. The affected people will, as a result of this transition, find themselves going from a position of importance to being sidelined or marginalized unless they are given possibilities to balance their losses with new opportunities. Gaining compliance depends, from this perspective, upon providing real opportunities that can counterbalance losses in human capital.

Here, again, the question of trust comes into the picture, as it is necessary that opportunities are perceived as real. As discussed previously, trust is not to be assumed or taken for granted. Unfortunately, ex-pats can unwittingly do much to damage the formation of a trustful relationship through intercultural communication misunderstandings. In addition, the Hungarian perception of foreign power holders, in which category the ex-pat manager falls, is at least tinged by the country's long history of foreign dominance and covert resistance. The picture is further complicated by the keen awareness, on the part of Hungarian managers, that ex-pats are paid considerably more than themselves, a situation that is difficult not to resent when Hungarian managers hold comparable positions on the organizational chart and work at least as long hours as the ex-pat. In the case of direction by a foreigner, a worst case scenario would be that of a home-office expert who enters the company abruptly, gives orders, and leaves again after a short stay. Such a person would run a considerable risk of being perceived as arrogant and not to be trusted. Under such circumstances, it would seem irrational to give one's all to the project in question.

Conclusions

As one of my interviewees so aptly said, 'One of the key concepts of Hungary is ambiguity. Nothing is very transparent, even for insiders'. This not withstanding, it falls to me to attempt a somewhat intrepid analysis of research results involving Hungarian culture.

Theoretical implications

To begin with the theoretical side, research results would suggest that the newer, and not so wide-spread, interpretation of organizational dynamics in terms of inter-personal communication and identity formation (as, for example, put forth by Stein Kleppestø, 1998), as an alternative to organizational culture theories is particularly applicable in some cases. For example, when it comes to issues involving trust formation, this perspective would be particularly applicable since the formation of trust in the Hungarian context is in large part a product of interpersonal interaction.

This is not to say, however, that pre-existing organizational cultures are without impact, as research results clearly show in terms of carry-overs of practices from the past, or that national culture plays no part in the dynamics of organizational life. The very dynamics of trust formation, to use the above example, is so highly influenced by national cultural experience as to be invisible for foreign managers, while it is taken for granted by Hungarians. That wide-spread attitudes and beliefs based upon historical experience, i.e., national culture, influence the frames of reference used by different groups involved in this study is most clearly shown in the difference between interpretations given by foreign managers and Hungarian experts. The relevance of informal networks to the issues mentioned was not, for example, visible to foreign managers while it was repeatedly mentioned by expert informants as a major element in explaining some of the issues from an Hungarian perspective.

On the theoretical plane it can be said, then, that this study demonstrates the efficacy of applying the perspective that people act and react according to what they consider to be appropriate frames of reference, be these called organizational culture or national culture, or ascribed to some other level of cultural aggregation. This perspective also accounts for the variance reported between and among different organizations and individuals.

Implications for management

It was suggested at the beginning of this chapter that those issues most deeply rooted in national culture are those that should be given particular consideration by foreign owners and their representative managers, adapting practices to suit the local context. At this point it is not so much the issues that were used in the research method as the practices that should be focused upon, and as practices are based upon assumptions, the latter must also come under scrutiny.

On the deepest level of national culture, or core culture, the only element found to affect functioning within foreign-owned production companies was that of trust. The prevailing world view that trust can only be reliably established through proven long-term association is one that is involved in issues 1, 2, 3, and 5. Thus it is of major importance for foreign managers to understand its dynamics, consequences and limitations within the workplace, especially since it is not a disposition that is likely to change quickly.

On the structural level, which according to Gullestrup is a part of the manifest culture, are to be found a number of present-day realities that may not be readily visible to foreigners, but which should not be overlooked in relation to company practices and assumptions. They include educational job specialization, household income structures, and language barriers. While local companies can do little to actively change these given structural difficulties, with the exception of offering language courses and perhaps extensive, but expensive, educational programs, they would do well to take them into account when planning new strategies.

On the organizational level, a category also belonging to the manifest culture, are found such phenomenon as dependency relationships, problem-solving through networks, and a kind of human capital, all relatively invisible for the unsuspecting Western manager. They are pre-existing organizational structures and practices involving shared perceptions within the company from previous times, and should be addressed and taken into account in times of radical company change.

Implications for innovation in industry

The occurrence of issue no. 5, involving a lack of compliance with direction coming from outside the company, and the cultural explanations found for it hold two implications for innovation in industry, one on the macro, national level and one on the micro, company management level.

On the macro level, if the most viable solution is to put matters in the hands of local company members, as was the only reported solution found to have been successful in the case study companies, know-how will also come to reside with locals within industry in general. In the case of new technological installations, such know-how is considered crucial to the development of technological capacity, including the capacity to innovate further technological refinements or improvements (Lall, 1990, p20; Vimani and Rao, 1997, p29).

On the micro level, individual managers would do well to consider histori-cally conditioned attitudes concerning suggestions for innovations in the area of technological refinements or improvements–and to create new management ap-proaches better suited to the cultural context. Consider, for example, the high probability that the very persons who are most likely to lose human capital as a result of new management structures and systems are also those who have in the past shown the capacity to innovate workable alternatives to systematic irrationalities. It would seem, then, that this group of people would be ideal candidates for enlisting in innovative activities, given their demonstrated abilities to innovate. In addition, enlisting their abilities would counter two problems: Firstly, it would tend to replace the lost human capital of individuals, giving them, secondly, less reason to resist changes within the company.

While the particular confluence of culturally influenced dispositions giving rise to issue no. 5 indicates a furtherance of know-how acquisition, and therewith an increased capacity for innovation, some of the same dispositions are involved in other conjunctures that would tend to hinder the realization of innovation at the company level. For example, trust formation is also an element in issues 1, 2 and 3. To take issue no.1, a tendency to avoid taking initiative and responsibility is obviously related to the realization of innovative potential. In coping with this issue, foreign management must not only avoid motivational programs that resemble those used in Socialist times, and hopefully create others that are better attuned to the local cultural context, but must also somehow overcome constraints posed by a pervasive mistrust in official systems both on the macro and micro levels. Solutions would vary according to specific cases, but would necessarily entail considerable reliance upon emic perspectives and most likely also the liberty to deviate from corporate prescriptions.

Notes

1   For a descriptive comparison of Western and pre-1989 Hungarian management orientations, see Baca (1995, p198), 'Intercultural aspects of foreign-owned production in Hungary' in *Uniqueness in Unity: The significance of cultural identity in European cooperation.* Proceedings of 1995 Sietar Europa Symposium.
2   Due to the methodological approach used in this study, the Western management practices of interest are not determined a priori, but taken up as a consequence of their involvement in common issues arisingin sample companies.
3   Interviews within Hungarian-owned companies were carried out by collegues whose research goals were different frombut non unrelated to the present research.

References

Baca, Susan (1995), 'Intercultural aspects of foreign-owned production in Hungary' in Bozena Machová and Sláva Kubátová (eds) *Uniqueness in Unity:*

The significance of cultural identity in European cooperation, Prague: SIETAR Europa, pp. 194-202.

Geertz, Clifford (1973), *The Interpretation of Cultures,* Basic Books: New York.

Gullestrup, Hans (1992), *Kultur, kulturanalyse og kulturetik* (Culture, Cultural Analysis and Cultural Ethics, forthcoming in English), København: Akademisk Forlag.

Hare, Paul and Ray Oakey (1993), *The Diffusion of New Process Technologies in Hungary,* Printer Publishers: London.

Hofstede, Geert (1991), *Cultures and Organizations: Software of the Mind,* Berkshire, England: McGraw-Hill.

Kleppestø, Stein (1998, forthcoming), 'A Quest for Social Identity: The Pragmatics of Communication in Mergers and Acquisitions', in Torp et al, (eds), *Cultural Dimensions of International Mergers and Acquisitions,* Berlin: Walter de Gruyter.

Kuada, John and Hans Gullestrup (forthcoming), 'The Cultural Context of Corporate Governance, Performance Pressures and Accountability' in Istemi Deming (ed.): *Corporate governance, Accountability and Pressures to Perform: An International Study,* Greenwich, Connecticut: Jai Press Inc.

Lall, Sanjaya (1990), *Building Industrial Competitiveness in Developing Countries.* Paris: OECD.

Sachmann, Sandra (1991), *Cultural Knowledge in Organizations: Exploring the collective mind,* London: Sage Publications.

Virmani, R.R. and Kala Rao (1997), *Economic Restructuring, Technology Transfer and Human Resource Development,* London: Sage Publications.

Index